SCOTTISH REGION
A History 1948-1973

BRITISH RAILWAYS REGION BY REGION

SCOTTISH REGION

A History 1948-1973

ALEXANDER J. MULLAY

TEMPUS

Frontispiece: The *Sunday Post* is Scotland's most popular Sunday newspaper, and its readership would have no difficulty in recognising this railway scene from its 'Fun Section' of 5 December 1965, even although it seems outdated at first glance. At the time, express trains running through Wullie's own county (this author is guessing Angus) were still powered by former LNER Pacifics, so this caricature was curiously appropriate. Railways were *expected* to be old-fashioned, is the underlying message. (Oor Wullie picture by permission, D.C. Thomson Ltd)

First published 2006,
This edition 2007

Tempus Publishing Limited
NPI Business Park,
Chalford, Stroud, Gloucestershire, GL6 8PE
www.tempus-publishing.com

British Library Cataloguing in Publication Data.
A catalogue record for this book is available from the British Library.

ISBN 978 0 7524 3686 9

Typesetting and origination by Tempus Publishing Limited
Printed in Great Britain

CONTENTS

ACKNOWLEDGEMENTS

As always, thanks go to the ever-helpful staff of the National Archives of Scotland, whose West Search Room is an Aladdin's Cave for the transport researcher. Also much appreciated is the assistance rendered by the staffs of the National Library of Scotland, Edinburgh City Libraries, Special Collections at St Andrews University Library, Dumfries and Galloway Library and Archives Services, and the Chartered Institute of Logistics and Transport.

Individuals who are thanked for assisting the author include Dr Ian Buxton, Maurice Green, Alasdair Law, Mike Macdonald, Charles Meacher, Lynn Mentiply, Alan Robinson, Stuart Sellar, Hamish Stevenson, and W.A.C. Smith. In particular, I would like to thank Stuart Sellar for patiently reading much of the MS, and for his helpful comments and constructive criticism.

INTRODUCTION

For half a century from 1948, Scotland's railway system was operated, for the first time, as a complete administrative unit in its own right, but also as part of the nationalised system for the whole United Kingdom. The Scottish Region of British Railways soon developed its own character, with its own problems and potential. Yet it suffered the same fate as the rest of the British system: lack of modernisation in the first ten years, the later supply of diesel and electric traction equipment which was not properly tested, the Beeching Axe, and the asset-stripping prior to privatisation. This is the first-ever telling of the story of Scotland's British Railways.

Much of this account of British Railways (Scottish Region) has had to be terminated in the mid-1970s, after which time the official records are closed at the time of writing. The author hopes for the reader's indulgence here; it is after all interesting – fascinating in places – to see how (and try to work out *why*) Scotland's railways were administered in the manner they were up until the mid-seventies.

The first eight years of nationalisation saw the UK's railways take a rudderless course. Career railwaymen were in charge on a day-to-day basis, and their decisions were untrammelled by the influence of socialist politicians on the one hand or profit-seeking businessmen on the other. Unfortunately this lack of contact with sympathetic politicians was to blight Britain's railways for two decades. Those eight years, 1948-55, saw practically no recapitalisation of railway assets, little in the way of publicity measures intended to engage public sympathy and support, and worst of all, there was a slaughter of unprofitable branch-lines of which Dr Beeching would have been proud. These comprised branch-lines which had never experienced diesel

traction, and which closed with the same high staffing levels and unimagi-
native timetabling which had been in force since Victorian times.

Indeed, there is evidence that Scottish Region was the most impoverished
region of all, the poorest of the poor. By 1958, ten years after nationalisation
and three years after the announcement by the BTC of the Modernisation
Plan, Scottish could show only 5 per cent improvement in traction renewal.
The worst of the English regions in this regard – the Western – registered
9 per cent, but had more than three times as many Diesels operating. The
best region, the Southern, could show 73 per cent renewal!

Following the 1953 Transport Act, ultimately introduced with the intention of reprivatising parts of the British transport scene, principally on
the roads, Scottish Region found itself governed by a Board composed of
businessmen. Needless to say their presence did not guarantee the introduction of any more positive attitudes into railway management. Requests
for modern diesel power on branch lines and calls for revised accounting
practices for assessing a railways' worth were only two applications made to
the Regional Board in 1955 by representative members of the public and
by the forerunner of the Convention of Scottish Local Authorities. They
met only with rebuffs, however; indeed, at least one of these petitioners was
treated with a shameful lack of candour by those in charge of Scotland's
railways at that time, as will be related.

Within a few years, with the Boards run by professional railwaymen once
more, and with service withdrawals continuing unimpeded, the rail enthusiast is tempted to conclude that it mattered not if Britain's nationalised
railways were administered by railway managers, or by businessmen who
had made their reputations and fortunes in other walks of life. The former
category lacked the political connections to seek some measure of the capital injection necessary for an industry exhausted both by war and by only
sporadic investment in the ten years beforehand. The businessmen were not
used to the idea of supplying services when they might not immediately
appear profitable.

What the railways needed after 1948 was a strong political overseer
– a Labour politician who would have given serving railwaymen a lead
to follow in managing a socially engaged railway, while creating a political matrix for such a conversion. But that would be to bring forward the
1968 Transport Act by twenty years. Unfortunately, the minister responsible
for the latter was a mere Parliamentary Secretary at the time of nationalisation (Barbara Castle), and the memory strains to recall the identity of
the Minister of Transport in 1948. It was in fact Alf Barnes, not exactly a

towering figure in the political pantheon. The fact that the reader needs to ask, simply proves the point: the nationalisation of the railways was done almost by rote. Incidentally, probably the best-known peacetime Minister of Transport before Mrs Castle was probably the Conservative Ernest Marples, who made no secret of his enthusiasm for motorways.

There was no guardian angel for the railways at Westminster in 1948, nor would there be for two decades. And perhaps not even then.

What follows is essentially a chronicle of the first twenty-five years of Scottish Region. While it has not always been possible to maintain a single narrative thread – for example, a separate chapter was deemed necessary for maritime and road-related aspects of the story – every effort has been made to make this history of the Scottish Region readable as a direct account.

The author is critical of the Board's attitude to rail closures in Scotland, and makes no apology for this. While the system inherited in 1948 did include duplication of lines and services, these were by no means the first to be dispensed with; indeed, the 1951 closures seemed to intentionally feature rural areas, and it was not the remit of TUCCs before 1968 to consider the *quality* of replacement transport services.

Not only that, but there is evidence of a curious determination among the most senior rail administrators to close as much of the railway as they possibly could. For this reason, the biggest closure of all – the Waverley Route – is considered in some detail in this book, as it stripped hundreds of square miles of a railway service. Yet the viability of the line, present or potential, does not appear to have been discussed by the Scottish Regional board at all. This was not just some kind of prejudice against the Borders area; the Glasgow-based Board was equally prepared to close the Glasgow Central (Low Level) lines – now the Argyle Line – and even commissioned a study on how best to sell off the trackbed under the city.

While it is easy for the historian to display hindsight in assessing how the nation's transport assets were handled, surely the governors of the nation's railway system could have shown something known as foresight.

A brief note on currency: financial totals in this book are rendered in decimal, even if before 1971. Each amount is followed by the approximate 'levelling up' to present-day values. For example, in 1948 a bottle of whisky cost £3.50 (actually £3 10s in those days) but has been rendered as £3.50 (£39) in the text. Also, see the note in the Bibliography. The British term 'milliard' is used for thousands of millions, instead of the US 'billion'.

one

THE POLITICAL WILL

With whisky retailing at no less than 70*s* a bottle (£3.50 in today's currency, but at least ten times as much at today's values), it is no surprise that the *Glasgow Herald* noted that New Year in 1948 was being greeted mainly with sherry and port. The weather added to the dreichness of the scene, the West of Scotland experiencing so much rain over Hogmanay that the Old Firm match had to be postponed by twenty-four hours.

Irrespective of the weather, the chimes of midnight ushered in a new era for Britain's railway system; for the first time, rail transport was nationalised in the United Kingdom. The year 1948 was to see, for the first time, public ownership of the railway companies, comprising 52,000 miles of track, 20,000 locomotives and 1,230,000 goods wagons – all part of a Labour programme of placing the 'means of production, distribution and exchange' in the UK in a position to be directly controllable by democratically elected politicians. Also swept up into the Government's arms were seventy hotels and inns, 50,000 tons of shipping, 1,640 miles of canals, and no fewer than 50,000 houses, nearly all of these previously railway-owned.

Just as in 1923, when Scotland's five main railways were 'grouped' into two London-controlled super-companies, there was an initial 'identity crisis'. *The Herald* reported that telephonists receiving calls at the former LMS and LNER offices on 2 January answered with the words 'Railway Executive!'

Historians have expressed surprise at how little determined opposition there was to the concept of nationalising the nation's vital arteries. Ernest Barry wrote in his book *Nationalisation in British Politics* that 'It was noticeable at the time, and has since been emphasised by historians, that no serious objections were raised, and no anti-nationalisation campaigns organised, before 1949'.

The Economist magazine had commented in 1945 on the mildness of the Government's proposals (which would hardly have pleased the Labour faithful), while even *The Times* hanselled the first day of the new British Railways, 1 January 1948, with what Berry calls 'a faint cheer', commiserating the new organisation on having to inherit so much run-down equipment.

No lengthy recitation of statistics is necessary to illustrate the latter point, although the full impact of war conditions, following a period of ever-reducing investment, makes unhappy reading. The four main railways emerged from the effects of the Second World War with only 70 per cent of their targets achieved on track maintenance – perhaps not so shocking nowadays, but unprecedented in the mid-twentieth century. One passenger carriage in eight was under, or awaiting, repair in 1946, while the proportion of locomotives out of service had gone up by a third since 1938, and now stood at one in twelve. Goods wagons under or needing repair had increased in number by no less than 281 per cent since 1938!

In financial terms, the Railway Executive estimated that the impact of the war, including direct damage from enemy action, came to £179 million (£3.75 milliards). The economist Denys Munby summed it up in bloodless academic terms, by describing this as 'net disinvestment on the railways for many years on a massive scale'. In 1946 Chancellor of the Exchequer Hugh Dalton stated that 'the railways are in very poor physical shape'. Nobody argued with that.

One of the few critics of nationalisation of the transport industry was L.T.C. (Tom) Rolt. He purchased a copy of the Transport Bill in 1946 in order to find out what was going to happen to his beloved canals, but:

> my interest in transport generally led me to wade through the whole text of a measure which, according to the political dogma then prevailing, was going to rescue road, rail and canal transport from the thrall of 'private enterprise' and dedicate them to the especial service of humble British citizens like myself.

Mr Rolt's readers would, however, recall the author's classic work *Narrow Boat*, with its excoriation of the privately owned railway companies in their casual, indeed almost hostile, treatment of the canals they inherited in the 1923 'grouping'. And that included his favourite line, the Great Western! The new measure would separate railway and canal ownership and create an administrative structure for all Britain's canals.

One organ which was not making positive noises in 1947 was the *Railway Magazine*, which predicted that 'there is no reasonable prospect that the dull uniformity of standardisation will be offset by greater efficiency in operation'. More imaginatively, the magazine commissioned a painting by Reginald Myers of what a contemporary locomotive would look like in Post Office red, possibly to mobilise public opinion against such an outrage. They even took advice from the Postmaster General (a Labour appointee) to ensure a faithful rendering. It showed an LNER B1 numbered 1948 (by that company's numbering, it should have been a K3) and named *The New Era* – a more apt title might have been *The end of civilization as we know it*, which would have fitted the magazine's editorial leaning. In this author's eyes, the B1 looked far more attractive than in the begrimed, if lined, black which became the norm. Soon, the magazine was complaining about the Bill becoming law, on 6 August 1947, 'with practically no newspaper publicity'.

This is an interesting echo of a comment made by the editor of the North Eastern Railway (later LNER) magazine in 1923, complaining that the press was allocating to the grouping 'perhaps .0001 per cent of the space they sometimes devote to a really interesting murder'. The media never changes, it seems, in its treatment of railway matters!

While many branches of rail unions were organising social events to welcome the new dawn of 'workers' control' in 1948, the former owners had an understandably different view of the future. In an editorial, the *Glasgow Herald* deplored 'the disappearance of a huge block of stock which had for generations provided an acceptable form of investment for a large number of people in all walks of life'. The editorial writer need not have despaired: compensation offered to transport shareholders by the Government was not ungenerous. Clement Attlee, by now Prime Minister, had promised 'proper compensation' to private railway shareholders ten years earlier in 1937, while future Prime Minister Harold Wilson was quoted by economic historian T.R. Gourvish as arguing that British Transport stock (which replaced previous share allocations) was over-valued by no less than 20 per cent. This could well explain the Labour Government's apparent exasperation with the railways – a network the administration was anxious to bring into public ownership, but was not prepared to recapitalise and re-equip. Taxpayers' money – if Wilson was to be believed – was simply being channelled into shareholders' pockets instead of into railway managers' budgets.

For assisting in the winding-up process, the directors of the 'Big Four' railways received one-off payments from the BTC 'as remuneration for the services rendered by them', former LNER Board members receiving £5,250 (£115,000) each, with £6,250 (£137,500) going to those on the

LMS Board. 'Reasonable expenses' incurred during the transition to nationalisation were additional to this, as well as any payments their shareholders
decided to issue to them as valedictory gratuities. Southern Railway directors received £60,000 (£1.25 million) between them from shareholders
(although GWR directors refused such an offer), and they could then look
forward to the sale of their overrated company stock. Does any of this 'feeding frenzy' sound familiar to the modern reader?

Meanwhile in a 1947 issue of the *LNER Magazine*, chairman Sir Ronald
Matthews thanked the company's staff for their work over the years, and
concluded with a morale-boosting message: 'the railways have never failed
the country and they will not fail it now'. He viewed the railway system as
entering into another time of trial, almost as if fighting a continuation of
the Second World War. His staff were too busy partying to notice!

Indeed, while the idea of nationalisation nowadays seems unthinkable
even to Labour politicians, it was demonstrably popular with voters. The
number of Labour votes counted at the 1945 General Election weighed
in at over 12 million. In 1950, after the most intensive nationalisation programme in Britain's history, there were 13 million voting Labour, and in
the election in the following year (which Labour lost, thanks to the quirks
of the national electoral system), 14 million votes were cast for the party
which brought the nation's railways under public control.

The British voter obviously understood the benefits of nationalisation,
and how the process worked. Although Eastern Region reported an incident at King's Cross in the first week of 1948, when an inebriate attempted
to order the crew of a newspaper train to take him to Yorkshire, this was an
exceptional incident. The mantle of ownership sat lightly on the shoulders
of the British electorate.

Telephonists answering as 'the Railway Executive' from 1 January were
perfectly correct – direct government control of the rail system was still
in place, with a politically responsive committee communicating directly
to the operating departments of the existing four rail companies. The new
transport legislation inserted a British Transport Commission at the peak of
the hierarchy, effectively creating a new tier of bureaucracy, but also bringing together all varieties of inland transport except air traffic. There were
now five separate executives communicating directly with the transport
undertakings themselves. Joining the Railway Executive were similar bodies
dealing with docks and inland waterways, hotels, road transport, and London
Passenger Transport, in a democratically answerable organisation under the
new BTC. This had no more than six full-time members, including the

chairman, and was described by the *Economist* magazine as 'astonishingly small for the task'. Indeed, it would become even smaller with the death of Lord Ashfield in November 1948. Some BTC meetings took place with only three commissioners present.

Appointed to head these few was Sir Cyril, later Lord, Hurcomb, a career civil servant not known for his operational railway expertise, although the new edition of the *Dictionary of National Biography* credits him with 'negotiating' the 1923 grouping. His entry in that worthy reference book states: 'without being an expert on any subject, he learned enough to be taken seriously by experts'. This non-expert grandly announced that he 'hoped' to visit the new BR Scottish Region at the end of January 1948. Why it should take him a full month to travel to the north of the British system was not explained, his examination of his new fiefdom beginning with visits to London termini on 1 January. He did, in fact, reach Glasgow and Edinburgh within a fortnight, staying two days north of the Border.

On one matter Hurcomb can immediately be credited: he refused to allow the new nationalised rail system to be christened 'Great British Railways', even although the exclusion of lines in Northern Ireland would have legitimised such a misnomer. For a misnomer it would have been; 'Undercapitalised BR' or 'Politically Outcast BR' might have been more appropriate, as we shall see.

With the new British Railways divided into six regions, there was a possibility that railway matters, and those of associated transport, could be administered on a devolved basis, in a way that had not been possible in Scotland since the boardrooms of the pre-grouping companies were mothballed in 1923. Although a regional structure was agreed for the railways from the outset of the nationalisation process – although not enshrined in law – the hierarchical structure above it does not appear to have been thought through properly.

The new BR was governed at a policy-making level by the BTC in London, with the Railway Executive continued to make operational decisions, passing these along to regional chiefs who were effectively downgraded. Interestingly, the BTC was adamant that these regional heads could not be described as 'General Managers'. But the demarcation lines between BTC (policymakers), Railway Executive (executing policy) and Regions (executing policy within regions) were not exactly clear-cut. One legal critic (future Home Secretary David Maxwell Fyfe) said of the Act: 'There is much confusion as to its effect and its method of working ... a public corporation intervening between the government and the people'.

At one of its earliest sittings, the BTC's agenda included an item on the collapse of a staircase at Alloway Station in Ayrshire – something which could and should have been dealt with by regional managers. It was felt necessary too, to inform the BTC in November 1947 that North Leith was having its passenger service terminated, although trains appear to have been withdrawn in the previous year, and this was no doubt hurried through to avoid a referral to the new TUCC. Indeed, the Commission might have referred it themselves. Nevertheless, despite early hiccups, Scotland's railways were to be run, for the next seven years at least, by railwaymen. How they fared will soon be revealed.

With 3,730 route-miles, the new Scottish Region was almost the same size as the Western Region (3,782 miles), both representing 19 per cent of total BR mileage. Western was, however, busier, with some 30 per cent more train miles worked (in 1946, see Table I). On the other hand, the Western needed some 45 per cent more staff to operate this higher level of traffic, so perhaps Scottish was not so badly designed after all.

Obviously, the two main constituents of British Railways Scottish Region were the former LMS and LNER networks north of the Border and, in this 'marriage' of rivals, Scottish was unique. Indeed, the new Southern and Western regions were almost identical to the grouped railways SR and GWR, while the new North Eastern Region harked even farther back and simulated the pre-1923 North Eastern Railway. Interestingly, at one time it was proposed that *all* former LNER lines south of the Border be called the 'North Eastern Region', which would have looked strange in Norfolk.

In retrospect, it is significant that the establishment of a Scottish Region of the nationalised British Railways seems to have been uncontroversial, just as there had been little public outcry in 1921 when Scottish rail users and investors faced the diametric alternative, the 'lengthwise' splitting of the system north of the Border into East and West Coast camps, both with headquarters in London. Admittedly, at that time, the Scottish Home Rule Association had prepared an open letter to the Ministry of Transport on this perceived loss of Scotland's railways, but their claim of an 'overwhelming demand of the Scottish People for direct control of their own affairs' was unsubstantiated. The SHRA, not being a political party, was not involved in the electoral process anyway, and the Scottish National Party did not exist at that time. At least the Association wanted to see 'friendly co-operation with English railway systems' if an exclusively Scottish rail network had been attainable.

That there was no major public reaction to the grouping should not be wondered at: public opinion had much less influence on politicians than nowadays. There was no such thing as the public opinion poll; decisions affecting people's lives were taken just as often in the Boardroom as in the Commons chamber. Indeed, the United Kingdom was not even fully democratic in 1921, some seven years before female emancipation was completed.

In contrast, the creation of a Scottish railway region in 1948 was a sign of changing times in the history of British governance. The raft of legislation brought in by the new Labour administration – nationalising coal, public health, steel, as well as railways – meant that both legislators and administrators had to be fully aware of differences between English and Scottish legal systems and had to draft accordingly. Even the wartime coalition government, led by a Conservative prime minister, found that its 1944 Education Act would not apply north of the Border, and a separate act had to be passed for Scotland the following year. In a small, almost imperceptible, way, the setting up of BR Scottish Region was the first step on a road leading to devolution, and who knows where beyond?

Just as there was a perceived requirement for an exclusively Scottish Region of the new British Railways, so its ultimate governing body, the British Transport Commission, recognised a need for a totemic Scottish representative. Recruited to the new body in 1947 was Old Etonian Sir Ian Bolton, a Glasgow accountant with, needless to say, no operational railway experience. One area of expertise in which he excelled was in company liquidation, a point to remember as the Region's history unfolds. Bolton, a former LMS director, represented Scotland on the BTC alone for seven years, when he was joined as a part-time member of the Commission by Donald Cameron of Locheil, another Glasgow accountant, who was also distinguished by his lack of experience in transport administration.

The Railway Executive, the next tier down in the transport hierarchy, had received an unusual tribute to its efficiency in 1940 when the newly appointed Minister of Transport, Stonehaven-born Sir John Reith, bustled into his new post, not long after leaving the BBC, expecting his supercharged organisational powers to be required to their utmost. In fact, he was immediately advised by both his predecessor and his officials that 'the railways run themselves through the Railway Executive Committee', as his biographer put it. 'Magnificent, if incredible' was Reith's verdict, and he was quickly on his way to a new appointment. More's the pity. While remembered nowadays for his Calvinistic – and sometimes eccentric – personal beliefs in an increasingly materialistic world, his vision of the BBC as a non-commercial public service which has kept abreast of the highest technical standards in the industry would not have been an inappropriate model for a nationalised railway service. Reith had even postulated the establishment of a British transport commission in a speech to the House of Lords in 1942.

The RE had Scottish representation in the presence of Sir Wilfred Ayre, a Fife shipbuilder, who was recorded as having 'a particular interest in Scottish affairs', although he was only a part-time member and had no known operational experience of railways. At least the Executive mainly comprised career railwaymen, even if the choice of chairman – Sir Eustace Missenden, formerly of the Southern – is seen by historians (such as T.R. Gourvish) as a missed opportunity; the potential for the appointment to bring in a forceful individual who would fight the railways' corner in the 'corridors of power' was not realised.

The Region had unusual characteristics which differentiated it from its five fellows. No other region operated such a variety of shipping, for example short-range ferries, Britain-to-Ireland packet steamers, plus a wide range of seasonal pleasure craft on both salt and fresh water. And from seas and lochs, so to the mountains. Of the seventeen highest railway summits on BR, five were in Scotland, including the highest on the standard gauge network – at Druimuachdar, 1,484ft up on the Perth-Inverness main-line. The other four were, in order of height, Currour, Slochd Mhuic, Dava, and Beattock. Four of these were on trunk routes where London expresses were operated. At the other extreme, Scottish had the dubious privilege of operating two underground railways – with steam power. Both of these railway operations, existing at opposite poles of operational difficulty, would have benefited from the use of electric traction. Yet, in this nation of developing hydro-electric schemes, not one mile of BR Scottish Region was electrified.

Five other Scottish railway companies were nationalised along with the 'Big Two', all of them having been operated for the previous twenty-five years by the LMS and LNER:

Forth Bridge Railway	Previously worked by LNER
Dumbarton & Balloch Joint	LMS
Dundee & Arbroath Joint	LNER
Grangemouth Branch Railway	LMS
Princes Dock Branch Joint	LMS

In the first of these, the FBR, eight of the ten directors had been appointed by the two companies in the ratio of 3:1, with the LNER the larger subscriber as well as being responsible for the operation of trains over the bridge and its day-to-day maintenance. As recounted in this author's book, *London's Scottish Railways*, the two rail companies discovered, when taking over the FBR in 1923, that it had been operating illegally since 1873, as the law relating to the appointment of suitably qualified directors was not being observed. The LMS and LNER appear to have carried on the tradition! Nationalisation was one unarguable improvement.

What is perhaps surprising about the above list of railways taken into public ownership is that there were so few. In October 1948, the Ministry of Transport conducted a survey of nineteen British lines not 'vested' at the beginning of that year, with a recommendation in each case that they should continue to remain independent, as with the Manchester Ship Canal railway system, or be regarded as moribund, like the Festiniog. Curiously, the document states that, 'there are no non-controlled railways in the Scottish Region'. So much for the Glasgow Underground, surely the busiest narrow-gauge system in the UK! There were literally dozens of industrial lines which would compare with those surveyed south of the Border – and that survey was in itself curiously flawed, omitting the Snowdon Mountain and the Port of London lines – but it seems possible that the lack of Scottish content in the 1948 report reflected the reduced role of the Ministry of Transport in Scotland. Even before devolution, the Scottish Office included a Minister with responsibilities for transport north of the Border, particularly for roads and airports.

The new Scottish Region was also affected by the creation of the other four Executives. Road transport nationalisation, such as it was, meant the ending of the railways' financial interest in what was, up until then, Scottish Motor Traction, and this loss of revenue was substantial. So substantial, indeed, that the accountants winding up the 'Big Four' railway companies in 1948 had to seek special dispensation to prepare accounts lacking the final dividends payment, as the bus companies operated to a different financial year. The BTC granted this with the noticeably bureaucratic reservation that it would only be allowed 'if the amounts were arrived at by applying the normal accounting practice of each of the main lines involved'.

Hotels were allotted their own Executive, no doubt much to the disappointment of railway managers, but would not be lost to BR for more than seven years, and it is arguable that they should have stayed with the transport undertakings which had fostered them. Ferries and pleasure cruising were split unevenly between Executive and Commission in a way that can only be described as confusing, and will be dealt with later. Docks and harbours were a major loss – in prestige, if not revenue – but inland waterways were a different matter.

Central Scotland's three canals, the Monkland, Forth & Clyde and Union, had been rendered largely redundant by the railways which had come to own them in the nineteenth century, but these waterways barely survived railway ownership – the Monkland certainly did not – and the new Scottish Region was probably glad to avoid responsibility for them. In practice, there does appear to have been a delay in establishing a canal administration, and a BTC document advised in December 1947 that, 'existing arrangements on [railway-owned] canals and docks will continue for the time being'.

'As from January 1st 1948, the administration of the railways in Scotland will function as a single entity': these were the opening words of the document which was to be the 'Holy Book' of the new 'Railway Region of Scotland' as it was quaintly termed. Compiled by BTC Secretary Miles Beevor, and issued by the Executive on New Year's Day 1948, its title was *Instructions, No.1 Scottish Region*. Its pages were white within a buff cardboard cover, bibliographical details which might appear to be too trivial to mention, except that Scottish was alone in not being colour-distinguished. The second in the series treated the LMR to pink pages in its booklet, with the NER in tangerine, Eastern in light blue, Southern in green, and the Western in a bright daffodil shade! *Instructions* included location of HQ, posts particular to the Region – for example, a Chief of Police – and regional boundaries, illustrated by map. Interestingly, these showed that the boundary with the NER on the East Coast main-line would be immediately south of Burnmouth, rather than Marshall Meadows signalbox as it became (and had been the Area boundary in LNER days), and the 'frontier crossing' on the Border Counties line was north of Saughtree, although the actual border was crossed south of there, at Deadwater, and the LNER Scottish Area had reached almost to Hexham.

It must be said that this apparently casual drafting was in fact the result of careless specification in the original documents drawn up to define the regions. In November 1947, the Executive provided the BTC with its draft proposals for the six regions required by the Commission, and the boundaries 'specified' therein were decidedly curious – for example, Burnmouth was definitely specified as the Scottish/NER frontier on the East Coast.

In the appropriately named 'Debatable Land', the rail boundaries proved anything but permanent. The regional boundary with the LMR on the Waverley Route was shown as south of Harker, and an RE document issued in March 1948 specified this as Brunthill down distant signal, near the bridge crossing over the WCML. Within ten years it was moved northwards by no less than 11 miles so as to give the LMR a free hand in rationalising its approaches to the Kingmoor yard, and, one suspects, to the considerable military installations in the area. Down at Carlisle, Kingmoor depot was definitely in Scottish Region while the former NBR and LNER Canal depot was not. This may have been because the former North British branch to Silloth was being taken over by the North Eastern Region. Curiously, both it, and the Canal depot, were to pass to the LMR within six months, with ASLEF asking for an explanation for the depot's transfer.

Demarcation was simpler at Gretna Green, with the Sark river crossing marking the meeting place of the 'nations'. Decorative 'frontier' signs were not erected here until 1951, on either side of the bridge which represents the national and regional boundary – at least nominally. In a further clarification issued in March 1948, the boundary 'immediately south of Gretna' was specified as 'located at the Gretna Junction down distant signal, which will be in the Scottish Region'. This would extend 'Scotland' quite some way south of the river! All this was more than twenty years after similarly appropriate signs had been put in place at Lamberton, north of Berwick on the ECML.

Although there were to be adjustments in BR regional boundaries in November 1948 and April 1950, neither 'simplification', as the first of these was called, affected Scottish Region. As mentioned above, the Waverley Route was annexed by the LMR to the extent of an extra 11 miles, ten years later.

One of the first decisions the new Scottish Region might have been expected to make was to choose its own headquarters, and here the struggle between Edinburgh and Glasgow, familiar to all Scots, would have asserted itself. Certainly, the latter city had four main-line stations to the capital's two, but only because the rail builders of the nineteenth century had not seen the need for a through station, allowing the running of trains from London to, say, Aberdeen via Glasgow. In fact, the official *Instructions* specify Glasgow as the site of the regional HQ, but the first *BTC Monthly Report* makes it clear that no jobs would be lost in the Scottish capital – a neat compromise!

In 1946 the LMS and LNER employed 1,904 office staff in Glasgow and 605 in Edinburgh, so it made sense to settle HQ status on the existing majority. When an Edinburgh MP raised the new office arrangements with Minister Alf Barnes, he was told that the numerical superiority of railway administrators was the crucial point in the selection of Glasgow, not least because the LNER had located their goods offices there.

Incidentally, nationalisation certainly created no redundancies at senior managerial level; where the 'Big Four' companies (and the Cheshire Lines Committee) had been administered by 182 officials earning more than £1,750 (£35,000) in 1947, now 197 were needed, forty-four of them in the offices of the BTC and the Executive. In fact, on 15 September the Commission actually minuted that 'the numbers of office staff should, in the first instance, err if at all on the generous side'. Another sign of centralisation, if nothing worse, was that the overall salary bill for such posts increased by some £11,000 to £550,996 (£11 million) as 1948 got into its stride.

The HQ of the new organisation north of the Border was founded in 302 Buchanan Street in Glasgow, the staff magazine pointing out that this address had been in continuous use as railway offices for ninety-nine years already. It had housed the LMS Northern Division HQ from 1923-48, and was partly reconstructed in 1937. Edinburgh retained its former LNER Area HQ office accommodation at 23 Waterloo Place until the opening of the new HQ in 1967, although the new Chief Regional Officer was based in the west. He was specifically given the responsibility of deciding which departments were located in each city, or elsewhere on the system. One curiosity lay in the delegating of the region's Marine Superintendent, Captain Harry Perry, formerly of the LNER, to the new Railway Executive Docks Managers Committee, while the Region's representative on the Marine Committee was William Yeaman, the new Commercial Superintendent. Also puzzling was the continuation of LMS and LNER hotel superintendents' postings, as discussed in a later chapter. The *Instructions* did not suggest how these phantomesque staff would be paid!

Taking the post of CRO was Thomas Forbes Cameron who, although educated in Edinburgh, had begun his railway career as a traffic apprentice on the old North Eastern Railway in 1912. He had returned to Scotland in 1943 as acting Divisional General Manager on the LNER, so he had a healthy mix of 'foreign' and Scottish experience. Perhaps this was not quite 'foreign' enough for everyone on the BTC; the Commission's Secretary, Miles Beevor, had already suggested that 'distinction in the armed services' might prove a useful qualification for CRO appointment, and in September 1947 Beevor's chairman, Sir Cyril Hurcomb, sounded out Sir Robert Inglis on his availability. We will meet Inglis later in relation to Glasgow's transport problems; at the time of Hurcomb's approach, he occupied what the *Railway Gazette* described as 'the highest administrative position in the Control Commission for Germany (British Element)': effectively transport supremo in occupied Germany. Inglis's response to Hurcomb's approach is not recorded in the BTC documents.

Presumably, many believed that the unique demands of the Scottish regional post, requiring the tactful integration of former LMS and LNER managers, meant that a high-profile appointment from outside either of these companies was necessary. Diplomacy was served by appointing an LNER official and placing him in a former LMS office! In any event, Cameron's LMS counterpart was at retiring age anyway.

Cameron's new annual salary of £3,750 (£75,000) was greater than either of his Eastern or North Eastern Region counterparts, although only half that of the CRO of the new London Midland Region, the biggest of the six. Four Scottish posts – those of the Operating and Commercial Superintendents, Solicitor, and Civil Engineer – were salaried at £2,500 (£50,000), more than the basic salary for the CRO of the neighbouring North Eastern Region.

Historian, and former railway administrator, Michael Bonavia, damns Thomas Cameron with faint praise by saying that, although efficient, this 'did not always appear in his rather lugubrious assessment of situations'. Nevertheless, he credits Cameron with amalgamating former LMS and LNER senior staff entirely successfully. Bonavia did, however, comment on Cameron's curious insistence on retaining a flat in Edinburgh's North British Hotel and commuting over to Glasgow daily by car!

two

1948: THE FIRST YEAR

Britain's railways had been nationalised for about five hours when the first accident occurred, and it was in Scotland. A goods train incorporating petrol tanks was passing through Inver tunnel, on the Highland main-line north of Dunkeld, when a number of the vehicles became derailed. According to the somewhat lurid, and difficult-to-decipher newspaper reports (the incident is not mentioned in the authoritative *Railway Yearbook*), two tank wagons were left suspended only by their couplings over a 60ft drop, until 'employees of the Petroleum Board' succeeded in draining off their loads. There were no casualties. How wagons derailed in a tunnel ended up hanging over a chasm was not clear from the reports.

English newspapers were also quick to report that Scotland was the scene of the first strike on the nationalised railway system. Only two days into the new working regime, 300 blacksmiths were made idle at St Rollox after boilermen took industrial action in a dispute over 'piecework rates'. More positively, the *BTC Monthly Report* recorded that, since the workers had theoretically taken control of Britain's rail system, absenteeism was greatly reduced.

Meanwhile, BTC documents circulating in that first month of BR's existence noted that the unique problem of amalgamating LMS and LNER staff and working practices north of the Border was being addressed by Cameron's management team:

The departmental officers appointed by the Executive have settled down to their new responsibilities and are energetically tackling the many problems which are arising, with a view to the integration of the former LMS and

LNER Railways [sic] which constitute the Scottish Region, including a preliminary survey of the district organisation.

The new region was exactly a week old when its motive power managers received a memo from the south on a subject which seemed to crystallise the concept of a unified British railway.

Entitled 'Interchange of Locomotives Between Regions', the document, which can be seen in the National Archives of Scotland, records that the chairman of the BR Mechanical Engineers Committee had decreed that 'it was desirable to obtain a preliminary comparison of the performance of the different standard locomotives in service'. It should be briefly explained that the term 'Standard' referred to the classification used by the former companies – for example, the LMS had reduced its locomotive stock to seventeen classes, outside which there would be no new construction. This was a whopping reduction on the number of classes inherited by the LMS in 1923; the company history gave up listing them after 400! 'Standard' was also the designation used for the 70000 classes, led by the Pacific *Britannia* introduced three years later, but does not apply here (see the next chapter).

The Mechanical Engineering Committee, one of eighteen in the Railway Executive, comprised an impressive list of names from Britain's steam railways. chairman Robin Riddles presided over Oliver Bulleid from the former Southern Railway, the GWR's F.W. Hawksworth, A.H. Peppercorn from the LNER, and H.G. Ivatt from the LMS. The names of R.C. Bond and E.S. Cox would be familiar to all railway historians, while Scottish Region was represented by G.S. Bellamy, who was previously the Mechanical and Electrical Engineer for the LMS's Northern Division.

Testing of existing locomotive types was to be undertaken from 19 April onwards, with engines being exchanged between regions, and set to work on routes their designers could never have imagined them operating on. Riddles, formerly of the LMS, was in overall charge of what became known as the 'Locomotive Exchanges' – hardly an appropriate term for the comparative testing of a unitary body's equipment – with RE deputy chairman Sir William Slim being asked to handle publicity. Yet, documentary evidence suggests that a locomotive design team headed by the same R.A. Riddles was already drawing up preparations for new BR designs, so the Exchanges seem, in retrospect, to have been quite unnecessary. Not only that, but more scientific testing could have been undertaken at Rugby testing plant, opening in the October of that year.

The memo dated 8 January is itself of some interest to transport historians in that it specifies that the former LNER express locomotive to be tested was the 'latest 3-cylinder Pacific', in other words, one of the new A1s or A2/2s. Confirmed by the first *Monthly Report of the BTC*, these references contradict existing accounts of the 1948 Exchange trials; authors writing on this subject have always assumed that the streamlined A4 was requested as the LNER representative. But the former company's authorities in the new Eastern Region were having none of this request for a new-fangled Thompson or Peppercorn locomotive, and by April the *Railway Observer* announced that the A4 Pacific would be participating. The Eastern lines would be represented by Gresley's A4s, and nothing else! The machinations necessary to do this are not mentioned in Cecil J. Allen's candid, indeed sometimes almost scathing, account of the 1948 Locomotive Exchanges, so the ER presumably relied on no one having read the original memo too carefully!

In passing, the A4s gave a flawed performance in the trials, showing a tendency to run hot when under test; but the hill-climbing of the newly renumbered 60033 *Seagull* on the Devon banks of the Western Region was an eye-opener. Nevertheless, even the most uninformed 'train-spotter' could have queried if a streamlined locomotive could be regarded as 'stand-ard' and whether it was likely to form the basis of a new class. The lack of such discussion in the technical press suggests that railway enthusiasts were happy just to enjoy the spectacle.

Scottish interest in the trials was restricted to testing on the Perth-Inverness main-line. Here, three types described as 'mixed-traffic' were pitted against one another, not just for performance rating but also for coal and water consumption. On the face of it, the fact that one of these engines was a Pacific (4-6-2 wheel arrangement) while the other two were 4-6-0s, would seem to give the Southern 'West Country' competitor a dis-tinct advantage over its LMS 'Black 5' and former LNER B1 rivals. So it proved, with the Pacific *Yeovil* generating the highest horsepower rating on all of the five tested stretches (for example, no less than 1,950hp in the up direction between Dalwhinnie and Druimuachdar; the '5' was next highest with 1,160, and the B1 recorded 1,115). Mr Allen was however critical of *Yeovil's* high fuel consumption, an area in which the B1 performed well. In other words, the test produced a 'swings and roundabouts' conclusion of no help whatsoever to BR administrators. 'Black 5s' remained the mainstay on the Highland main-line where they had in no way proved their superiority against visiting loco designs.

Incidentally, *The Scotsman* had championed the B1 on the grounds that its livery – LNER green – perfectly matched the Highland scenery, as compared to the black of the LMS Class 5, or the malachite green of the SR Pacific. The latter's livery was 'altogether too gay and skittish to blend well with country through which the line runs'. One assumes that the journalist had his tongue firmly in cheek! But in view of the negative response to the Exchange in Scotland, these observations were probably just as informed as any other.

Nothing much resulted from these trials nationally either. If operational conditions were deemed worthy of including in the testing process – as opposed to the calibrations obtainable at Rugby – it would surely have been preferable to assess the selected locomotives on a single route – say Settle-Carlisle – and any subsequent transfers could be made on the basis of demonstrated need.

An even more productive exercise would have attempted to even up existing imbalances in motive power on different parts of the system. Within a few years, for example, Gerard Fiennes of the Eastern Region borrowed what he described as a 'spam can' (a SR Bulleid Pacific) which proved far superior to the former LNER 4-6-0s still employed on the Great Eastern. Similar trials of LNER Pacifics – too heavy for their own company's metals in East Anglia – could have been conducted on the Midland and West Coast main-lines with a view to permanent transfers, *not* an exchange, of some thirty or so engines.

Many of the 'West Country' and 'Battle of Britain' Pacifics were to spend their working lives sauntering at the head of light semi-fast passenger trains west of Salisbury, while 'Black 5s' were regularly rostered to express duties on the West Coast main-line as were B1s on the former Great Central and Great Eastern systems. Equally, Haymarket would daily supply Pacifics to haul five or six bogies on 35mph schedules from Edinburgh to Perth or via the Waverley Route to Carlisle while Polmadie's mixed-traffic engines wrestled with excessive loads over Beattock. This is a point to which I will return!

To say that the renumbering and 'rebranding' of BR locomotives in 1948 was complicated is to understate the case. A crest for the new concern was not immediately forthcoming, so 'BRITISH RAILWAYS' was the legend soon applied to tender and tank locomotives alike. In the case of some smaller tank locomotives, this necessitated the 'BRITISH' being transferred on *above* and in some cases, diagonal to, the 'RAILWAYS'.

Numbers were another confusing area. The LMS had used four-figure numbers for its ex-Midland Railway and more recent 'standard' classes, so these were soon being prefixed with 'M', particularly when outshopped from St Rollox. Former Caledonian and Highland engines carried five-figure numbers starting with 14000, and the first of these digits was soon to be upgraded from '1' to '5'. There was no need to renumber former G & SWR loco stock, as the last representative of that company, No.16905, was withdrawn in April, within four months of the dawn of public ownership. The LNER had already begun renumbering its stock in 1946, starting with its Pacifics, all of which were to have 60000 added, but most of that company's stock bore four-digit numbers, soon to be simply prefixed with a '6'. In effect, Scottish was ignored in this scheme, its operation of locomotives numbered with four, five and six, emphasising the region's dual origin, something which Tom Cameron and his staff were supposed to be unifying. In practice, no one north of the Border seemed too concerned – perhaps the Scots are accustomed to being divided!

Liveries were more complicated, and not exclusively a problem for Scottish Region, as there was no question of each region having its own (although that might have been worth considering). Instead, the previous practice was continued, of painting different types of locomotive according to the work they undertook. Unfortunately, it has to be said that the BTC did not noticeably assist in launching the corporate image of British Railways. Express passenger engines began appearing in blue as well as green, with mixed traffic types bearing green or lined black, although the national 'picture' can only be described as confused. It was no wonder; when the Railway Executive put up a national liveries plan to the Commission on 31 December 1947, the reaction the next day (New Year's Day was no holiday in the south in those days) was woolly and unhelpful. The minutes for the BTC's meeting, on 5 January, show that the Commission 'reserved any conclusion [although?] in favour of a suitable shade of green for passenger steam locomotives [and] distinctive colouring for locomotives used on the principal express passenger trains, and for dining cars'. The last point was dropped in the following month; restaurant cars would be liveried in the same colour as other passenger carriages. A separate livery would have been logical, however, as restaurant cars were transferred to the Hotels Executive by the following July. One livery suggestion included in this document, and apparently accepted by the BTC, was 'golden ochre' for main-line Diesels! Sir William Wood, former LMS President, and now a Commission member, muddied the waters even more, expressing approval for LMS 'red' *or* LNER green *or* Caledonian Blue, the last of these colours to be restricted to no more than 125 locomotives likely to haul the most prestigious of expresses. This must have been an exasperating time for railway managers!

Nowadays, any kind of corporate redefinition would be placed in the hands of public relations consultants, whose logos, slogans, and branding would never be challenged by anyone, as happened in recent years with the nonsensical renaming of the Post Office.

Nevertheless, as if to convince the public that BR knew what it was doing with its new stock, Leith Central Station hosted a 'fashion parade' of liveries in May 1948, with the 'modelling' being done by A3 No.60091 *Captain Cuttle*, A2 No.60501 *Cock o' the North*, B1 No.61245 *Murray of Elibank*, and one of the few named 'Black 5s', No.45157 *The Glasgow Highlander*. An unusual item of rolling stock was the US-designed stainless steel 'Silver Princess' coach being tested at the time on such services as the 'Flying Scotsman'. In describing the event, opened by the Lord Provost of Edinburgh and attended by 6,500 members of the public over three days, the *Railway Observer* neglected to mention which colours were worn by each engine, although we do know from other sources that the A3 was resplendent in a purplish shade of blue – not specified to the BTC – and the A2/2 in LNER green. Nationally, the picture was just as confused.

As late as May, the technical press was carrying an announcement about liveries for both locomotives and carriages. The former would be blue, with red, cream, and grey lining, for 'the most powerful express locomotives', green with similar lining for 'other' express engines, and lined black for mixed traffic units. Carriages would be 'plum and spilt milk' for most express duties, but chocolate and cream for the Western. Suburban stock on every region except the Southern would have maroon livery with golden yellow/black/golden yellow lining. Fourteen routes would have train sets made up in these colours, the Scottish interest being centred on the East and West Coast main-lines and Glasgow-Aberdeen. The public was invited to send comments about these to 'Box A' at the Railway Executive, 222 Marylebone, London NW1!

Consistency in painting carried out at Scottish Works was seriously lacking. St Rollox began to apply lettering in white, and with BR name totems different from anywhere else. Cowlairs was painting B1s, D11s, even K2s, in green, even when renumbered, with lettering (LNER, naturally) in yellow. Kilmarnock Works painted all lettering in 'straw colours'. Inverurie used BR totems from mid-March and applied green to the B12 4-6-0s, which were now black south of the Border. Lochgorm (Inverness) removed all existing number-plates as routine, while these were now being universally fixed down south. Meanwhile, the new A2 Pacific *Tudor Minstrel* was seen operating trains between Waverley and Glasgow with a builder's plate reading 'LNER 1948'! What was it that the *Railway Magazine* had predicted about 'the dull uniformity of standardisation'?

The year 1948 saw the restoration of some pre-war traditions, such as the 'Flying Scotsman' service running non-stop between London (King's Cross) and Edinburgh (Waverley), albeit on an unambitious schedule. Similarly West Coast expresses were bound by a 60mph speed limit, at least officially. While A4s headed the non-stop service over the Border in Berwickshire, the West Coast lines saw the introduction, virtually from BR's first month, of diesel-electric power. And with no hint of golden ochre!

Just before nationalisation, Derby Works had turned out, with English Electric traction equipment, the first of two 1,600hp Diesels. Numbered 10000 and 10001, they were designed by H.G. Ivatt, who then received authority to construct two entirely new members of Stanier's 'Duchess' class to operate in comparison with the new form of motive power. The new Pacifics incorporated such innovations as roller-bearings and improved firebox arrangements, all designed to improve the engine's ability to undertake lengthy rosters with a reduced 'turnround' time.

If the LMS had intended an exhaustive comparison programme of testing – why else produce two updated examples of Stanier's pre-war steam design? – the nationalised railway management had no such intention, it seems. It was in fact in a Glasgow newspaper's correspondence columns that the matter received detailed consideration. A Mr Menzies wrote to the *Herald* strongly backing the Pacifics, pointing out that the Diesels could only equal one of their steam rivals if coupled together. This meant that their combined weight was 50 per cent more than that of a 'Duchess' Pacific, while their length was twice as great, possibly necessitating a reduction in the number of coaches hauled, where platform length was an issue. Interesting points these, and they were echoed by Railway Executive chairman Sir Eustace Missenden in a paper he wrote two years later (see Bibliography), but Mr Menzies had bestirred a formidable opponent.

Cecil J. Allen was visiting Glasgow in that first week of 1948, on a speaking engagement undertaken with O.S. Nock to lecture to Scottish schoolchildren on the wonders of the modern railway system (presumably not British Railways, then). Mr Allen also wrote to the *Herald*, taking up cudgels on behalf of 10000/1, pointing out that their greatest advantage was their guaranteed availability. Perhaps he was premature – the whole point of constructing an improved version of the 'Duchess' (Nos 46256/7) was to investigate whether technical improvements could increase steam locomotive mileage, and the new BR administration do not appear to have prosecuted the comparisons as thoroughly as the LMS had been preparing to.

Detailed results would have been interesting: as it was, what mileage figures emerged were inconclusive and disappointing from the steam enthusiast's point of view. The two new Pacifics, with their modifications designed to lengthen annual mileages, ran approximately 5,080 miles a month (No.6256) and 4,070 (No.6257). In comparison, unmodified No.6240 accomplished 6,018 miles a month. No 'Duchess' achieved more than 90,000 miles annually, not even the last two, intended to reach the 100,000 mark. As a matter of interest, Scottish-based A4 No.60009 *Union of South Africa* ran a higher total mileage than any of its LMS rivals – 1.85 million approximately – at an average of 5,530 monthly. It enjoyed some three years more 'life' than the 'Duchesses', but that fact merely reinforces the theory that the LMS Pacifics, with their limited water capacity tenders, were never able to achieve their full potential.

In contrast, the two Diesels are recorded as having notched up 50,000 miles in three months, creditable indeed when their availability figures could be affected by staff unable to remedy minor problems, the equivalent of which would not 'fail' a steam locomotive. On the other hand, construction costs, which would have favoured the Pacifics, do not appear to have been compared; not long afterwards, in January 1950, Missenden costed a Pacific express passenger locomotive at £17,000–£18,000 (£350,000), compared to a 1,600hp Diesel, effectively one of the Ivatt locos, at £70,000–£80,000 (£1.5 million). Incidentally, steam looks underpriced, even for the time (*Britannia* cost over £20,000 to build in 1951) when adjusted up to present currency levels, but, the cost of the two LMS main-line Diesels came in at £66,000 the pair, of which £5,000 was regarded as recoverable, covering the forging of reusable jigs. Missenden should have good reason to remember this costing – as RE chairman he was asked by the BTC in May 1948 why there had been a four-fold increase in the cost of building these pioneering locomotives. Apparently the £15,000 cost per pair had escalated to £66,000 'as the original cost was based on the assumption, since proved erroneous, that the work to be undertaken by the Railway Company would involve costs very similar to those incurred in building locomotive tenders. The estimate was prepared on a cost per ton basis accordingly'. Steam, on the other hand, would benefit from considerable economies of scale, all the resulting economies being achieved entirely 'in house'. Missenden's doubling of Diesel construction costs suggests a poor memory, or a determination to build in an excess factor!

Certainly, when operating together, the two Diesel units were perfectly capable of keeping the (admittedly very slow) schedule on the 'Royal Scot' between Euston and Glasgow; after all, they were almost equal to a later 'Deltic' in terms of power. They even achieved the 'Royal Scot' journey non-stop on 1 June the following year, which a 'Duchess' could never do. Although not based in Glasgow, these pioneering Diesels were nevertheless an almost daily sight at the city's Central Station, and the comfort of their cabs must have been an eye-opener for former LMS footplate crews. Locomotive engineer E.S. Cox records that 10000 'rode like a charm from the first day'.

Not surprisingly, they seemed able to inspire affection among those who built and tested them. In a letter to the author, Alan Robinson, a member of the Electrical Section of the CME's department at Derby, tells of a cab ride from Glasgow southwards on the 'Royal Scot' working, 'We were checked all the way from Eden Valley Junction [just south of Penrith] to Crewe. All the same it was some ride!' Although a steam enthusiast, Mr Robinson recalls how his departmental colleagues were determined to out-shop at least one of the Diesels before the LMS lost its identity on 1 January 1948. And it was the British taxpayer who had to pick up the bill, which went 400 per cent over budget (see this author's *Railways for the Nation*). Nevertheless, 'They are the only Diesels for which I have any affection', Mr Robinson says.

The apparent consensus in 1948 in favour of renewing steam's grip on Britain's railways is worth considering at greater length. As we have seen, the former LMS had been experimenting with diesel power for main-line services, while the erstwhile LNER Board of Directors had decided, in July 1947, to invest in a fleet of twenty-five diesel-electric locos similar in power rating to LMS 10000/1. Incidentally, the principal base for this fleet was to have been Leith Central, despite the fact that it was an active passenger station. The LNER proposal was curious, even suspicious, considering that the company was in the middle of a renewed construction programme for no fewer than eighty Pacifics. The Diesel plan could have been bluster, an attempt by this company, at the forefront of opposing nationalisation, to project an image of an enterprising concern whose directors and share-holders deserved maximum compensation.

In contrast to all this, Robert (Robin) Riddles, the former LMS locomotive engineer responsible for designing the fustian 'Austerity' 2-8-0 and 2-10-0s for the War Department, prevailed with his plans for a reinvigorated programme of steam traction on the new British Railways. In this, he was undoubtedly justified by the unpredictability of oil imports as the years of peacetime rolled on. A plan to convert 1,229 steam locomotives from coal to oil firing in the late 1940s had to be abandoned before it reached three figures, with no less than £1.22 million (£27 million) already spent on storage depots.

In a report to the BTC on 16 February 1948, the Commission's Secretary Miles Beevor (no doubt still celebrating having an A4 recently named after him!) stated that a shortage of rail tank wagons was the limiting factor, and that no more than 108 engines could be converted in the foreseeable circumstances. When the conversion programme was up and running, it was anticipated that 4,000 tank vehicles would be required, although use could be made of those previously carrying aviation fuel. The NAS copy of this report carries an additional handwritten comment indicating concern over increased annual costs if the scheme continued, and this may well have been written by Sir Ian Bolton.

Suffice to say that there was a Ministry directive to abort the conversion plan in December 1947 (two months before Beevor reported to the BTC), with some depot installations continuing until the following March. The only such conversion in Scotland, only 90 per cent complete, was at South Leith (according to the report; the actual location was Craigentinny, opposite the carriage depot) where three vertical tanks, with a total capacity of 250,000 gallons, were erected. Carlisle Canal also underwent some preparatory work. As only one former LNER engine was converted, a WD 2-8-0 apparently operating out of Doncaster, it seems unlikely that oil-fired locomotives were found on former LNER lines north of the Border. On the former LMS, the most northern conversion was at Carlisle (Durranhill), but this was no longer a working MPD, thus necessitating two servicing sessions between rosters, and no refuelling would be possible until the engine had returned to England. The cause of diesel – or any oil-fuelled form of locomotion – can hardly have been advanced by all this.

Although not a problem at the time, the plentiful supply of oil would prove rather more variable in years to come. In 1957, when the first DMUs began to operate between Edinburgh and Glasgow, their introduction was restricted by a political retraction in oil supplies, caused by the Suez crisis. Riddles' critics could point out that there had been a major coal shortage in 1946/7, but he could argue that, in the long-term, coal-fired steam had a guaranteed, indigenous, fuel supply.

All this was in line with the thinking at the top of the Railway Executive. In January 1950, chairman Sir Eustace Missenden specified the availability of coal as a major factor in renewing steam traction on BR – the first

'Britannia' Pacific emerged one year later – but fuel availability was not the only doubt the chairman entertained as to the future of diesel traction on main-line work. Missenden believed that 1,600hp was the most that could be generated within the profile of a single-unit locomotive, and that twin-working would be undesirable where train length might be a problem, just as Glasgow's Mr Menzies had believed.

The chairman predicted that Diesels might find their place on the system as shunting engines, or in working secondary routes in support of electrified main-lines, and (only possibly) operating railcar services. 'It is most unlikely that Diesel traction will sweep this country as it has done in the USA' – this was the opinion of the operating head of Britain's railway system just five years before the publication of the Modernisation Plan! As late as 1953, the Executive proposed a new construction programme for push-pull stock for steam-hauled branch services, in preference to DMUs. This Riddles-inspired proposal 'infuriated' BTC chiefs, according to Dr Bonavia.

Incidentally, the Austerity freight locomotives designed by Riddles occupy a small but significant niche in post-war railway history. When hostilities ended, the LNER purchased 200 of these units, but when the Railway Executive decided to acquire a further 553 locomotives – on loan to BR, but intended originally, Riddles is alleged to have said, to be dumped at sea after the war – the Executive benefited from buying 'in bulk', acquiring these for a unit price of around £2,700 each. Nevertheless, this appears to have left BTC chiefs unimpressed, and was seen as placing too high a reliance on improvised, non-standard equipment. Indeed, the NAS records contain a later RE request for an extra thirty-nine 'Austerities', with forty-three tenders, costed in March 1949 at £200,000, making the unit cost nearly twice as expensive as the previous purchase, and that was before the individual reconditioning cost of £2,300 was taken into account. The records are unclear on this, but it would appear that this later order – and one minute reference specifies 'LMS-type 2-8-0s' (possibly Stanier 8Fs, or was this a reference to the LMS origin of their designer, Robin Riddles?) – did not go ahead. BR was to operate 753 Riddles-designed 2-8-0s and 2-10-0s, and needless to say these most plebeian of locomotives were still defying their watery destiny well into the 1960s.

The Scottish angle to all this, was, firstly, that no less than 422 of these 'Austerities' 2-8-0s were constructed at NBL Glasgow (BR numbering 90000-90421) and, secondly, that the larger 2-10-0s (90750-74, again NBL) operated north of the Border almost exclusively. The latter point was a little surprising, since all former NBR yards had never seen freight locomotives larger than a J37 0-6-0 (apart from ROD 2-8-0s operating during and immediately after the First World War).

So serious was the coal shortage by the end of the Second World War that the amount of steam locomotive mileage was having to be monitored and restricted. In 1947 the 'target mileage' agreed for the following year for steam-hauled passenger duties was fixed at 3,107,360 – 6 per cent up on 1947, but 4 per cent down on the previous year's figure. Three expresses on the East Coast Main Line were stripped from the timetable in 1947, while excursion trains were not permitted. The authorities began to reassess this rather harsh restriction as soon as nationalisation was in place. On 22 January 1948, Transport Minister Alf Barnes wrote to Hurcomb relaxing this ban, particularly for children's outings, but continuing it for sports events, or for local holidays on days when factories were working:

> as we are anxious that this should not be construed as indicating a change for the better in our economic situation ... rather it should be presented as a decision not to continue an emergency measure made necessary last year by the exceptional need to build up stocks of coal. I have agreed to consult the Chancellor of the Exchequer as to the form and appropriate time for such an announcement.

Bringing the Chancellor into a discussion on excursion trains indicates a rather different world from nowadays, when the Treasury no longer even pronounces on interest rates! Within ten days of Barnes's letter, BR was disputing the continuing ban on sporting specials, and with some success; by the time the FA Cup Final came around, nearly a million people were transported by special trains in the four months up to May 1948.

As we have already seen, Robin Riddles believed that the steam locomotive had plenty of life left in it, but acknowledged that, in the longer term, electricity was the principal motive power of choice. After being appointed at Riddles's behest to the highest salary for any technical official employed by the Executive, and only £500 less than some of the committee members, C.M. Cock undertook the chairmanship of a joint BR/LT committee on the provision of electric traction, as he was well-qualified to do, following his career on the Southern.

The Cock committee failed to reach any long-term conclusions about what form electric traction should take on Britain's railways, except the possibility of using a comparatively low-powered fifty cycle system, which was soon tried out on the Lancaster-Morecambe-Heysham line. No recommendations were made about moving away from the 1500V dc overhead system for all regions except the Southern, and this was installed on the former Great Eastern lines and over the Pennines at Woodhead. Yet as early as 1956, BR decided on the 25kV ac system as standard, with its facility for using lighter catenary. Unfortunately, Cock's lack of direction led to an impossibly pessimistic estimate of the costs of electrifying Glasgow's suburban lines, denying the least profitable region on BR an electric train service until the 1960s.

How was the new Scottish Region faring as 1948 opened out? Documents circulating between Executive and Commission in the summer analysed all regional performances for the months of March and April in both profitability and operational efficiency, and Scottish came out well in one set of figures, but not so well in the other.

While all six regions took £9.76 million (£195 million) in gross passenger revenue, out of a total national income of £28.29 million (£565 million) from all rail operations, and including ships and hotels – these figures showing increases, both in forecast and in comparison to the same period in the previous year – Scottish was not performing to the national standard. Rail operations showed the heaviest net loss in Scotland in the four weeks to 18 April, the system losing no less than £369,000 north of the Border. Nearest to Scottish was the Western, with a loss of £306,000, while the LMR and Southern lost only £28,000 and £18,000 respectively. In contrast, both the Eastern and North Eastern showed a profit of at least £70,000. Scottish (and the Western) could argue that large parts of their systems were dependent on holiday revenues, and this appeared to be supported by the returns from hotels and restaurant cars, which made a loss in all regions. The Hotels Executive which would take over these aspects of 'railway' operation, was not commissioned until July. On the LMR, the loss on hotels was much greater than that on rail services, no less than £34,000.

Punctuality was, however, something else again; in the four weeks to 20 March, Scottish express trains showed very good 'on time' statistics compared to the average for the six regions. Although only 58.4 per cent arrived at their destination punctually in Scotland, this was half as good again – and on the second largest sample – as the national average of 40.7 per cent, with the Eastern (a partner region in the running of Anglo-Scottish expresses) coming in at only 22.9 per cent. The Southern recorded 55.8 per cent punctuality with its express steam services and 60.6 per cent with electric but, with the technical press commenting frequently on the poor quality of locomotive coal available, the all-steam Scottish Region's figures appear all the more impressive.

Scottish did well with all other (non-express) passenger services, recording 79.6 per cent 'on time' arrivals, compared to 82.5 per cent for steam on the Southern and 89 per cent for LMR electric. Surprisingly, Southern electric only achieved 68.7 per cent, with North Eastern electric services registering 78.4 per cent. Scottish steam proved superior to comparable services on all other regions except Southern.

Bearing in mind that the unique problem facing Scottish – namely, the amalgamation of two rival systems – was sufficient for the BTC to have considered requesting the release of a senior military transport officer from occupied Germany, it hardly needs to be emphasised that Cameron and his management team had achieved a considerable amount in a short time.

While locomotive trials were being carried out in various parts of the United Kingdom early in 1948, most south of the Border, rail managers and footplate crews found themselves facing a trial of a very different kind in August of that first year of BR operations. It was created by freak weather conditions in south-east Scotland, but it was to have repercussions throughout both Scotland and England.

Although it might be thought more appropriate for a meteorological history than one dealing with railways, a brief account of the 1948 floods is necessary here. The facts are that rainfall had already been heavy in the Scottish Borders in the first week of August 1948, but on Thursday 12th, phenomenal weather conditions occurred. Around 400 million tons of water fell on the Tweed Valley in a twenty-four-hour period, equivalent to more than 5in of rain over an area of 130sq. miles. Streams and rivers were turned into torrents, and embankments took on the consistency of melting chocolate. Older residents still recall the sight of animal carcasses floating past their houses. It was a miracle that no human life was lost.

The area's railways were overwhelmed. The East Coast main line was cut in thirteen places, with seven bridges swept away and six landslips. The Waverley Route suffered four landslides, while the St Boswells–Reston and Jedburgh branches were so badly damaged that they lost their passenger services forever, the former of these two branches being cut in two and never reconnected. A train with fifteen passengers was reported stranded overnight at Chirnside on this line.

Michael Bonavia personally visited the area during this crisis, expressing amazement at the extent of the damage. The following November, the BTC approved remedial work costing £720,000 (£14.4 million), approximately one-sixth of which was for bridge replacement by McAlpine's. For the first few days of the emergency, all East Coast traffic had to go through

Carlisle, where the queues of trains awaiting a platform space were reminiscent of wartime. Two days after the emergency, the 13.15 southbound from Edinburgh (Waverley) was five hours in transit before it cleared Carlisle, and still had to reach Newcastle before turning south. Obviously, former LMS traffic was also affected. The Tweed Valley line escaped surprisingly lightly considering it was in the centre of the storm; the only real damage was a landslip at Carham. Once this was repaired, rail managers were able to look at the line as a useful deviation for the ECML, which was clearly going to be out of commission for some time (in fact, three months).

With the repair at Carham being completed by the 16 August, the Tweed Valley line was reopened, allowing the rerouting of such East Coast expresses as the 'Flying Scotsman' – scheduled to be non-stop between Edinburgh (Waverley) and London (King's Cross) – via the northern half of the Waverley Route and the Tweed Valley. What happened next was an extraordinary passage of improvisatory railroading excellence: express enginemen decided that 'non-stop' should be exactly that, even if it meant breaking records!

Previously, the British record for a journey without stops had been set by the LMS over the 401 miles between Euston and Glasgow Central, but BR's improvised diversionary route from King's Cross to Waverley via the Tweed Valley line in 1948 was some 7 miles longer. It required crews to zealously husband their water supplies as the water-troughs nearest to Edinburgh were at Lucker in Northumberland, some 88 miles to the south. Southbound trains, faced with a trying gradient of nearly 10 miles up Falahill Bank, had no prospect of 'rushing' the climb, and the Valley line had to be negotiated at no more than 25mph.

In the circumstances, just getting through would have been enough, but a number of 'top link' drivers thought differently. The decision to run non-stop did not come from on high – it was made in the engine-crews' mess-room and on the footplate. Seventeen such trips were made between 24 August and 18 September, eight of them northbound, when the A4s concerned had already clocked 300 miles without a break.

In the book *Non-Stop!*, this author discussed the work of Haymarket drivers in bringing the non-stop 'Flying Scotsman' through the 1948 floods by the Tweed Valley line. It was generally assumed that 9 September was the date of the final non-stop trip northbound, as related by the late O.S. Nock, but subsequent evidence suggests otherwise. On 21 August, Alan Robinson (quoted above for his experience with LMS Diesels), was a young clerk in BR's CME department at Derby, taking advantage of his travel privilege by journeying to Edinburgh via London on the famous train. He records his memories thus:

> Whilst I shudder at the very thought of contradicting O.S. Nock, we did have a non-stop run on the 21st [September], via Kelso, behind No.60024 *Kingfisher*. As a callow youth of 17 I did not have the gravitas to ask for the names of the crew! That day remains as one of the highlights of my love affair with railways. I did not record the arrival time [at Waverley] – my memory is of just after 7 p.m. [rescheduled arrival time] Certainly I was walking around Haymarket shed at 7.45 p.m. according to my notes.

Nobody had expected records to be broken. All this was the result of team spirit, pride in the job, public spiritedness, call it what you will. If the rest of the history of British Railways was going to be like this, there need not have been any fear for the future as far as operational matters were concerned.

three

OLD CUSTOMS DIE HARD: SCOTTISH REGION TO 1955

The last Scottish locomotive to be retired from normal service was a J36 0-6-0 No.65345, withdrawn from Thornton depot on 4 June 1967. She was a mere sixty-seven years old, younger than some of her sisters, such as No.65224 *Mons* (seventy-two years) or No.65210 (seventy-four). In other words, despite the promise of a new dawn under public ownership from 1948, and despite the thousands of millions of pounds poured into the rail system following the announcement of the Modernisation Plan of 1955, professional railwaymen were still operating Victorian steam locomotives daily in the twentieth year of nationalised British Railways.

Longevity of steam locomotive classes was scarcely a matter of comment in early BR days – neither railwayman nor layman expected unbraked coal trains to be hauled by anything other than six-coupled steam engines older than the men driving them – and that was saying something; footplate crewmen did not reach 'top link' status until well into the second half of their careers. In 1953, when the Railway Executive was taken to the Court of Session for allegedly setting fire to an Edinburgh lineside building through a locomotive's emission of sparks, the engine was claimed by the pursuer to be old and not properly maintained. When the RE demurred on this, the locomotive's number and age were demanded, two facts which the defendants declined to give in correspondence.

The point about all this was that the lack of new traction on BR was no secret even from those with no interest in railways. Parliament was told in 1946 that the average LNER locomotive was thirty-two years old, but even into the 1960s express trains were powered regularly by thirty- to forty-year old locomotives. The passenger coaches they hauled were little younger; the BTC learned ten days into nationalisation that 23.6 per cent of coaching stock was thirty-five years old or more.

What is perhaps surprising about this extension of the life of the successors to George Stephenson's finest was, firstly, that there was little concerted effort to deploy express steam power as effectively as possible and, secondly, that the decision to introduce 'Standard' class units seemed to have such little logic behind it. To take the second point first, 999 'Standard' steam locomotives were built in BR workshops between 1951 and 1960. They numbered twelve classes, designed to undertake a variety of jobs but to have high route availability and with technical features permitting easy maintenance.

Despite being literally designed by committee, most of the designs were successful – in the case of the 'Britannia' Pacifics and 9F 2-10-0s, conspicuously so – but the ordering policy was curious. It would surely have been more appropriate to have 'road tested' a few examples of each design from each of the issuing works, before deciding on the numbers to be ordered, and whether they (like, say, the Class 4 4-6-0 of the 75000 class) should be ordered at all. And why produce the 'Clan' Pacifics when the larger 'Britannia' had such high route availability anyway? The 'Britannia' did not operate on Perth-Inverness and the Fort William lines, but neither did the 'Clan' design, with the exception of a one-week tour of duty on the West Highland for 72001 in 1956.

The creation of this 'Standard' class in particular raised a question about its provenance – and this was very much a Scottish question. The 'Clan' Pacifics were lighter versions of the 'Britannias' and rated only at 6MT to the larger engine's 7 when the 'Clans' were outshopped in 1952 (although this power classification changed within a few years, to 7P6F and 6P5F respectively). According to the RCTS history of the 'Standard' classes, the 'Clans' were originally, and appropriately, intended to operate on the Perth-Inverness main-line, but this plan was changed as the 'Black 5s' already working there were so new. For this reason, these even newer Pacifics were not fitted with the necessary token-catching apparatus, which was necessary for exchanging signalling 'tokens' at speed when entering and leaving single-line sections. Yet the traditional concept of cascading motive power stock involved fairly new engines – in this case, the Class 5s – being redistributed after being replaced by even newer units, and the railways had been doing this for decades.

Having Pacifics operating on the Highland main-line might have been interesting, and the 'Clans' certainly should have been allocated there. Standard Class 5s began working the route as early as 1952, undermining the RCTS theory for the non-deployment of 'Clans', while loading tables from 1957 include a listing for Class 6P locomotives, 'Clans' occupying this category along with the former LMS 'Jubilee' or ex-LNER V2 classes, neither of which were seen on this line either. One of the BR Standard design team, E.S. Cox, believed that the 9Fs would also have found their way to this line if steam power had been required for longer.

The *BR Magazine* gave a warm welcome to the first of the Clans (named in alphabetical order, this meant *Buchanan*), although the weather at the beginning of 1952 was anything but warm, and the locomotive's first visit to Edinburgh is believed to have been halted by a foot of snow encountered at Midcalder. Soon, driver-turned-author Norman McKillop was sampling the new Pacific with a footplate ride on a Glasgow-Liverpool service, and registering approval. Mr McKillop was particularly impressed by the boiler, persuading the fireman to over-generate steam to the point of testing out the safety valves. The now-retired driver, forever associated with the A3 Pacific *Spearmint*, sensed that the Clan's maximum was 80mph, and it would have been interesting to know if he felt that the new locomotive's employment on express passenger work out of Polmadie was the ideal use of a lightweight Pacific when the Highland main-line and the routes to Stranraer were deprived of such increased motive power.

This author recalls seeing a 'Clan' on a train of sugar beet empties only a few years after its construction, so to say that these attractive engines never found their niche is an understatement. Interestingly, after the appearance of the ten 'Clans', another fifteen were planned for both the Scottish and the Southern regions. Their appearance would have compounded the question as to why they were built at all, as the Southern already had more Bulleid Pacifics than it had appropriate work for – and no fewer than fifty *more* of the Bulleids had been built under BR anyway.

To cap it all, for every two standard units built, no fewer than three non-standard pre-nationalisation types were turned out in the first eight years of BR, many of them from private manufacturers. That these orders were for such stalwart designs as the LNER B1 (136 built for BR) and the LMS 'Black 5' (100) suggests that there was no need to build entirely new designs with the same power rating.

But the programme to build Standard steam locomotives in the early 1950s should not be allowed to camouflage the fact that there was precious little else in the way of financial regeneration benefiting the railway network at this time (see Table II for the Scottish aspect to this lack of recapitalisation). In the words of economic historian T.R. Gourvish, 'The early years of nationalisation were a bleak period in terms of investment, and many writers have traced some of the railways' enduring problems to this situation'.

This forces a return to the other point outlined above, namely the uneven allocation of existing express passenger power between the former LMS and LNER systems. This was not of course a peculiarly Scottish problem, and had its roots in the curious decision by the former company, the LMS, to perpetuate the Midland Compound 4-4-0 design in the 1920s, despite its being overshadowed by the appearance of such larger and more powerful types as the GWR 'Castle' 4-6-0 or the LNER A1 Pacific even at that time.

While the Compounds could produce performances far beyond their design capability, and were highly respected by drivers on both sides of the Border, their reputation was built on the efforts of a hard-pressed fireman. A Compound travelled 400 miles non-stop with the Edinburgh section of the 'Royal Scot' in 1928, a distance that no Gresley Pacific was to equal for twenty years, but the comparatively tiny tender hitched to the engine had no corridor connection with the train (and, needless to say, no proper toilet facilities, or access to such facilities, for the three men working this eight-hour journey on the footplate) and had to be specially strengthened with heightened coal-rails to carry sufficient fuel. In other words, despite this one-off accomplishment by No.1054, this locomotive design was certainly not suited to long-distance work as the fourth decade of the twentieth century approached.

Although the LMS hurriedly tried to reverse its 1924 decision to invest in 1914-vintage 4-4-0s for express work by ordering the larger 'Royal Scot' 4-6-0s in what O.S. Nock called 'a shipwreck hurry', the Western and Midland lines on the former LMS system were never to attain the level of motive power provision required in the 7P and 8P categories, right up until the arrival of Diesels in numbers from around 1960.

Ten years after nationalisation, the former LNER lines were able to call on no fewer than 202 Pacific locomotives of power classifications 7 and 8. These comprised classes A1, A2, A3, and A4. The W1 4-6-4, operating alongside the other King's Cross streamliners, is not included. This was no less than four times the number of former LMS Pacifics available for the West Coast main-line in January 1957. The former Midland lines had no Pacifics at all unless one counts the 'Britannias' – of which the magnificent total of eight worked out of Manchester and Leeds from around 1958. Cecil J. Allen said at this time: 'I dare hazard that not a few of the [former] LMS operating authorities heartily wish they had as many class 8 and 7 locomotives to play with as their neighbours on the other side of the country'.

Just to accentuate the imbalance, the former LMS passenger rail network connecting London with Birmingham, Liverpool, Manchester, Leeds, Sheffield and Glasgow, was operated by the same number of 8P Pacifics as there were 7 and 8Ps allocated to two former LNER sheds at Newcastle-upon-Tyne! There was a slight favouring of 'Britannias' and 'Clans' to the west, although the first fifteen of the former class went to the former Great Eastern, a line which no LNER CME had seen fit to provide with Pacific power.

Transfers of locomotives within or among regions was an obvious national approach to solving the problems of utilising aged or underpowered locomotive on one line (invariably ex-LMS) while other areas enjoyed a surplus of power. For an example of the latter point, Edinburgh Waverley's services to the likes of Dundee, Perth and Carlisle were frequently Pacific-hauled, even when some of the services concerned were little more than stopping trains.

Norman McKillop once wrote, without comment, about operating his beloved A3 Pacific *Spearmint* on an Edinburgh-Perth train which comprised seven carriages as far as Dunfermline and four thereafter. The author can recall travelling on a Waverley Route 'express' north from Carlisle with an A3 heading six coaches. In contrast, passenger services between Edinburgh (Princes Street) and Carlisle were headed, for part of their journey at least, by Class 4 2-6-4 tank locomotives, and a fine turn of speed they had too! Their train would be attached to a Glasgow or Aberdeen section at Carstairs or Symington for the journey southwards. Just to increase the imbalance, Princes Street often saw ex-LMS Pacifics working in from Glasgow on 'filling-in turns'. This would be an indication of utilising heavy power units to their maximum on a 'dead end' line, meaning that an engine unused as a substitute for a number of departures for the south would be sent off on a return trip to Edinburgh simply to keep its mileage figures up. It certainly made for interesting visits to Edinburgh's Princes Street – Pacifics on the locals, 'tankies' on the expresses! But from the railway managers' viewpoint, it was less amusing to have to accept this persistent imbalance in top link power penalising the former LMS lines just because of a bad locomotive ordering decision, taken apparently below Board level, in 1923.

One sensible transfer of surplus power from east to west did take place in 1951. Three two-year-old A1s were sent from Edinburgh's Haymarket to Glasgow's Polmadie in 1951 and operated as far south as Crewe. This was precisely the kind of reallocation of power which should have taken place throughout the system, with more passenger work being undertaken from

Edinburgh, Newcastle, and Peterborough depots by V2s and B1s, freeing Pacifics for work on the hard-pressed Western and Midland lines. Former LMS depots could have transferred the prolific Class 5s to release their former LNER counterparts to take existing Pacific rosters. Typically, the A1 transfer barely lasted two years, and should really have involved Carlisle (Kingmoor). It was surely tactless to send an A1 Pacific called *North British* to Polmadie, that ultimate Caledonian fortress!

Mention has already been made of the former Highland Railway main-line between Perth and Inverness, with its summit of 1,484ft at Druimuachdar. It was, not surprisingly, susceptible to bad winter weather conditions, although, in that respect, it was not alone in Scotland. In December 1952 Scottish conducted a 'census' of its snowploughs, a document which still makes interesting reading. At that time there were 354 ploughs on the Region – from 'cow catchers' implements fitted below buffer-beam level, to 'nose' ploughs, some of them capable of sweeping two lines simultaneously. In all, 381 locomotives were adapted to operate ploughs, and 154 of them, nearly 40 per cent, were based at Perth and Inverness. Fort William had seven appropriate locomotives, and Oban four. In the south of the country, Carlisle (Kingmoor) had forty-one adapted engines, but the number at Canal was not specified by the Region as that depot was nominally in the LMR. Northwards, Hawick had three J36s equipped to tackle trouble on the Waverley Route. West of Carlisle, Stranraer surprisingly shedded only two suitable locomotives, both of them 2F 0-6-0s, and Newton Stewart two – this for an area where only the pen of David L. Smith could do justice to the horrendous conditions which could lead trains to be abandoned even on the former G & SWR main-line to London (as had happened in 1940), never mind the two routes to Stranraer.

The most prolific locomotive adapted for snowplough work was the 'Black 5', no fewer than 128 being so equipped when necessary. On the former GNSR section, eleven D40 and fourteen D41 4-4-0s could be utilised. Not that any shedmaster would choose such a lightweight loco with a bogie, or a Mogul with a pony-truck for that matter, for major track clearing. It was widely understood that, if charging a bank of snow, you reduced the risk of derailment by putting an 0-6-0 – lacking pony truck *or* bogie – right behind your largest plough!

When the LMS and LNER attempted to control the burgeoning network of bus services in Scotland in 1928, by buying a major proportion of company shares, they came seriously unstuck. Instead of enjoying a firm hand in the boardroom, the two companies, by investing £200,000 in Scottish Motor Traction (SMT), merely strengthened and emboldened a formidable rival.

More details can be found in this author's *London's Scottish Railways*, but suffice to say that the negotiations on the railways' side were so ineptly handled that a considerable delay resulted in the reorganisation of a new SMT company, in which it was agreed that the LMS and LNER would invest, during which time the original bus company's capital quadrupled. This inevitably downsized the purchasing power of the £100,000 each railway company was investing in the new organisation, so their financial influence in a reconstituted SMT, formally set up in the summer of 1929, was reduced. With only two seats on the Board of Directors, the LMS and LNER negotiators were shown to have been naïve and indecisive when exposed to the harsher economic climate outside their own sheltered duopolistic existence. Not surprisingly, there were nearly a dozen withdrawals of passenger services in Scotland within the following three years, while SMT went from strength to strength.

While the LMS and LNER failed to control bus services in Scotland, they at least ended up benefiting from them financially. In 1946, Scotland's railways 'earned' £452,000 (nowadays worth approximately £11 million) from their initial 'one-off' £200,000 investment in Scottish Motor Traction in 1929, to which they subsequently added. This did not include separate, although smaller, dividends from Alexander's and Highland (LMS only).

To lose this kind of annual return after the following year represented a major loss of 'unearned' profit, as well as finally removing any measure of control or influence that the railways might have held over their newer rivals. Indeed, in 1948, SMT entered into what might be described as 'voluntary' nationalisation, with its stock being sold to the BTC at a more than reasonable return. The Commission split the company's passenger-carrying operations (renamed Scottish Omnibuses) from the former SMT engineering division, which retained the famous name.

If this is perhaps more detail than the railway-orientated reader feels is appropriate in a history of Scotland's railways, it will nevertheless be necessary to feature Scottish Omnibuses again in this narrative. Within ten years, this company, supposedly under the same transport 'umbrella' as the railways, was quick to criticise the latter for daring to introduce modern Diesel units in competition with buses on such lucrative routes as Edinburgh-North Berwick and Edinburgh-Peebles. It would also argue successfully for grants from BR to cover for closed rail services, even when trading in the resulting monopoly situation. Additionally, BR paid rates on all its landed property, contributing to local authority spending on roads and thus benefiting its transport rivals.

It was not only in Scotland that railway companies were feeling the heat of road competition. Throughout the UK, the rural railway lost popularity, not just because of its comparatively high fares and often unappealing station facilities – although these were important factors – but because railway lines had often been built far from the communities they were intended to serve. Gatehouse of Fleet, in Galloway, was an obvious example, its station being some 7 miles from the town, which was situated on the main road from Dumfries to the Irish Channel ports. David L. Smith, historian of the old Glasgow & South Western Railway and its LMS successor in that corner of Scotland, has recorded that one rural stationmaster was astonished at the amount of fares the local bus conductor could take in a single day in a community where the railwayman had always assumed that people preferred to stay at home!

There were strong historical reasons why railways had been unable to locate their stations close to the towns or villages they nominally served, and landowner hostility was often responsible. Even when the iron road reached the proximity of a town, it often failed to penetrate to the town centre. Haddington, Duns, and Selkirk were cases in point, while at Kelso the station was not only situated on the wrong side of the Tweed, but stood atop a steep hill.

In the circumstances, it was no surprise that the flexibility of the country bus could render a railway station superfluous. Even where branch termini were conveniently situated, as they were in Aberfoyle and Brechin, the trains still could not match a transport service that actually transected the High Street and stopped outside the Post Office, school, and Town Hall.

As for rural freight services, an official Scottish Region report concluded in 1958 that 'country stations are no longer necessary to rural economy, and farmers can get along perfectly well without the aid of transport which requires them to convey their goods to and from the nearest station which may be anything up to 10 miles distant'. This particular document (see Bibliography) went on to recommend the closure of the line being examined – the St Boswells-Greenlaw stub of the former Berwickshire Railway – despite the fact that the (freight-only) receipts for 1957-58 came to £11,215 against staff costs of less than £3,000. While the latter figure does not include costings for a daily goods train, there would still appear to be some considerable margin for profit, particularly since the locomotive utilised each morning could also undertake other work on the Waverley Route for the rest of the day. Yet here were professional railwaymen *recommending* closure of a line whose income comfortably exceeded standing costs. No doubt closure would have gone ahead too, except for the fact that, as documents in the National Archives reveal, Berwickshire County Council and the local branch of the National Farmers Union had been promised that the line would remain open as an alternative to the loss of Lauder's goods station earlier that year.

Because of this preoccupation with operational factors in assessing line viability, to say nothing of any lost profit from holding an investment in the buses themselves, the immediate post-nationalisation period saw a major escalation in rail closures, especially in Scotland. Dr Bonavia has said that there was 'no determined policy on the part of the Executive' to close lines that were not remunerative, so the Scottish closure rate must therefore have been higher than the rest of the UK's.

In the first five years of BR, there were no fewer than thirty-seven withdrawals of Scottish rail passenger services, including two former North British services in England. There were seventeen in 1951 alone, a peak year for the withdrawals. Among the counties affected were East Lothian, Selkirkshire, Wigtownshire and Berwickshire, all of whose county towns lost their rail services. In the case of Berwickshire, where Duns and Greenlaw rivalled one another to celebrate capital status, equality was ensured by having *both* communities wiped from the Scottish map of rail passenger services.

Other branches closed included Brechin, whose rail terminus could hardly have been more centrally situated in the town, and Leith Central, the largest terminus built from scratch in the UK in the twentieth century (and closed after less than fifty years service). Meanwhile, to withdraw passenger services from Aberfoyle, as happened in 1951, was a public statement that the new Scottish Region had no interest in promoting tourism. Not only is Aberfoyle the gateway to the Trossachs from the south, the station was perfectly situated next to the main street, and today its site is used by coaches and a tourist information centre.

At least the Area Board, when newly established four years later, was able to bask in the news that 'assets' had been recovered from the Aberfoyle and Kilsyth branches to the extent of £126, presumably not including track, since freight was still running on these lines up to 1959. Indeed, in 1954, Scottish leased out Gartmore Station on the Aberfoyle branch for the filming of *Geordie*. Cinemagoers saw actor Bill Travers leaving for the

Melbourne Olympics amidst scenes of great enthusiasm, and returning in disgrace to a station which had presumably been stripped bare of 'valuable' assets. In contrast, clearing the Fortissat branch released £3,263 worth of assets in the same year.

By 1964, Scottish was able to boast of £128,240 worth of recoverable items from the Peebles demolition, the largest in Scotland up to that time. One suspects that these figures were more comprehensible to the account-ant than to the average railwayman – the £3,400 worth of equipment 'recovered' from the Peebles line per mile was twice that on other lines, but it was not the only 'recovery' figure which had the power to lift eyebrows (see Table V).

Demolition of the Lauder Light Railway was announced in 1960 as gen-erating nearly £30,000 (£417,000), a remarkable figure for a 10-mile single line built with minimal earthworks and buildings as permitted by the 1896 Light Railways Act. Dornoch's branch came into the same category (and the recovery figure was not that much more realistic). Here, the 'lightness' of the line's construction had meant that the replacement of time-served Highland Railway locomotives in the 1950s posed a particular problem for BR. This had been solved by drafting in two post-war WR pannier 0-6-0 tanks, Nos 1646/9 from North Wales and Bristol respectively.

Meanwhile, for many years, the Lauder Light had been making do with former Great Eastern tank locomotives running with empty side tanks and improvised tenders in order to distribute the locomotive weight as evenly as possible on this fragile branch (this was before the introduction of light BR 2MT Moguls at the eleventh hour). Yet its closure to freight in 1958 apparently promised a rich harvest of recovered materials, despite the fact that, according to the LLR's historians, Messrs Hajducki and Simpson, all bridges and station buildings were left intact after closure (two of the latter consisted of timber and corrugated iron sheeting). They do however record that many of the sleepers recovered had only been laid recently. Even so, the recovery figure seems far too high, and the thought that it was being 'spun' as an argument for closure is suggested by a letter quoted by the historians mentioned above. It came from the Regional Chief Commercial Manager, Stanley Raymond, later to become head of the British Railways Board, no less.

Raymond claimed in 1958 that the 'recovery of redundant assets' on the Lauder line would represent a definite benefit (presumably to the tax-payer), through not having to provide an uneconomic service, and through a grotesquely exaggerated recovery figure (although this was not specified publicly). Because of the dubiety of these figures (see Table V), it has to be said that, if there was an economic case for closing a potentially important line into the Trossachs, or down the valley of the Leader Water, it was not being made by Stanley Raymond on this occasion.

An added source of puzzlement is the similarity in recovery figures per mile, whether the closed railway was single or double-track. This suggests that the actual materials making up the permanent way – rails, sleepers (especially if concrete), ballast – were budgeted as reusable, with the principal income coming from the sale or rental of lineside accommodation, inflated no doubt on grounds of increased amenity. This would explain why the recovery fig-ure for the Peebles line, with its numerous crossing-keepers' cottages, was so high, although whether these qualify for the exact description in the Board Minutes of 'readily recoverable redundant assets' is questionable. In any event, this estimate surely included bridges which were not in fact removed. And, it has to be said, the supposedly highly lucrative Lauder branch comprised no such accommodation at all (Table V gives a chronological listing of intima-tions to the Board relating to 'recovery of assets').

That this was a new preoccupation for rail managers is suggested by the very contrasting fate of the Invergarry-Fort Augustus branch. Closed to all traffic at the end of 1946, this formerly independent line, operated succes-sively by the Highland, the North British, and the LNER, was the subject of a special submission to the BTC by the Railway Executive in February 1948. The Commission was told that, 'an estimate is being prepared of the cost of recovering the track material for scrap. *If such recovery proves worthwhile...*[author's italics]'. The later view held by Scottish Region that closed lines could yield a rich source of materials would appear to date from 1955, the year when the Regional Board began to hold meetings under the chairmanship of Sir Ian Bolton.

The management's apparent enthusiasm for closures – although it would perhaps be fairer to call it resignation to losing out to road competition – did not permeate down to the average railwayman. The *BR Magazine* was overwhelmed in 1954 when it asked for its readers' views on the increased rate of closures, with Mr W.A.C. Smith of Glasgow, well-known for his rail-way photography over many years, quoted by the editor as saying:, 'I have yet to see any determined effort made to increase patronage in borderline cases ... I remain unconvinced that everything possible is being done to fight competition from buses'.

The short-sightedness of the management's closure activities was con-firmed by the withdrawal of Penicuik branch passenger services in 1951, in an area where the population trebled in post-war times – making the town larger than, for example, Hawick (whose station the rail administrators would get round to closing as well) – but where the Midlothian road system had seen almost as little investment as the railway. Perhaps Penicuik's example of negative thinking in the Lothians should have come as no surprise. The nearby burgh of Dalkeith had seen its passenger terminus closed by the LNER in 1942, yet the station site could not have been more central to the town, and was converted into a bus station as soon as BR put it on the market.

In 1955, the newly constituted Area Board learned that the closures of branches and stations had saved £348,052 (£5.4 million) and £37,225 (£580,000) respectively since 1948. At the same meeting, the Board members agreed to recommend the establishment of a marshalling yard at Millerhill at an estimated cost of £2.9 million (£45 million), producing a projected annual saving of £95,000 and an anticipated return of 3.2 per cent annually against outlay. As will be discussed in more detail later, this was a disastrous decision. But then, closing railways to save £50,000 a year hardly makes much sense either, when road infrastructure is not required to make money, and a more enlightened approach to rail provision could surely be expected, then as now. To be fair to railway staff, this is a criticism not so much of them but of the politicians. Unfortunately, it was not to be until 1968 that a Transport Act would reach the statute book to enable local authorities to subsidise, and become involved in, transport matters in their area. Meanwhile, the railways continued to be a political orphan, with no one at Westminster, where the Conservatives took power once more in 1951, claiming parentage.

Sir John Elliot may have published an economic analysis of Scottish Region which this author finds unbelievable (see below), but he could not be faulted for his attitude to Westminster's stewardship of the nation's railways. Elliot had begun his transport career as a public relations officer on the Southern Railway between the wars. Although he was later successively CRO of both Southern and London Midland regions, and followed Missenden as chairman of the Railway Executive before taking over the London Transport Executive, he does not appear to have had operational experience, nor to have spent any of his career working in Scotland. In 1953, safely appointed to his new post in London, Elliot ticked off his political masters: 'a word of friendly advice to our legislators ... if they cannot now compose their ideological differences as to how the nation's transport system should be organised, then the responsibility for inefficiency resulting from disappointment and frustration at all levels will be largely on their shoulders'.

In one of its last annual reports, in 1979, published before sectorisation took place in 1982, British Rail described itself as, 'a mixed enterprise operating commercial and non-commercial services'. Presumably this hybrid status was not perceived by BR managers until after the passing of the Transport Act in 1968, and there was precious little sign of any non-commercial thinking among senior Scottish Region staff before that year, the twentieth since the railways were taken over by the representatives of the people. It was unfortunate that one of these representatives made a living out of closing down failed companies, but Scotland's railway network was surely rather more than that.

Addressing LMS shareholders in 1940, company president Lord Stamp had announced that the Far North lines of the Northern Division had just seen a 40 per cent increase in traffic, and he wondered if anyone felt that the retention of such lines in peacetime had not found its full justification at a time of war. That there had been critics in the south who were unhappy at the comparatively unprofitable nature of much Scottish mileage ceased to be a problem for rail managers after 1948. Instead, it would become a problem for politicians, and the kernel of the problem would not change or go away.

At the end of its first year, BR's Scottish Region made a profit of income over expenditure of only £200,000 (£4.45 million). Unimpressive certainly, although the new Western Region, whose identity had scarcely been disturbed in its gentle transition from the Great Western Railway, had succeeded in generating only £500,000 profit in 1948. The loss of dividend income from SMT cannot have helped Scottish Region. As mentioned earlier, in 1946 this investment in passenger road services brought in approximately £452,000 for LMS and LNER, some £11 million at today's prices, in return for an initial £200,000 investment in 1929. And things did not improve for Scottish. Although the Region's accounts broke even in 1951, that boom year for closures, it was only in this year and 1948, during the first quarter-century, when no loss was made. In particular, it should not go un-noticed that even a good financial performance by Scottish Region in 1948 and 1951 did not lead to any investment 'reward'. The financial years of 1949 or 1952 did not see any substantial capital investment which might have accrued from the previous year's working profit. This was an organisation where no profit was required, and where any working surplus should presumably go back into capital. But this did not appear to happen.

It is interesting to compare the profitability of passenger services on Southern and Scottish Regions during a single week, the week ending 11 October, in 1952, since the latter operated no electric trains at the time, and would not do so for another nine years, despite the availability of hydro-electricity. The Southern Railway on the other hand had begun electrifying suburban services in London, and out to the South Coast, from the mid-1920s, and the post-1948 Region was the beneficiary:

Type of train	Scottish Revenue	Southern Revenue
Express	£26,348	£37,869
Semi-fast	£14,894	£82,755
Stopping	-£50,349	-£9,997
Suburban	-£8,850	£115,138

The final figure quoted, for Southern suburban services, was for electric trains only, and helped the region to a handsome £225,765 profit over its passenger services in their entirety. In contrast, Scottish made an overall loss, and it is not clear if the 'express' element of the regional figures included expresses to and from England. Labour historian P.S. Bagwell has cited Southern electrification as almost the *only* substantial example of infrastructure investment in pre-war railways between 1920 and 1938, which totalled £125 million less than it should have, according to his calculations (levelled up to modern values, £6.07 milliards). This implies that the 'disinvestment' by the GWR, LMS, and LNER assumes even greater proportions for each of these companies, and of course, for Scotland. A review of motive power modernisation some years later, in 1958, makes it clear that the Southern was still by far the most 'modern' region, and Scottish the Cinderella (see Table VI). This places in particular perspective the failure of the post-1955 Scottish Board to work amicably and constructively with the North of Scottish Hydro-electric Board in seeking to electrify the lines in the Far North or in the West Highlands, using renewable energy, as we shall see.

A more surprising assessment of Scottish Region's economic performance came from the aforementioned John Elliot, and was delivered to the Institute of Transport in October 1953, not long after his post of Railway Executive chairman had been abolished. In this presidential address, Elliot cited Scottish Region as an outstanding financial success, telling the Institute's members that 'it was clear [in 1947] that the railways in Scotland could best be operated as a single unit, as was first proposed by the Government of the day in 1921. The substantial economies of £3 million [£45-£65 million] *a year* and improved working secured in Scotland since 1948, have proved the advisability of this course [author's italics and parentheses]'. It is difficult to see exactly, and Mr (later Sir John) Elliot failed to indicate, where these enormous savings were achieved. No major passenger termini, offices, or MPDs were closed in Scotland between 1948 and 1952 to eliminate duplication of facilities, and the numerous branch closures of those years, as noted elsewhere in this book, targeted such rural communities as Aberfoyle, Brechin, Jedburgh, Selkirk, and Whithorn. As for improved working, such internal services as Glasgow-Aberdeen were 20 per cent slower than in pre-war years, while many Glasgow suburban services were running at an equally incredible 3 per cent of capacity, if BTC figures were to be believed (see the next chapter). Not only that, but the Region made a working profit only once, and broke even once, in those five years, with the working expenses increasing year on year, finally topping £40 million in 1952.

Certainly, the BTC decreed on 23 September 1948 that there was 'ample scope for securing substantial economies in Scotland', and asked the Railway Executive to report on this, but the implied dismantling of duplicated facilities was not achieved as easily as must have seemed apparent from London. Indeed, as remarked earlier, the first-ever *BTC Monthly Report* had guaranteed that there would be no redundancies when the former LNER Scottish Area HQ in Edinburgh was downgraded and, of course, remained open. In May 1949, Secretary of State Arthur Woodburn announced a reduction in the number of 'district administrative centres' on the new Scottish Region from thirty-seven to twenty-seven over the previous year, but did not itemise the saving accruing. He also announced £400,000 (£8 million) worth of plant modernisation in three different depots, all in Glasgow.

Interestingly, BTC chairman Lord (then Sir Cyril) Hurcomb seemed to hold a more relaxed view of Scotland's potential economies than his own commission, telling the Railway Students' Association on 20 October 1948 that, 'it will take time before the full effects and economies of the change [in Scotland] can be worked out in detail'.

One can only assume that Elliot was boasting of savings of £3 million *in total* over the 1948-52 period, although the printed account of his speech in the *Journal of the Institute of Transport* does indicate 'per year' and this was faithfully reported in the technical publications, such as *Trains Illustrated* in December 1953. The report in the *Railway Gazette* contented itself with a comment on the overdue unification of Scottish railways.

Even if the longer time-span was intended, this would equate to around £11 million (modern) saving for any one of those years, and the reader can only speculate about where such economies were accomplished; in particular, it seems surprising nowadays that two major HQ buildings were kept on in the city-centres of both Edinburgh and Glasgow, with the Railway Executive anxious to assure railwaymen that there would be no redundancies. Although in theory there was no longer a centre in Edinburgh administering the LNER Scottish Area, and a counterpart in Glasgow to run the LMS Northern Division, the offices remained in both cities for almost two more decades, and we have already seen that there was an overall increase in both the number of senior rail executives nationally, and in their salaries bill.

Looking back, it would appear that the tradition of not permitting questions following a presidential address, which was practiced at such learned societies as the Institute of Transport, has allowed a serious error to enter the historical record. But this was not the first time that Elliot had produced statistics to raise the eyebrows. On a visit to Scotland in June 1951 as chairman of the Railway Executive, he announced that, since nationalisation, 'the annual saving in Scotland overall' was £12 million (£220 million)! Since gross revenue in 1950 was £35.2 million in Scottish Region against £35.6 million costs, it goes without saying that Elliot's figure is difficult to understand! The statistic was published in the *Railway Gazette*, but one must assume that the intended figure was £1.2 million, stipulated, again, without detail of how it was reached, except through 'economy in the operation of many local services, [but] this could only be brought about by cancellation of many services'.

Curiously, the RE chairman visited Aberfoyle on this Scottish visit, no doubt to satisfy himself that the recent withdrawal of the occasional one-coach branch train was making a substantial contribution to this enormous saving on Scottish Region. In 1955, the Scottish Board, as mentioned earlier, was told that closures had saved £348,052 (£5.4 million) since nationalisation. It is interesting that depriving innocent rural communities of their trains was seen as the key to making fiscal improvements. This policy was to be seen more openly at work when the Board Minutes became available.

In 1955, when the new Area Board began to meet, and the Government had braced itself for a (long overdue) Modernisation Plan with a £1.2 milliard bottom line, Scottish was BR's worst-performing region, posting a loss of £10.6 million (£165 million). This followed the allocation of what economic historian T.R. Gourvish records as 'central charges'. At that stage, these could not have included much in the way of capital investment, begging the question of whether Scotland's railways were unprofitable because they lacked capital regeneration, and whether matters would have been a great deal worse if 'capital charges' had included more in the way of costly motive power improvements, electrification, or re-signalling schemes.

Operating a railway lacking investment must have been bad for morale, particularly following the false dawn of nationalisation when railway staff might reasonably have anticipated a more sympathetic attitude to rail transport from government. Cecil J. Allen detected an atmosphere of disillusionment when he wrote in 1951 an article called 'What can we do about it?' in the magazine *Trains Illustrated*. He was concerned with a journey which began in Glasgow and turned into a passenger's nightmare, and his thoughts are worth reproducing here. In November 1951 Mr Allen planned to travel south from Edinburgh (Waverley) on the 5.14 p.m. 'North Briton' express as far as York. Unfortunately, there had been a collision in Queen Street Station (still lacking modern signalling and track circuiting) between A3 Pacific *Spearmint* and its train, which had 'marooned' the coaching stock in the Glasgow terminus, and Edinburgh Control had to hurriedly assemble a rake of coaches to start the service from Waverley, but without the advertised restaurant car. Commendably, departure was delayed to allow Glasgow passengers to catch up by a substitute service, but less commendably, a North Berwick train was allowed to leave Waverley just ahead of the express which, as a result, was delayed all the way to Longniddry, with departure from Dunbar being no less than twenty-nine minutes late. The crew of A1 Pacific *Bon Accord* reeled off the miles thence to Newcastle so quickly that the train was only thirteen minutes late on Tyneside. Scottish Region had done reasonably well at short notice, in contrast to their North Eastern colleagues who had three hours to find a restaurant car which would actually be open for business, but in fact compounded the problem by attaching a closed car at Newcastle.

When the LMS and LNER had begun operations in 1923, both companies realised the importance of publishing a staff magazine as a means of bringing together staff and managements from more than fifty companies between them, and from almost one end of the United Kingdom to the other. It would seem natural, therefore, that the new British Railways would be even more anxious to unify its widespread workforce by publishing a staff magazine reflecting the geographical and historical disparity of its employees but, curiously, this did not appear to be a priority for the new national management. Not until April 1948 had the BTC set up a committee to investigate the establishment of a truly national staff magazine, which 'should be sold to the staff and not given away free-of-charge'.

Meanwhile, the *LNER Magazine* was converted in 1948 into the *British Railways Magazine (E, NE, & Scottish Regions)* without any seeming 'makeover', but this would clearly not capture the interest of former LMS employees north of the Border. Nor ex-LNER employees either, if the content was anything to go by! One of the first issues in 1948 featured 'Our friend the potato', an account of the work of the stationmaster at Holbeach in Norfolk in ensuring the speedy dissemination of the local root crop. The report on the emergence of 'Coronation' stock, still in its 1937 livery, from the carriage sheds at Ballater in April 1948, perhaps indicated better days to come – indeed, Scottish Region officials apparently still harboured the hope of seeing streamlined, or at least 'high speed', trains operating once again, as we shall see. (Incidentally, former LMS staff had their own magazine: the unfortunately entitled *Carry on*).

It was not until January 1950 that the *British Railways Magazine (Scottish Region)* finally made an appearance, retailing at threepence (1.5p). This contained a morale-boosting message from Railway Executive chairman Sir Eustace Missenden, and a regional insert. In six editions, the journal claimed a monthly circulation of 116,000. The first Scottish insert included an article, simply entitled '302' about the 'new' regional HQ in Glasgow's Buchanan Street, and there was a biographical profile of T.F. Cameron.

Editorial standards improved over the next few years, with a good mix of historical and technical subjects, not forgetting the social side. In 1952 there were dignified articles on the railway elements of the late King's funereal progress from Sandringham to Windsor, and that year's Harrow disaster, involving an Anglo-Scottish express. The latter item was accompanied by a technical description of what soon became known as AWS or ATC equipment, and it is lamentable to think that this kind of cab signalling had been available, either in mechanical or electrical versions, for over half a century. In 1950 the *Railway Yearbook* had said of ATC that 'on the main lines, not very much has been done in this direction'. Two years later, in the aftermath of Harrow, the same publication stated that 'AWS would undoubtedly have prevented this accident'.

By 1955, not a mile of Scotland's railways was electrified. The only Diesel locomotive seen daily north of the Border was the occasional shunting locomotive, or even more occasional Nos 10000/1, all of LMS provenance. No major stations had been rebuilt, colour-light signalling was restricted to less than 1 per cent of route-mileage, and cab signalling was unknown.

Just to put this lack of investment into a safety context, a glance at the working arrangements at Glasgow's Queen Street terminus is illuminating.

In a transport magazine published in January 1956, contemporary author George Robin described the signalling arrangements at the station, one of Scotland's busiest, and these, needless to say, consisted almost exclusively of semaphores. These were controlled from a 97-lever box above the tracks, although there was a three-aspect colour-light signal facing trains approaching the station through the 1,011 yard tunnel, making up half of the infamous 1 in 42 gradient down from Cowlairs. Conditions in the tunnel were described by Mr Robin as 'deplorable', and the safety features built into the trackwork at this potentially dangerous site were, it appears, mechanical, consisting of treadles and track bars. He added: 'the operation of a treadle, 42 yards beyond the northern tunnel portal, records that the engine has cleared [presumably the banking engine at the rear of the train]. If violent slipping occurs beyond this point, the driver *should* be able to prevent his train from running back' [this author's italics].

There was a record of exactly this happening at least three times in the quarter-century after 1925. On one occasion, in 1928, four lives were lost and no fewer than sixty-five people were injured. In BR days, A3 No.60100 *Spearmint*, as already mentioned, had suffered a brake failure when descending the bank and collided with the train being shunted for it (see Accidents, listed in Table XIII). At the time of Mr Robin's article, official loading figures for the incline went no higher than 200 tons for an 8P Pacific, with N15 bankers being allowed 190 tons, and a V1 tank 160. All this was fairly academic since no locomotive was allowed to take more than a single coach up the gradient to Cowlairs.

Powered track circuiting would of course have warned signal staff about any train failing to clear the section, and could have prevented at least one of these accidents. Track circuiting was some fifty years old by the 1920s, but was not functional here until Remembrance Day, 1956. Cab signalling, in the form of AWS, did not appear on this line until 1958. Yet it was the first main-line on Scottish Region to be so equipped (estimated at £203,885 in March of that year). It would not be able to boast continuously welded rail for even 75 per cent of its length until 1967. To this day, the line has not been electrified, although diesel multiple units have operated here since 1957, but not exclusively, and Queen Street tunnel was still obscured by smoke.

While BR's motive power policy was built around the steam engine at this time, an earlier form of motive power could still be seen at work on the system: the horse. Financial documents now in the National Archives show that the cost of maintaining Scotland's railway stables came in at nearly £16,000 (£355,000) in 1948, with shoeing costs alone account-ing for £1,867 (£41,600). By 1954, horses were costing Scottish Region £7,016 (£111,000) in the first six months of the year, indicating a reduc-tion of costs, although unfortunately there is no indication in the file of the number of four-legged 'loco' numbers involved. £1,330 (£21,280) was spent on shoeing in those six months. Clearly there was a major increase in this aspect of equine maintenance.

This may be the first time that these figures have been published, as these BR accounts were protected by the thirty year rule of confidential-ity. Perhaps civil servants believed that rascally Russians were desperate to discover the cost of using horses in Scottish goods stations!

four

THE BOARD TAKES OVER

1955 was a milestone year in the history of Britain's railways. Looking back, the announcement of the Modernisation Plan on 24 January catches the eye, and its importance was indisputable. But in that very month, an organisational development was triggered that had a crucial significance.

The Transport Act of 1953 brought about the dissolution of the Railway Executive along with all the other Executives, barring London Transport. One of the minor applications of the legislation was to return hotels to railways control, but the most important consequence for the railways was the legitimisation of the regions and their new governance by Area Boards peopled by appointed, non-professional, members. The Act was described at the time by one legal expert as 'the first measure of denationalisation to reach the Statute Book'.

From a Scottish point of view, it was noteworthy – for having a Scottish point of view. In abolishing the Railway Executive, the Act stated that there was 'a requirement that the scheme shall provide for an authority for the whole of Scotland (with or without authorities for areas in Scotland)'. This legitimised Scottish Region – although the 1947 Act had *implied* the need for a regional structure – and there are numerous references in the Act for the Transport Minister to consult with his colleague, the Secretary of State for Scotland, in implementing its provisions. The British Transport Commission became the direct governor of British Railways, and quickly set about creating six regional committees to oversee the work of the new General Managers – formerly the Chief Regional Officers. As chance would have it, Scottish was to have three GMs in succession in its first year.

The new Boards were modern counterparts of the old companies' Boards of Directors. Stepping into the positions of Scottish Board chairman and vice-chairman respectively were the two Scottish BTC representatives, Sir Ian Bolton and Donald Cameron of Locheil, and there were five other 'directors'. The first meeting of the Scottish Board took place at 302 Buchanan Street, Glasgow, on 17 January of that new year, with General Manager T.F. Cameron present 'below the salt', along with the Region's legal adviser and the new Regional Secretary.

The minutes of the new Board record that it was felt necessary for a map of the Scottish Region to be made available to the interested public – although the Region had been in operational existence for seven years already – and it was decided to publish this in the *Glasgow Herald*, along with what the Board members clearly regarded as lesser newspapers, such as *The Scotsman*, *Times*, and the official Edinburgh and London *Gazettes*.

The Board had no fewer than eight sub-committees, dealing with mechanical engineering, civil engineering and signalling, staff, estates and rating, shipping, stores and general, traffic (commercial and operational), and new works. The chairman was automatically *ex-officio* on each of these committees, whose quorum, curiously, was one. Scottish Region was now, nominally and practically, in the hands of a professional liquidator.

A number of special meetings of the Board itself appear to have been held over the next four years, dealing with detailed matters, such as Connel Ferry Bridge Tolls, services to the Highlands and Islands, battery-powered trains, Prestwick Station, and liaison with Scottish Omnibuses.

There were limits to the Board's power – it could only undertake capital projects up to £25,000 (£415,000) without reference to the BTC, and make appointments salaried at up to £2,100 (£35,000) per annum. The amount of capital expenditure was doubled within eighteen months. In turn, the Board authorised Cameron to spend up to £5,000 without prior reference, and to make appointments up to £1,750 per annum. By midsummer, Cameron had retired and been succeeded by the fifty-five year old A.E.H. Brown, but by the year's end the assistant general manager, James Ness, was occupying the new GM's chair following Mr Brown's untimely death after a short illness. For the first time in over thirty years, decisions on Scottish rail provision were being taken locally by Scots or at least by Scottish residents. In 1959 Bolton retired, to be succeeded by his deputy, Cameron of Locheil, but when the latter retired after a further five years, the general manager (by then, W.G. Thorpe) assumed the chair. Cameron of Locheil did not leave the committee until the end of 1972 but continued to serve on a Board where an employee was the titular head. By 1964, and certainly until 1971, the Board could have reasonably been renamed the

'Management Committee'. Bolton's part-time seat on the BTC was meanwhile taken by Frank Donachy, a mining trade unionist, until the abolition of the Commission in 1962, although Donachy then went on to serve on the British Railways Board part-time until the end of 1967.

One of the earliest matters dealt with by the Scottish Board was the gruesomely celebratory report on rail closures (mentioned earlier, and to be considered again later), which saved £50,000 a year, but with no allowance for changing demographic factors, or any recognition of how these lines could have been improved as potential feeders to the remaining system. More positively, the Board considered the application of the newly announced Modernisation Plan in Scotland.

When the 1955 Modernisation Plan was first aired, there was only one Scottish Region passenger train initiative listed in the initial press reports, and this was in fact the only claim to traction re-equipping which Scottish Region could make at that time. In July, the Scottish Area Board minuted that a Diesel multiple-unit service between Edinburgh (Waverley) and Glasgow (Queen Street) would be introduced, costing £651,800 (£10.15 million) to implement. Curiously, the *BR Magazine* for March 1955 had failed to mention this innovation in its coverage of the Modernisation Plan, citing instead a plan, although no more than an intention, to electrify Glasgow suburban services. It also dealt with the prospect of atomic power for Britain's trains, something which was 'not being overlooked', but which would probably take the form of a nuclear-fuelled national grid feeding rail electrification schemes, 'rather than engines carrying their own [atomic] power plants' – for which we are all thankful!

A year later, in March 1956, *The Scotsman* newspaper published a special supplement on the subject of British Railways modernisation. As usual with such publications, it was paid for by advertising, with each advertiser benefiting from a supporting article giving an uncritical review of the company's products. Despite this bias, the reader could assimilate details of BR's new Board, its engineering, passenger, freight, and shipping, operations, topped off by a brief historical piece written by C. Hamilton Ellis.

But there was precious little about modernisation. Platitudes abounded, but not many definite proposals. It would be unrealistic to expect illustrations of new diesel and electric locomotives or multiple units, but some kind of prediction about their introduction might have been appropriate. The proposed Edinburgh-Glasgow 'Inter City' service, approved by the Board eight months previously, was barely mentioned. A lengthy article on freight centred on the proposed marshalling yards, and there was considerable detail, although no illustrations, of the new utilities at Alloa and Thornton. With the front page of the twelve-page supplement given over to less than exciting details about the members of the new Scottish Region Board, *The Scotsman* initiative must be seen as something of a failure in public relations terms. Only the inclusion of a photograph of James Ness, by then the new General Manager, caught the attention, particularly printed alongside an assurance that the same youthful-looking Mr Ness used to work for the North British Railway (he was fifty-two in that year). The newspaper recorded that Scottish offered no fewer than thirty-five camping coaches for holiday accommodation – hardly an index of modernity, but an interesting detail nevertheless!

The paper also included an advertisement for the North British Locomotive Company, boasting that it had just received a number of BR orders, one of them for a 2,000hp main-line Diesel, needless to say, not for Scottish Region. NBL, the reader learned, was 'ready to meet any demands'. Did that include refunds, the historian is tempted to enquire, cynically.

The announcement in the summer of 1955 that 171 main-line Diesels were being introduced on to BR, stated specifically that they would oper-ate from the Eastern and London Midland Regions, a statement which, Board members were told, 'has led to adverse press comments in Scotland'. Curiously, one usually authoritative transport magazine repeated the dubi-ous press-release statement that locomotives of power ratings greater than 2,000hp 'are not required at this stage of diesel development on British Railways'. Bearing in mind the wasteful over-provision of passenger space within train rakes at that time – some first-class carriages conveyed as few as thirty-six people – and the poor ratio of passenger numbers to the tare weight of express trains resulting in lengthier formations, the question arises: if not then, when?

A curious report reached the Board in May 1955, emphasising the lack of any stated policy toward public transport provision among the most senior figures in, and even above, the industry. Chairman Sir Ian Bolton reported that he had met a Colonel Armstrong who was pressing for 'lightweight' Diesel trains to be based at Carlisle to serve the extreme south-west of the region. Unfortunately, the colonel, according to Bolton, 'had not been able to put forward any reason for supposing that this would lead to any addi-tional rail travel'. In that case, what was the Modernisation Plan, with its promise of comfortable DMUs, all about, one is tempted to ask? Only three years earlier a RE committee on 'Light Weight Trains' had recommended the experimental introduction of DMUs on rural lines on a 'large scale', and one of the areas identified for such an innovation was the Waverley Route running north from Carlisle, and serving communities in both Cumberland and Dumfriesshire. This idea came to nothing and did not seem to be recalled by Bolton when he was interviewed by Armstrong. The reader's puzzlement grows with the Board's minutes recording that, 'the chairman had made it very clear [to Armstrong] that the railway policy was 'to serve the more populous districts first with Diesel cars''. This is an interesting comment because it simply did not happen. Whatever the Board's policy towards dieselisation actually was, at a time of piecemeal investment, particularly as far as Scotland was concerned, it is not clear from the Board Minutes of the time. For example, after rebuffing Armstrong so heartlessly, the Board recorded in December 1955, that it would like the General Manager to borrow a lightweight DMU (probably from the LMR, although the potential lender was not specified), 'as an earnest of the Commission's willingness to endeavour to stimulate traffic in areas of small population before deciding on the withdrawing of services ... a loan would have a good effect on public opinion'. This is the exact opposite of what had been minuted only six months earlier, regarding the utilisation of DMUs; serving the 'more populous districts' in May; stimulating traffic 'in areas of small population' by December! In fact, Bolton's specification of urban services as being more worthy of capital investment was called into question by a report from BTC Comptroller Reginald Wilson, who in March 1953 showed that four services on Glasgow's south side had lost £220,000 (£3.5 million) in a single year (capable of wiping out the first year's profit), and were running with no less than 97 per cent of the seats unfilled. The routes concerned were the Cathcart Circle, as well as services to East Kilbride, Kirkhill and Uplawmoor. This must have staggered Scottish Region (the Area Board was not of course in existence at this time). If trains on the Circle could not break even, perhaps nothing could! Wilson believed that 'poor utilisation of staff and equipment' was responsible, although the former – staff – could reasonably point out that the much of the latter – equipment – dated back to the pre-1923 days when the line was worked by the Caledonian Railway (legally the Cathcart District was an independent company, and entered the LMS fold six months before its Caledonian operator).

Yet, despite Bolton's statement to Colonel Armstrong, there were apparently no plans for diesel introductions on suburban trains in Scotland's largest city. Services on the Cathcart Circle carried on with steam traction for another seven years; the 'underground' Glasgow Central Low Level line was actually to close in 1964 with steam still in use! Perhaps this explains why the chairman did not tell the colonel in 1955 that 'the railway policy was to serve the *more profitable routes* with Diesel cars', as Scottish Region was still digesting Wilson's unpleasant surprise.

The opinion of non-transport experts, regarding the question of rail viability, seemed to be running ahead of that of railwaymen themselves in the 1950s. In the first year of the decade, the MP for Midlothian and Peebles, dismayed at the closure of Symington-Peebles branch to passengers, asked the Minister if he was aware of the trend in Scotland for the population to gradually move from the overcrowded west central belt to the east. Alf Barnes promised to 'study' this point, one which has continued to the present day, and has seen the city of Glasgow shrink to around half of its population in 1945.

In March 1956, the Area Board considered a letter from the Association of County Councils in Scotland asking that 'no further branch railway lines should be closed to passenger or other traffic until the possibility of running diesel train units or battery cars had been explored'. The Association also made the reasonable suggestion that a branch line's total turnover from both freight and passenger should be sufficient to prevent closure being considered, if these exceeded running costs. The Board's minutes do not record what reply was made to these eminently sensible suggestions, from 'lay' members of the rural community, but we can take it to have been negative. Yet, precisely this kind of accounting was adopted by Scottish in 1972 after initially naming a closure date for the Kyle line (see Chapter 6). The Association was not easily put off, however, suggesting in December 1956 that rails should not be lifted on a closed line until 'adequate [replacement] transport services' had been ensured. Replying on 16 January 1957, the Board argued that leaving infrastructure intact could lead it to deteriorate and prevent economical re-use elsewhere on the system. Additionally, material could be lost to theft and vandalism. The Board's secretary also reasonably pointed out that it was the responsibility of the Transport Users Consultative Committee (TUCC) to assess the transport alternatives in the event of a closure. The fact that British Railways had to point this out to a major local government forum is perhaps significant.

TUCCs were established by the same 1947 transport legislation which created British Railways. The committees had two roles: to make appropriate recommendations to the Minister of Transport on rail and other services provided by nationalised transport undertakings, and to offer an impartial process for considering complaints from the public and local authorities about passenger train withdrawals and line closures. The committees could make representations direct to the Minister on either of these points, and in particular concerning any possible hardship caused by a closure proposal. Unfortunately, judging by the BTC's recommendations to the Minister in December 1948, it seems entirely possible that the concept of an independent consultation on proposed rail closures was not really understood in Glasgow. As members of the TUCC Scotland, the BTC received the names of Messrs Bolton and Cameron, along with Mr Hastie, Freight Manager of the Scottish Division of the Road Transport Executive – in other words, two of those proposing the closures and one who would almost certainly benefit from them! To be fair, the 1947 Act required at least one BTC member to hold a seat on each TUCC. An unusual aspect of the law gave the Minister the right to disband the Central committee, but not its Scottish and Welsh counterparts.

When originally launched in 1947, the TUCC system placed no particular emphasis on Scottish or Welsh rail closure proposals, where geographical isolation, and lack of alternative road services, might have been factors worthy of greater consideration. This might explain why the entire Whithorn peninsula south of Newton Stewart lost its passenger service in 1950, and why Jedburgh and St Boswells-Greenlaw lost services overnight two years earlier. In the latter two cases, this was a direct result of the flood damage mentioned in an earlier chapter, but different factors affecting each branch should surely have been investigated here. For example, a freight service continued to Jedburgh, and the occasional excursion train could visit in complete safety, while the Greenlaw line closed with track dangling over a gaping chasm, and was left like that for some time!

Prior to 1947 a semi-formal network of twenty-eight joint committees had sprung up in England and Wales after the 1921 Transport Act allowed discussions between the 'Big Four' railway companies and local authorities on localised transport needs. Yet there was no equivalent in Scotland. As we shall see, the new Regional Board, whose officials lacked any experience of dialogue with their local government counterparts, dealt with such enquiries with less than complete candour.

Another problem relating to the TUCC's remit was that they had no powers to recommend alternatives to closure; for example, they could not suggest allowing a branch line to run at a manageable loss if it served a public need, nor could they make suggestions for more economical operation. After October 1968, the committees received the power to assess the *quality* of possible alternative transport facilities, but that sensible alteration came too late to save almost any Scottish railway.

Significantly, a court challenge to Section 6 of the Act came about in June 1950, when Fife County Council disputed BR's right to withdraw passenger services on the Newburgh-North Fife line. Surprisingly, the council effectively won an immediate interdict postponing withdrawal of the service, with Lord Blades commenting that 'a nationalised undertaking could not take the law into its own hands', although he conceded that BR could still lodge a defence. The report on this action in the Court of Session appears incomplete, but the resulting defence was obviously based on recent legislation, and the line closed within a year. But it says little for the new TUCC system that it should be challenged so soon by the very section of the community – local government – which it was intended to benefit.

Additionally, and even more regrettably, the TUCCs were not always seen as impartial. In 1962 the TUCC's decision not to oppose the much-lamented decision to close the Peebles line, led to accusations of lack of impartiality – the head of Scottish Omnibuses was a member of the committee (at the chairman's invitation), and that company was on record as complaining about the introduction of DMUs on the route four years earlier. No wonder there appears to have been a lack of public confidence in the TUCC system.

Meanwhile, farther south, author Tom Rolt attended a meeting to object to the withdrawal of passenger services on the former GWR line between Cheltenham and Honeybourne, only to observe:

> the members of the [TUCC] committee, and the local officials of the Western Region coming in together, laughing and joking among themselves … It struck me then that we were wasting our time.

In his detailed appraisal of rural transport options (see Bibliography), David St John Thomas was kinder in his summing-up of TUCC failings: 'TUCC staff are of course answerable only to the committees, but it would be scarcely surprising if they had greater sympathy with railway officials than with people they represent but with whom they are less closely in touch'. He added that those serving on such committees, or servicing them in a clerical capacity, need not have any transport expertise, or personal knowledge of alternative transport services available in the event of a rail closure. The reader however can be excused for thinking the opposite – that TUCC members had *too much* transport expertise! In Scotland, the committees in later years were often chaired by the convener of the local authority which, in urban examples, might well be the head of a rival bus or tram network operated by that very authority. To be fair, there are examples of interests being declared, as in 1962 when the erstwhile Lord Provost of Edinburgh chaired the inquiry discussing the proposed closure of the South Side suburban line, but that particular inquiry produced its own, needless, complications, the urban circle being inappropriately lumped together with the Rosewell branch service. And closure went ahead anyway, on the casting vote of the chairman – this, despite the fact that the Town Council had voted overwhelmingly against closure.

Bearing all this in mind, it is difficult to assess the remarks made by regional chairman Sir Ian Bolton on 27 May 1958, when he said, 'It will be easier to withdraw services than it was. Until quite recently we did very elaborate closing of lines in Scotland – possibly more so than in any other region'. Puzzling indeed, since the consultative and statutory procedures undergone in Scotland (to which Bolton was presumably referring) were standard for the whole United Kingdom. What is more worrying is the audience which Bolton addressed when he made these remarks. He was speaking at a joint meeting of Scottish Region and Scottish Omnibuses, the 'nationalised' successor to the railways' old jousting partner, Scottish Motor Traction. Bolton's words could almost be interpreted as 'We're closing railways as fast as we can, dammit', although that is possibly unkind. Certainly, the minutes of the meeting suggest a strained atmosphere, with the SO representatives demanding a written record at the end of the meeting.

One interesting point was that the bus representatives at this meeting complained about diesel services being introduced on the North Berwick and Peebles lines, pointing out that these burghs were already receiving perfectly good bus services. The fact that rail revenues had increased by 65 per cent and 111 per cent on these respective services may have influenced the bus representatives to speak as they did! They also claimed that rail fares had not gone up enough at the lower end of the spectrum, resulting in an inevitable loss on shorter-distance rail services. What the railway representatives made of this is not at all clear!

When the *BR Magazine* had cited electrification of Glasgow suburban routes as the only Scottish traction change listed under the 1955 modernisation plans, the writer probably had in mind the internal Regional report of 1954 on rail electrification in Glasgow. Whether he had actually read it is another matter entirely; archive copies show that it carried 'confidential' status. Its message was not a particularly promising one. Following the 1951 report by Sir Robert Inglis on Glasgow's passenger transport services, electrification of BR lines in Scotland's largest conurbation was taken as inevitable. Scottish Region set up a working party to look at the details, with costings, and its report appeared in July 1954. The committee's remit was narrower than that of Sir Robert, a former LNER official recalled from a major transport posting in Germany, who envisaged electric trains approaching the city from all directions. In contrast, the committee considered only the North Clydeside lines from Airdrie westwards to Helensburgh, Milngavie and Balloch, and the Glasgow Central lines to Kirkhill, the Cathcart Circle, and Neilston High. Neither Inglis nor Scottish included the Central Low Level Lines in their considerations, and this was probably a case of only reinforcing success. In the previous year, 1953, Queen Street Low Level handled nearly four times as many passengers as Central Low Level in three times the number of trains. Incidentally, if the reader is puzzled about the omission from these pages of any mention of the Glasgow Underground, it is because this narrow-gauge system was built and operated by the city authority.

The committee was distinctly lukewarm on the financial viability of electrification. Estimating capital costs of £9,470,860 (£153.4 million) for the conversion, of which £3,533,000 (£59.2 million) would be spent on rolling-stock – to be built in BR workshops – the report concluded that 'the net position would be worsened to the [annual] extent of £67,087' (£1.08 million). That was despite a predicted 50 per cent rise in annual receipts and an impressively precise 52.77 per cent improvement in mileage figures. The full cost of conversion would be £10,967,492 (£177.7 million) including signalling and track improvements which would also benefit other traffic, for example West Highland trains or freight, all of which were specified to continue with steam haulage. Conversion of station lighting from gas to electricity was included in the costing, logically too, and its omission from the eventual electrification on North Clydeside was to be a source of complaint for some time.

The report's authors admitted they were unable to quantify such factors as the possibility of rail traffic's share increasing because of worsening traffic congestion, particularly on the Clyde bridges, and the spread of peripheral housing schemes whose inhabitants would require transport links with the city centre. The novelty effect of electric trains was not mentioned at all, but proved to be a major factor in the case of the North Clydeside service, as we shall see. Finally, costs were based on the assumed adoption of 1,500V supply, with the heavy overhead catenary then used for power transmission, two factors which did not in fact come into the final equation; BR adopted 25kV ac as its standard for electrification from March 1956 onwards. One positive point was the promised elimination of 'smoke and dirt' from the

Queen Street Low Level line, making the omission of the Central Low Level lines – which had as much as smoke and dirt as any moderniser could wish to eliminate – more than a little puzzling.

It was not until 1957, with DMUs already operating between Scotland's two largest cities, that a programmed approach to traction re-equipping throughout the Region appears to have been finalised, when Scottish contributed to a BTC publication of April 1957 called 'Diesel and Electric Traction and Passenger Services of the Future'. This was effectively a five-year plan, although it was under extensive revision almost immediately after publication. By the following year, diesels accounted for Scottish mileage of 218, while steam covered 1,343 route-miles, and that excludes Anglo-Scottish services. Electric train mileage in this official publication was recorded as three! The publication presumably referred to North Clydeside mileage, not yet open to public traffic.

Table VI summarises the modernisation of Scottish by 1958, in comparison with the other five regions. Although traction improvements are only one yardstick to assess the progress of the 1955 Plan three years after its announcement, it will be immediately obvious from the table that Scottish was not faring well at that time. Western was the only English region with a comparable percentage lack of improvement in traction conversion, and even it was nearly twice as well off as Scottish. While the two regions shared an absence of both electrified mileage and a fleet of main-line Diesels, at least Western had more than three times as many DMUs, this for a Region virtually the same size as Scottish. The Eastern, North Eastern, and LMR recorded very similar levels of traction conversion at this time, but the Southern was out on its own in terms of modernity. This was slightly misleading as the erstwhile Southern Railway had taken up electrification well before 1948 but, whichever way the figures are examined, Cinderella status seems to have been conferred on the rail system north of the Border.

Needless to say, when BR later decided to close the Kirkcudbright branch in Colonel Armstrong's area – not to mention every wayside station between Kirkconnel and Carlisle, except Dumfries and Annan – no diesels, lightweight or otherwise, had been given much of a chance to revive rail usage in the counties of Dumfriesshire and Kirkcudbrightshire. The exception was a short-lived DMU feeder service from Dumfries to Carlisle to connect with the 'Caledonian'.

Nowadays, at least three of these main-line stations have been reopened, but the county town of Kirkcudbright, one of the most attractive tourist destinations in Scotland, lost its services just the same, and without any experimentation with more modern traction. An added bonus of operating a DMU on this particular line would have been the elimination of shunting passenger stock in and out at the terminus – Kirkcudbright had no run-around loop at its single platform. But the branch trains were steam-hauled to the end. This last point underlined the importance of the suggestion by the Association of County Councils nine years earlier that no rural service should be withdrawn without an attempt to improve receipts by introducing diesel services.

It seems to this historian that that there was no clarity whatsoever in the philosophy of rail transport provision. How could there be? This nationalised industry was being overseen by conservative figures torn between their personal dedication to the concept of public service, and the traditional businessman's need to run his business prudently and efficiently. At an operational level, it was being run by people who were impatient at not being able to see the trees for what they perceived as dead wood.

There was perhaps an added complication in this equation. As we know, Sir Ian Bolton represented Scotland on the BTC from 1948 to 1955 – alone for nearly all of this time – and then took the Chair on the new Board from 1955 until his retirement in 1959. As mentioned earlier, in passing, Sir Ian was an accountant, and appears to have specialised in company liquidations. While there are positive aspects to such work – a good liquidator may be able to fulfil existing orders and preserve employment – it is difficult to see such a specialist being able to bring anything but a sharply forensic view to, for example, the operation of an unremunerative branch-line. If the chairman could only focus a ruthless businessman's eye on rural transport services, it might be difficult for his committee colleagues to differ.

It would be stretching a point to say that Bolton wielded the scythe which removed so many rail options from the public domain, but his place in all this should nevertheless be seriously assessed. While heading Scottish Region, and up until 1965, Bolton was acting as liquidator, appointed by the Court of Session, for a Stirlingshire road haulage company called London Scottish Transport. His fee for this was £6,500 (£79,000) in 1964 alone. The irony of the head of the Scottish railway system closing down a rival road company should not have escaped the reader, but the main point about this is that Sir Ian could hardly be expected to leave his liquidator's hat in the Scottish Region cloakroom before each board meeting!

There is of course no suggestion that Sir Ian Bolton personally benefited financially in any way from replacing rail services with alternative road service provision or from the decision to sell off land 'liberated' from railway control. Like Brutus, Bolton was an honourable man; his Board's reaction to the *Broadford* accident shortly before his retirement, proves this (see the chapter on Scottish Region's maritime services). On this occasion Bolton personally recommended a working procedure which was undoubtedly safer than that operated previously, even although the Caledonian SP Company felt that to do so might attract litigation from a family bereaved by the previous method of operation.

Although not spelt out in the Board Minutes, Bolton probably realised that the recapitalisation of Britain's railway system offered by the 1955 Modernisation Plan was doomed to economic failure, as long as identifiable areas of the network were known to be loss-making. Since those areas, mainly branch lines, were not scheduled to be modernised, they would presumably continue to make losses, thus acting as a deficit against the capital account. Logically, the future of such lines could be summarised with the imperative 'Either close or spend'. Bolton's instincts towards eradication were correct as far as the Board's apparently negative intentions were concerned, although, as this book hopes to show, there was little consideration given to social factors, as one might expect from an organisation supposedly owned by the nation.

At the UK level, the BTC was planning to electrify the Euston-Manchester service – which already made a profit, according to statistician Sir Christopher Foster – while failing to institute a Beeching-like programme which logic would suggest was necessary to eradicate those lines generating a deficit. Otherwise, these would offset and nullify the Plan's intentions of making BR profitable by 1960. Foster, writing in 1963, has pointed out in his book *The Transport Problem* that a modernised British Railways was expected to, 'break even in 1960 [but] that was the year of the greatest deficit so far'. Perhaps this was the reason why the Scottish chairman was looking for 'easier' ways to close the railways in his charge. Ironically, his Region was the least modernised by 1958.

In his account of Scottish railway history between 1923 and 1948, this author commented on the lack of investment by the LMS and LNER in their freight services. Eighty shunting yards were inherited from the two grouped companies in Scotland by the new British Railways, but no new marshalling yards had been opened north of the Border during that quarter-century, there had been no major re-equipping of mineral wagons with continuous brakes, and even the majority of 0-6-0 steam locomotives which moved most of the nation's goods trains, remained built and operated by their respective pre-grouping companies.

This was partly because such companies as the Caledonian and North British had recognized the importance of the coal industry, which was then geared for an export market as well as supplying to domestic and industrial customers. The latter company had grafted a new railway – the Lothian Lines – virtually intact on to the existing infrastructure to ensure efficient passage of coal from the Lothians to Leith docks, and introduced Scotland's first control office to oversee this important traffic. Sturdy locomotives such as the NBR 'B', 'C', and 'S' 0-6-0s (later LNER classes J35 to J37), along with over 150 former Caledonian 'Jumbos', serviced Scotland's coal needs into the second half of the 1960s. The LMS had introduced 4Fs and the LNER, J38s, both 0-6-0 classes basically similar to the pre-grouping designs. Superficially, there seemed to be no need for change. There was of course a sound economic reason why the grouped companies minimised any investment in freight services in an overall British context. In 1930 the Railways (Valuation for Rating Act) had allowed railways and canals up to 75 per cent relief on the rateable value of premises 'used wholly for industry or transport purposes', but the railway companies were required to pass this financial benison on to their customers requiring the transport of coal, raw materials for steel making, timber props for mining, and agricultural goods. Although it appeared to apply only in England and Wales, this Act was to have the unfortunate effect of creating a disincentive to rail investment in freight transport, since the average return per train was now reduced. Not surprisingly, with the Act still in force at the time of nationalisation, the unfitted goods wagon (not fitted with a continuous brake but with a hand lever) remained a transport staple.

By the 1950s rail managers were desperate to open new marshalling yards, particularly those which would permit 'hump' shunting, but they were seriously out of step with road developments. The expansion of road transport following the denationalisation of British Road Services – a result of the election of a Conservative Government in 1951 – was to produce a very different climate for freight transport. Unfortunately, while rail managers were still trying to bring an Edwardian system up to date, the new Elizabethan age was a step too far for them at this time.

A 1945 document on postwar reconstruction, available for scrutiny in the National Archives, shows that the LNER Scottish Area called for a marshalling yard to be built at Alloa at a cost of £141,000 (£3.83 million), and no less than £2.25 million (£55 million) to be spent on a new yard at Portobello, although, confusingly, the latter was listed as only a 'second [level of] priority'. Cadder yard, the LNER's biggest in or near Glasgow,

required improvements in two respects, for new staff restrooms and locomotive watering arrangements. None of these went ahead, certainly not as
part of a concerted LNER programme.

Portobello never did receive a modern marshalling yard, but Alloa sur-
faced again in the 1950s. By this time it was costed at 'nearly £500,000'
(£8.1 million), and was approved by the BTC in August 1954. Ten years
later, the Scottish Board Minutes include an entry concerning the budget-
ing of £31,650 (£394,000) for the installation of wagon-sorting equipment
at Alloa yard, of which only £1,268 (£15,780) was actually spent. It appears
that the order was then formally cancelled, with the original expenditure
written off. As the yard had been operating for some years by then (although
its marshalling facilities would only last until 1973), it was a curious item of
bookkeeping altogether.

This level of spending was as nothing compared to the plans for the
yards at Millerhill and Perth. Media reports on the cost of the former were
accurate for once, the 'nearly £3 million' mentioned in the transport press
reflecting the report to the Area Board which costed the project at £2.9
million (£45 million). This would include taking powers to carry out a
road deviation and involved the closure of Millerhill Station. Net savings
were expected, to the tune of £95,000 annually. New goods facilities were
also promised for Dundee in that year.

Perth's new yard was costed at £1.65 million (£25.6 million) in a report
to the Board in May 1955, although that would include the cost of a re-
signalling scheme as well. But the public was told a different story, *Trains
Illustrated* announcing the cost as £1.5 million, but that was also to include a
new yard at Craiglockhart in Edinburgh. Unfortunately, by April 1966, only
eleven years later, BR was 'rationalising' freight traffic in the Perth area, and
the Scottish Board was considering a 'reduction in the status of Perth yard'.
In December of the following year, the Board was informed of the closure
of the Perth 'hump yard'. By this time the main-line along which it was
aligned had lost one of its northern destinations anyway.

Perth and Millerhill yards were to be located at what T.R. Gourvish
called 'former company exchange points far from the main centres of production and consumption'. While the 'company exchange' element was
certainly true of Carlisle's Kingmoor yard, and to a limited extent of Perth,
it was never so with Millerhill, situated within the former NBR and LNER
fortress and many a mile from former Caledonian or LMS metals. Gerard
Fiennes believed that the Millerhill investment should have been made
nearer Glasgow, if it was to be made at all. Nor was the yard opened speedily;

in 1961 the Board was disappointed to learn that the Up half would not be available for service until June 1962, and the Down not until November of that year. Within eighteen months, an official BR working paper designated the Waverley Route, along which Millerhill yard was aligned, as a closure target (see Chapter 8). Local railwayman Stuart Sellar points out that during construction there was a proposal to make the yard one sided only, but too much had already been built.

The extent of the ground-clearing at this Midlothian site dismayed even supposedly uninformed members of the public, as this author recalls, hearing critical comments on a Waverley Route express passing slowly through the blighted landscape around 1960. None of us passengers, far from the decision-making processes of the BTC or Scottish Region HQ, could see where on earth the traffic would come from to fill those arrays of empty tracks. At the time of writing, it is possible to *buy* Millerhill! It is listed on the BRB website as 'Yard. For Sale'.

To give an idea of the scale of these yards, that at Kingmoor was nearly 3 miles in length, eighty-five tracks in width, and intended to process up to 5,000 wagons a day. Although sited in the London Midland Region, Kingmoor's inclusion in this volume is easily justified. It was intended to cope with freight to and from three Scottish routes, and in 1959 Scottish Region budgeted £46,400 (£653,000) towards permanent way works and signalling alterations in connection with the yard. More than 200,000 tons of slag, much of it from Lanarkshire, was brought in to cover and desecrate perfectly good agricultural land, providing a base for sidings, many of which were redundant as soon as completed. Although enthusiastic staff told a transport reporter in 1962 that the yard would pay for itself in ten years, a visit to the site nowadays presents a very different perspective. The area of the Down yard seems to be given over to industrial developments, and the Down control tower is derelict.

This author's only happy memory of the yard's construction phase came on holiday when my late afternoon Carlisle-Dumfries local, headed unusually by a Fowler 2-6-4 tank, made a publicly unscheduled halt at the closed wayside station of Rockcliffe, for the benefit of Scottish construction staff employed at Kingmoor. It was something of an 'Adlestrop' moment; Edward Thomas's poem of that name was based on an unexpected stop at an unknown station.

At least the Alloa yard was targeting an identifiable source of cargo – coal – and this was equally true of Thornton yard in Fife. Not one of the features of the 1955 Modernisation Plan, the Thornton investment was planned

from the earliest times of BR, in 1948, although its location was conten-
tious, the green field area having being eyed by the National Coal Board
for a spoil dump. Construction did not begin on the seventy-eight acre
site until 1953, costed at £1.35 million (£22.4 million). When the facility became operational three years later, it was described by G. Freeman
Allen, editor of *Trains Illustrated* magazine, as a 'wonder yard'. Comprising
thirty-five parallel storage sidings, its hump area was fitted with the most
sophisticated wagon-selection equipment, prompting Mr Allen to proclaim
that 'railways are more than just in the fight to hold their rightful share of
the country's freight traffic ... they are going to win'.

Unfortunately, there was an almost immediate contraction in the Fife
coal industry, with Thornton handling only 1,800 wagons daily, just over
half its planned capacity. Gourvish was sympathetic to BR in this instance,
believing that production predictions issued by the NCB had not proved
realistic. Certainly, in 1957, BR's Scottish Area Board was minuting that
the pit closure programme under way at that time included some twenty
closures *more* than expected, and the lack of liaison between the coal industry and BR – its closest trading partner, but also a faithful customer – was
deplored in correspondence with the NCB.

Brake-fitted freight services were introduced in 1957 between Glasgow
and London, and Glasgow-Sheffield. The former of these, running between
Gushetfaulds and Kentish Town, was distinguished with the name 'Condor';
not an avian appellation, but a verbal contraction of 'container' and 'door
to door'. Early loadings were disappointing, but the 'Condor' caught the
imagination nevertheless. From around 1958 these trains were hauled
by ungainly looking Metro-Vickers diesels with an asymmetrical wheel
arrangement of Co-Bo (three axles on one bogie, two on the other). They
were not destined for a long working life, and in fact were not perpetuated
beyond the original 'Pilot Scheme' order of Diesels (and that was unusual)
but BR was right to exploit the service's publicity potential.

Significantly, the Glasgow to London and Sheffield freight services were
for containers, pre-loaded and simply swung on to flat wagons. These
should not be confused with the modern type of container; the 1955 version, usually made of wood, held only four tons of cargo. Incidentally, in the
following March, BR ordered 400 such containers from Cowlairs Works.
While meat transport was a targeted market, so was furniture, which seems
curious in these modern days of drive-hire vans. Unfortunately, when a
Royal Commission on Transport had reported in 1931, twenty-four years
earlier, it was highly critical of the freight-carrying performance of the

railways, pointing to the lack of containerisation on the railways at that time. In 1928, the 'Big Four' operated with only 1,574 containers; by 1955, this had reached 34,223 under BR; unfortunately this was the same 4-ton capacity container in service a quarter of a century earlier.

The freight world was changing, albeit painfully slowly; the 'Condor' was the future, not the marshalling yards. The historian can only express bafflement at the huge BR investment in gargantuan yards whose purpose was unclear and devoured good agricultural land, while simultaneously introducing fitted freights, that is, the type fitted with continuous brakes which could be operated from the locomotive, which could achieve higher speeds, and should bypass these expensive new facilities if their acceleration was to win business customers. Towards the end of 1955 the Board was noting the success of a new Renfrew-Inverness freight service, via Perth and Aberdeen, described as loading to capacity. To build on this success, more services were proposed – Aberdeen-Middlesbrough, Falkirk-South Wales via Edinburgh, Dundee-Liverpool – all of them 'valuable instruments of competition' as the Board Minutes record. The total weekly mileage for fast, fully vacuum brake-fitted freights on Scottish tracks came to 50,000 in May 1957, at a time when BR was pushing ahead with its enormous yard-building programme. Within two years, these services were rejoicing in names:

1800	Paisley-Inverness	'Hielan Piper'
1755	Dumfries-Aberdeen (Kittybrewster)	'Kitty'
1805	Stranraer-Edinburgh (Lothian Road)	'Lothian Piper'
1855	Edinburgh (Lothian Road)-Stranraer	'Galloway Piper'
2100	Aberdeen (Guild Street)-Kilmarnock	'Killie'
1845	Greenock-York (Dringhouses)	'Sweep'

Perhaps BR managers believed that, by introducing more fast freights, while dealing with bulk cargoes in the traditional unbraked stock hauled by low-speed locomotives, they were covering all the commercial 'bases'. This failed to take into account the growth in the capacity of road vehicles, as well as the move to supply the power industry with other types of fuel. But there should have been no lack of expertise in road vehicle management among BR staff in any of the regions. What makes the decline in rail's share of inland freight movements in the UK all the more regrettable, was that nationalisation removed what measure of control the 'Big Four' enjoyed in the running of road transport. In 1944 they had more than £3.32 million (£83 million) invested in two major road haulage firms in Newcastle and Glasgow alone, in addition to their own vehicles and garage investments worth a total of £6.7 million (£167 million). More details will be found in Chapter 7, but suffice to say that, under nationalisation, the railways were able to maintain their road presence, while obviously losing their investment in commercial freight companies. They had also lost their investments in road passenger concerns, and it is to passenger train services that we must now turn our attention.

A recently declassified report in the National Archives of Scotland charts the introduction of diesel passenger services (strictly speaking, DMU and railbus services) into Scotland in 1957-58, and some surprising facts emerge. Out of nine routes converted to diesel (and battery power in one case) at that time, all showed a marked improvement in producing passenger revenues – at first. Yet, no fewer than seven of them would close completely, and one partially, within eight years. Two of the closures would take place less than four years after re-equipping.

In an even shorter period, no less than one third of the services were returning negative revenues within two years – in other words the Diesels, despite their modern image at that time, and a handsome press build-up, inspired fewer passenger journeys than their dirty, unfashionable, steam predecessors (see Table IV).

An exception to all this was the Edinburgh-Glasgow 'Inter City' DMU service. Built at Swindon, and later designated as Class 126, these units were powered by mechanical transmission and were designed to be run in six-coach formations. A driving cab occupied the full breadth of the vehicle at each end, with a gangwayed half-cab driving car in the middle of the set. This later allowed shorter formations on such work as Glasgow-Stranraer and Aberdeen-Inverness. The inter-city services also sported buffet cars.

Interestingly, in 1961, this Diesel introduction was estimated as having cost £1,284,000 (£17.3 million), nearly twice the 1955 estimate, but the annual 'revenue improvement' was put at no less than £153,947 (£2.07 million) annually. Certainly, there was a recorded 28 per cent increase in turnover in 1957, and approximately 5 per cent and 8 per cent in the following two years. Loading figures were made to look greater because of the introduction of a more frequent, regular-interval, service, but of course that was one of the advantages of operating units with a driving cab at each end of the formation. When introduced on the Glasgow (St Enoch)-Girvan-Stranraer route in 1959, the 126s registered a revenue increase of 11.7 per cent, and that in the winter months.

These Swindon 'Inter City' DMUs entered service between Edinburgh and Glasgow on 7 January 1957 amidst an international crisis. Because of this, the Area Board ruled that there would be no inaugural run for local dignitaries and media, owing to fuel rationing following Britain's disastrous invasion of Egypt. The two city Lord Provosts were, however, invited to inspect the new stock at Waverley and Queen Street on appropriate occasions before the service began. The buffet cars were not available at the introduction of the service; the first two were not delivered until 25 February, with three more following in April.

The Class 126 units may have been noisy, smoky, and overheated – complete with onboard furnaces! – yet by present-day standards on the route they were reliable and commodious, with their buffet cars proving particularly popular. Cecil J. Allen experienced a westbound trip in the driver's cab not long after introduction and, while impressed, was surprised to find that the unit's maximum speed was 70mph, which he believed insufficient to allow recovery from delays.

Nevertheless, the 'Inter City' sets were an undoubted success; a 1961 review of DMU performance throughout BR found that the 126s achieved the highest weekly mileage (2,036 miles) of any sets under review, as well as 88 per cent availability, although fuel consumption was higher than on later, more modern, units. The fact that these diesels were built and tested at a BR works, in this case Swindon, must have made a crucial contribution to their success.

In contrast, Scottish was to suffer more than most regions from unreliable equipment in its deliveries of diesel and electric power units, many of them received direct by BR from commercial builders. This followed what was clearly less-than-effective acceptance testing, particularly on the LMR, carried out on behalf of Scottish. Of course, as the old saying goes 'If you want something done properly, do it yourself', and Scottish was remiss in this respect, as we shall see. It is entirely possible that the success of the 126s – one of the first main-line diesel schemes in the UK, and tested properly by their Swindon makers – may have blinded Scottish to the later need to properly assess the products of commercial companies lacking the pedigree of the Great Western!

Unfortunately, the memory of the 126s may be slightly tarnished by the fact that Scottish took too long to find replacements for them in the years up to 1971, but that was hardly the fault of these excellent Swindon products. Not until 1968 was the Board informed about tests with 'push-pull' stock which was to be the Region's substitute for the obvious future requirement – electrification of the route.

Although the official stock register shows these pioneering DMUs as allocated to St Margaret's, they in fact operated from the newly appointed

Leith Central depot, the station which lost its passenger services five years earlier, although identified by the LNER as a potential diesel depot as early as 1947. Local engineman Charles Meacher recalled that, so unreliable were fuel gauges on these and other early BR diesels, fuel tanks were allowed to fill to overflowing at Central, a site one storey above street level. Not surprisingly, this led to a surprising number of cases of 'rising damp' affecting tenement dwellers nearby in later years. No doubt this potential need for compensation was not taken into account in the costings for this traction initiative!

Edinburgh benefited – or was thought to benefit – from other early diesel introductions, such as Corstorphine-North Berwick via Waverley, and Waverley-Galashiels via Peebles. The conversion of the former Leith Central terminus to a DMU depot made further introductions in South East Scotland logical, and the public certainly appeared to respond positively.

The North Berwick trains showed a two-thirds increase in patronage when introduced the following year, using Gloucester-built DMUs (later class 100). Greater frequency was one of the additional benefits of dieselisation, and Sunday working was introduced on the North Berwick branch. All this was despite heavy snow in the first week of the new service causing a DMU to be abandoned on the branch. A second annual increase, this time of nearly 10 per cent, was a respectable performance but was still not enough to save the Corstorphine end of the service from withdrawal ten years later.

This was a baffling closure, since road congestion in that area was (and still is) a chronic problem and, with a station at Pinkhill, the branch also served Edinburgh Zoo, one of Scotland's greatest tourist attractions (Glasgow's Calderpark Zoo only received its own station as late as 1951). Corstorphine was also used as an occasional starting and terminal point for services to and from Berwick-on-Tweed and the Waverley Route to reduce platform occupation at Waverley. Perhaps the diesel service simply raised rail managers' expectations too high as far as this route was concerned, or was it a political decision? Significantly, the North Berwick end of the service is still operating, and electrified into the bargain. The politics of Scottish rail closures will be examined later. With Scottish Omnibuses complaining by the following September about what they saw as the unnecessary introduction of diesels on the North Berwick line, it can be inferred that bus revenue was seriously reduced that summer!

The next introduction in 1958 was a DMU service between Edinburgh (Waverley) and Galashiels via Peebles. Its initial success was unprecedented:

111 per cent up on steam revenue! Scottish Omnibuses complained about this one too! But the second year's improvement was only 4 per cent and from then onwards it was downhill all the way. Within three years, closure was decided upon, taking place in February 1962, although as early as 1960 the Board had considered abandoning the line south of Peebles, and combining the Rosewell and existing Peebles services. Needless to say, this experiment did not proceed.

Interestingly, a few years earlier, the local authority had objected to the removal of the remains of the former CR and LMS branch into Peebles from the west, a line already deprived of passenger services since 1950. Diesel trains were then requested on this line from Symington, serving also Biggar and Broughton. Scottish Region replied that 'no case existed for reversing its decision' on track-lifting; after all, the 1958 estimate for recovered materials came to some £2,000 per mile (see Table V). In a curious footnote, the September 1960 Board Minutes indicate that a £59,113 (£768,000) outlay had been incurred on the 'recovery of assets' from this line, 'against £38,139 (£495,000) authorised'. This seems to make no sense; even if the latter figure represented the net credit, and it is not dissimilar from the recovery figure intimated to the Board two years earlier, the £59,113 figure is unexplained. It probably does not indicate the cost of track-lifting, with two major viaducts left intact, at Lyne and Neidpath.

All this removed Peebles, one of Scotland's most beautiful towns and an outstanding tourist centre, from the British Railways map altogether. Needless to say, the road connections from Edinburgh to this town and to Galashiels were poor, the bus taking some ninety minutes for 30 miles in the latter case. Possibly the reason for the disappointing rail performance was the remoteness of some of the stations from the centres of the towns they purported to serve (although this was not a problem in either Peebles or Gala) and the railway 'missed' Penicuik, one of the fastest-growing communities in Scotland, altogether. Even diesels couldn't be blamed for that!

In strict chronological terms, the next motive power innovation in Scotland featured, not diesel traction, but battery power. Two railcars were built in 1958 at Derby, responsible for the chassis and bodywork, and Cowlairs, where the traction equipment was fitted, to produce a single 'BMU' superficially similar to the 'Derby Lightweight' so successful south of the Border. Archive papers record this as a joint initiative with the North of Scotland Hydro-electric Board, which had suggested this experiment, to ascertain if locally generated power could offer new transport options. Scottish industry showed an interest, the Edinburgh company of Bruce

Peebles offering to provide electrical transmission equipment. That this company was invited to attend meetings on the matter shows some broad-mindedness on the part of the Board; Bruce Peebles was the company suing for locomotive-generated fire damage to its lineside building!

The Hydro-electric Board's participation was certainly generous – a reduction of £5,600 on power consumption, a connection charge of £5,100 (although it is not clear if this was a discounted cost or a fee waived) and a straight donation of no less than £6,000. The line involved was the picturesque Deeside branch running south-west from Aberdeen to Ballater. This was BR's choice; the Hydro-electric Board seem to have been split between Dundee-Arbroath and the Peterhead branch. But Scottish Region quite reasonably insisted on having the last word on operational aspects of the experiment, so Ballater it was.

Seating thirty-one first class and eighty-six second class passengers, the two-car unit, utilising the 'Derby Lightweight' DMU shell being turned out in numbers since 1954, was to be moved to the north-east from Glasgow in almost wartime secrecy. Even the unit's numbering had taken on a cloak-and-dagger aspect, with the planned numbers M79182/3 being suspended and replaced by SC79998/9. Management instructions stressed that the units be transported out of Glasgow 'by special freight train during hours of darkness' and were then to be stored in the carriage shed at Ballater by daybreak. Cleaning was then to take place before a press launch, with the actual service beginning on 21 April 1958.

The reaction of the rival bus company was to be monitored by rail staff on the line, but only 'in such a way as not to draw the [bus] inspectors' attention that they are being observed by us'. Heartening to see bus competition being taken seriously, and being responded to positively! There seems no doubt that BR believed that this new equipment would stimulate extra custom, certainly to begin with, and to capitalize on this, stationmasters were urged to listen to the weather forecasts on the Scottish Home Service at 5.55 p.m. each evening, and then to chalk up a weather summary on a blackboard displayed prominently in their station. All very admirable, although the resulting flurry of requisition forms specifying blackboards indicates that no such thing existed at Ballater line stations at the time!

More seriously, the Ballater stationmaster was soon expressing his disappointment by memo at the schedule proposed for the new units – eighty-five minutes for nine stations in 43 miles, one minute *slower* than steam traction! 'I would have thought a speedier run in both directions would be possible', he advised his superiors, with good reason one imagines. On this occasion, the traffic planners were listening, resulting in one battery timing of seventy-one minutes, but with six stops. Unfortunately, there were to be other instances on Scottish Region where newly introduced traction was diagrammed to operate on steam schedules. No doubt there were sound operational reasons for this, allowing drivers and guards time to familiarise themselves with new equipment, and with the new concept of having only one man in the cab, but there were other ways this could have been achieved.

Unfortunately, the battery cars' introduction was not enough to save Deeside's rail connection, and the Ballater branch closed in February 1966. On introduction, the battery railcars, with diesel support, had increased revenue by nearly two-thirds, with a lesser increase, of just over 10 per cent, in the next full year (as shown in Table IV). To have failed after such an improvement was hugely disappointing, indicating that even a determined initiative such as this in 1958, conducted in an atmosphere of espionage, of moving units under darkness, of shadowing bus inspectors, would still come to naught.

It may well have been that the root of the problem was rail's failure to capitalise on its greatest potential weapon – speed. With one station – Torphins – generating only one ticket sale *per week*, there was a strong case for cutting out all intermediate stations except Banchory and Aboyne and aiming to deliver commuters into Aberdeen in less than an hour from Ballater. But, on the contrary, Scottish Region actually opened an additional halt on the line – this was one occasion when a more forensic approach to intermediate station services might have paid off. Certainly, the fares offered on the line were highly competitive, with the Aberdeen-Ballater Cheap Day Return fare costing only twopence (1p) more than the bus, offering good value for Ballater residents commuting to work in Aberdeen. Their 07.20 departure from the branch terminus had no road rival – the TUCC insisted on a bus running at this time before it would agree to closure in 1966, so a local company offered a 07.00 service. This simply meant commuters had to get up earlier; the bus took 103 minutes for the trip.

In retrospect, it seems highly regrettable that BR Scottish Region and the NSHEB did not work together more frequently and more closely, either by extending the battery experiment, or in harnessing hydro-power to provide the Highlands with electric trains – commonplace in such mountainous countries as Norway and Switzerland. Even France was 80 per cent dependent on hydro-power for its electrified railways in 1948.

In examining the respective Board Minutes for 1956, the researcher is struck by the air of caution – and in the Hydro-electric Board's case, of suspicion – in their relations. Scottish Region saw the NSHEB approach regarding battery cars as an opportunity to secure a cheap deal for one particular line, and the lack of depreciation cover built into the costing suggests that BR, from the outset, saw no long-term future in the Ballater arrangement. Meanwhile, the Hydro-electric Board Minutes indicate irritation among Board members, particularly Sir John Erskine, in BR's apparent initial refusal to examine German battery-car designs, as he had suggested, while seeking advice from German railways as soon as technical obstacles began to appear.

This was a lost opportunity for Scottish. A good working relationship with the Hydro-electric Board could have led to the electrification of lines north and west of Perth, as well as in extending the battery scheme, by working with a institutional partner which had shown itself to be both innovative and generous. The West Highland line was built with the kind of public subsidy normally unknown in nineteenth-century railway promotions; it should not have been impossible, in a post-war era when the Highland and Islands Development Board was established, to persuade even a London government that utilising locally produced power for rail traction was an environmentally sound idea.

The next three diesel introductions all centred on Edinburgh once again. In May 1958 the Leith North branch from Princes Street was converted, with traffic immediately increasing by 41 per cent. Yet, the following year saw a *decrease* in passenger revenue of nearly one-fifth over the 1957 figures. The files indicate that the timetable had been rationalised in that second year of diesel operation 'to reduce costs. Steps so far taken to recapture the business lost have met with indifferent success'. This is a less than adequate explanation, and it may well be that the corporation bus services in that area responded to the railway's improved performance in 1958 with a better service. But in any event, the Leith terminus at Lindsay Road was a good mile from the heart of the town (although it would be handy now for the new Ocean Terminal) while Princes Street had only a limited number of connecting services, none of them to other parts of Edinburgh except suburban stations on the Carstairs/Glasgow (Central) line. Within four years, the Leith line had closed, even before the doomed Princes Street terminus.

Two more Edinburgh services, both centred on Waverley, went over to diesel power that summer. These comprised trains on the South Suburban circle through Morningside Road, Newington, and Craigmillar, along with the Rosewell and Musselburgh branches. All showed immediate improvements in revenue, and sustained this into a second year. Yet the services were all withdrawn within six years. One clue for this disappointing outcome lay in the timetable, which remained geared to steam timings even after conversion to diesel. This author recalls a DMU journey on the 'Sub' where the driver took out his newspaper during a prolonged stop at Duddingston & Craigmillar Station while waiting for the timetable to catch up with the train! Additionally, the location of the Musselburgh terminus was too far from the town centre to offer buses on the A1 a run for their money. The new Musselburgh Station is even farther out!

The final two diesel introductions in 1958 were in a class of their own. Both were rural, operated amid beautiful scenery, and featured single-vehicle railbuses. These were the Gleagles-Crieff-Comrie service, operated by Wickham railbus, and the Speyside line between Aviemore and Elgin, where a Park Royal vehicle was introduced. With only around forty-four to fifty-two passengers being seated, depending on design, a railbus clearly could offer no solution to any overcrowding issues, and the public's reaction to their introduction may have posed exactly that kind of problem! The Gleneagles units generated an immediate 150 per cent jump in ticket sales and the Aviemore, 88 per cent. Yet in the second year, both earned less than the steam services they replaced! In neither of the cases was a full second year of accounts available for comparative purposes, so the regional document restricted itself to quarterly samples. With these showing the diesel as having had a strictly temporary attraction, the document quotes the ending of a local construction project in the case of the Gleneagles service as having a significant effect on revenue – presumably this had inflated the steam figures – and, in the case of Aviemore-Elgin, patronage had been affected both by bad weather and 'a variation in the renewal dates for season tickets'.

One suspects that the 1950s railbus attracted a volume of business which its limited capacity prevented it from satisfying, and Scottish officials who had served with the LNER in the late 1920s should have known this. Steam-powered Sentinel railcars introduced at that time had shown – for example, on the former NBR Carlisle-Silloth service – impressively increased revenue initially. Passenger journeys were up 31 per cent in July 1928 and no less than 127 per cent in the following month. But long-term, these increases proved unsustainable, and additional coaches could not be towed when traffic was heavy. No figures seem to be available for the traffic performance of three ex-LMS Leyland-built diesel railbuses operating out of Hamilton just after nationalisation, and all withdrawn by April 1951.

Significantly, well to the south in former GWR country, transport author L.T.C. Rolt argued for a railbus on the Honeybourne-Cheltenham route when faced with closure, only to be told that it would stimulate more patronage than the vehicle could handle. He dismissed this, as a reason for withdrawing the rail service altogether, as 'Alice in Wonderland thinking'.

Almost unperceived by railway staff at the time, the diesel railcar, and indeed the railbus, were ushering in a new era in rail transport. When one prominent railway enthusiast was asked in later years why he was less interested in modern rail activities, he replied by paraphrasing Gloria Swanson in *Sunset Boulevard*, stating that his interest was still 'big', but it was 'the trains that got small'. In particular, the idea in 1958 that, for example, a North Berwick branch train could comprise a two-car DMU, was novel, particularly when the loading figures circulated in only the previous year permitted 230 tare tons in either direction – effectively eight non-corridor vehicles. Nowadays, a Glasgow-Aberdeen express can comprise only two carriages. The tabular entry for the North Berwick branch lists nothing larger than 3P power for passenger services here, yet the author's first visit to this line in the late 1950s was behind a tender-first B1 – a 5MT.

In practice, the 1957 loading schedules (see Bibliography) were about to become redundant, on some lines at least. The 'Inter-City' Class 126 DMUs could tackle Cowlairs Bank with ease, although through services to King's Cross, to say nothing of trains to the West Highland line and to Fife, were still regulated by the table of loadings giving a theoretical maximum of 200 tons for a 8P steam locomotive with, as mentioned earlier, a N15 allowed to bank up to 190 tons, and a V1, 160. The tables are a veritable seam of interest to the enthusiast; why, one asks, was an 8P – a 'Duchess' or 'Princess Royal' Pacific – allowed to take 570 tons up Beattock Bank unassisted, but only 500 if stopping for assistance? Again, returning to the point that modern trains, running to a fixed-interval timetable, are a fraction of their former size, the permitted loading of seventeen coaches on the WCML north of Carlisle seems extraordinary, particularly when this limit could be exceeded 'on the authority of the Chief Operating Superintendent'.

On the East Coast, the tables reveal (to this author) a previously unknown hierarchy within the passenger locomotive ratings. For example, on the Dunbar-Berwick section southwards, the Gresley A3 Pacific, theoretically a 7P, was allowed to take 520 tons over Cockburnspath, 30 tons more than the seven rating, and making the older Gresley machine the equal of an A1 or A4. North of Edinburgh, the A3 and A4 again were treated equally, being allowed 420 tons on the Bridges line north to Aberdeen. An A1 could take twenty tons more, while the nominal 8P loading figure was 500 tons, permitted only to those members of the A2 class not converted from V2s (the A2/1s).

'Internal' services within the region included an instruction that Glasgow-Aberdeen trains were limited to twelve bogies of pre-grouping stock or eleven of BR, and must include a brake vehicle at each end of the train, presumably to allow a reasonable turn-round at both Aberdeen and Buchanan Street. Within five years, the new three hour timetable would see these coaching rakes reduced to half this length. Meanwhile, with trains to Oban and Mallaig comprising two DMU carriages nowadays, it seems extraordinary to see the tables permitting twelve-coach trains to the former destination and 400 tons tare to the latter in 1957.

Anglo-Scottish passenger expresses were of almost incidental interest to Scottish Board members in BR days, the Board Minutes showing a pre-occupation with internal lines. There are comparatively few mentions of cross-border traffic, but around the mid-1950s Scottish managers seemed to become aware of the rivalry posed by air services. This may not be as blinkered as it sounds – before the Second World War, the LMS and LNER had a financial interest in Railway Air Services connecting London with Manchester, Belfast, and Glasgow, while after the war, internal civil aviation was slow to develop in the UK; Edinburgh, for example, did not receive civilian flights until 1947.

In 1955 Scottish began talking to both the London Midland, and the East Coast regions, about a new generation of 'high speed' trains. The crying need was for an early-morning departure from Edinburgh and Glasgow, with a late-afternoon return, although combining the stock of two such services, out and back on the same day, certainly did not appear in the plans as the year came and went. Special livery featured prominently in the discussions, and the 1937 'Coronation' observation cars were being considered for a comeback on this proposed service on the East Coast main-line as late as March 1956 – with, incidentally, a supplement of half a crown (12.5p) to be charged. In the event, with the initiative being taken by regions to the south, the East Coast succeeded in establishing the first of these long-delayed services, introducing the 'Talisman' express between King's Cross and Waverley, in September 1956. On a 400 minute schedule with a Newcastle stop only, and with the load restricted to less than 300 tons gross, this was originally run as an afternoon train only, utilising, of course, conventional stock.

It was not long before a corresponding morning service was run to mesh with it, the stock being fitted with roller-bearings to allow a 786 mileage daily. In 1957 Timken roller-bearings were fitted to no fewer than four coaching sets, two of them spare, to enable 'there-and-back' running in a single day. *Trains Illustrated* hailed this as the first 'general application' of bearings to passenger stock in British rail history. Timken had only invented them sixty years earlier.

An additional variation in the 'Talisman' service in 1957 was to start the up morning service (to be called the 'Fair Maid') at Perth, although patronage proved disappointing. This should not have been surprising, since the down service missed an Inverness connection by eighteen minutes, hardly a stimulant to regular long-distance travel on the service. Nevertheless, both up morning and down evening trains developed a gratifying level of revenue south of Newcastle, and should have been introduced more than thirty years earlier, as soon as the 1896 'go slow' ordinance had been abandoned in 1932 (see this author's *London's Scottish Railways*).

The West Coast equivalent, the 'Caledonian', did not appear until the following year, initially formed by an 08.30 departure from Glasgow and 15.45 return. The short turnaround time at Euston drew criticism from the media, and even the Scottish Board members felt that an earlier departure time in the morning would be preferable. These were the men supposedly in charge! Though, to be fair, the 1948 *Instructions* booklets had nominated the LMR as the lead player on Anglo-Scottish services on the WCML. By 1962, a re-timing caused by delays created by electrification meant that it was now impossible to operate the service with a single train set, the up and down services now passing each other in the Camden area. It was a disappointing aspect of the 'Caledonian' service, when a departure from Glasgow could have been up to forty-five minutes earlier.

Nevertheless, with a 405-minute schedule for its 401-mile journey, the 'Caledonian' was actually faster than the 'Talisman' on the East Coast, and in many ways represented the swan song of the 'Duchess' class of locomotives. On one occasion in 1957 a southbound service reached Euston in 119 minutes from Crewe – averaging approximately 80mph and equal to the 1937 dash on the day when LMS Pacific No.6220 *Coronation* attained 114mph on the northbound leg of the working. Despite all this, the service did not survive the conversion of West Coast services into a standardised timetable suitable for electrification in 1964.

Two innovations in long-distance travel which involved Scottish Region in the mid-1950s were the 'Starlight Specials' and the Car Carriers. The first of these emphasised the concept of 'cheap and cheerful' travel to a generation which traditionally looked on overnight travel as something that could only be undertaken in a sleeping car, and was financially out of bounds to the retired or the student – two staple sources of rail traffic nowadays – as well as to the average worker. Passengers could now 'sit up' in a reserved seat instead of reserving a sleeping berth, while the return ticket from Glasgow or Edinburgh to London, initially £3.50 (£56.75) attracted an entirely new market – or rather, a belated attempt to recapture the market lost to buses from the late 1920s onwards; rail managers may have noticed that Scottish Omnibuses had doubled the number of London-Edinburgh long-distance services over the five years up to 1951. Any loss of sleeping-car revenue was compensated for by the economic utilisation of long-distance stock which would normally only have been used during daylight.

Introduced in 1953, the 'Specials' were an immediate success, running from April to September, with no fewer than twelve leaving Glasgow on a single night during the 'Fair' holidays in that first year. In their second summer, sixty-nine of them conveyed 28,000 passengers from Glasgow and forty-six carried 22,000 from Edinburgh, channelled at peak holiday times on eight-day or fifteen-day return tickets down both East and West Coast lines. The *BR Magazine* recorded with delight that, in that first summer, 'there were no complaints of double or incorrect bookings'. A dip in loadings occurred in 1955 when open stock was introduced, but the figures gradually recovered. At less hectic times, it was found possible to head a 'Special' out of Glasgow (St Enoch) round the Saltmarket curve to join the former LNER lines and thence head for London via Bathgate and Edinburgh (Waverley). This introduced the sight of a Gresley Pacific to the former G & SWR terminus some years before they began working in from Leeds in place of 'Royal Scot' 4-6-0s. At the southern end, Marylebone terminus was regularly used until the service was withdrawn in 1962.

The 'Anglo-Scottish Car Carrier' was another mid-fifties innovation in Anglo-Scottish travel. This initiative appears to have begun on Guy Fawkes Night in 1956 when two vans, each big enough for two cars, were added to the 22.15 ex-King's Cross and the 22.20 up from Waverley – a modest beginning, and northbound traffic can hardly have been encouraged by a requirement for all four cars to be loaded at King's Cross by 16.00, a mere six hours before departure! Waverley was a little more liberal, loading one car every fifteen minutes from 20.00 at Platform 8A. Petrol tanks were to be filled only for 50 miles driving, for no immediately obvious reason with, more understandably, no petrol to be carried in separate containers. The guard took charge of all keys once the vehicles were loaded. Fares for car and driver were £21.75 (first) and £18.75 (second), both returns, but not including sleeper supplements (£328 and £283 respectively in modern currency).

Scottish and Eastern Regions were clearly feeling their way in assessing this traffic, but their instincts were good. Soon, BR discovered that it could adapt a number of GUVs (General Utility Vehicles), with end-doors, to cater for greater vehicle numbers and to speed up loading. It became necessary in summer to create complete trains, formally named 'Anglo-Scottish Car Carrier' from the 1960 timetable, to satisfy demand. A number of Scottish destinations were advertised from time to time for these car-carrying trains, with Holloway as a later access point for London. By the early 1960s, with double-decker vehicles in use, sleeping cars and a restaurant vehicle would then make up the rest of the rake. However constituted, these trains, one of which was seen by this author loaded to nineteen vehicles, were regularly headed by steam well into the 1960s, and must have presented a severe challenge of locomotive haulage. In 1961, the last year of the steam-hauled 'Elizabethan', it was reported that the down 'Non-Stop' was frequently finding difficulty in picking up water at Lucker, the last troughs before the Scottish Border, because the 'Carrier' was running, late, just ahead.

Ironically, the 'Anglo-Scottish Car Carrier' was created around the same time that Britain's first motorway was opening. Nevertheless, it was a concept worth marketing, particularly given the slow spread of motorway provision – no six-lane highway crosses the Scottish Border to this date, on East Coast or West (where the infamous 'Cumberland Gap' still restricts Anglo-Scottish traffic). Edinburgh, Scotland's capital and greatest tourist centre, continues to be the largest city in Britain without a direct motorway connection to London.

While Scottish received its first diesel shunting engine (13005), allocated to Ayr on 21 November 1952 (although Kingmoor was running five by then, all former LMS examples), the slow introduction of diesels on to main-line services, both internal and Anglo-Scottish was, as noted earlier, a source of media criticism in 1955. By the end of the decade, matters were little better, the only heavy diesels regularly crossing the Border being the Ivatt twins 10000/1 and the Southern Region trio 10201-3 on temporary transfer to the London Midland. Interestingly, all these Diesel pioneers were rated at 6P for loading purposes, making them the theoretical equal of an ex-LMS 'Jubilee' or LNER V2, except No.10203, classified at 7P, the equivalent of a 'Britannia' or 'Royal Scot'.

Meanwhile, steam reigned supreme on the East Coast route north of Newcastle. English Electric Type 4s (later, Class 40) were not allocated to North Eastern until 1959 or Scottish depots until early 1960: Haymarket received its first, D260, on 19 February. And still the introduction of the 'Heralds' was delayed.

While no more than a footnote to British railway history, it is interesting nevertheless to observe that the 'Deltic' (Class 55) was to be named the

'Herald' class if a proposal from the PR departments of the Eastern, North Eastern, and Scottish Regions had been sanctioned by the Scottish Board in the summer of 1959. The Board Minutes make it clear that this suggestion did not find favour with its members, and the chairman, despite his LMS background, stated a personal preference for names commemorating famous racehorses, a practice enshrined in LNER policy from the mid-1920s with the A1 class (and later A3, and postwar A2) Pacifics. Sir Ian Bolton, retiring in September 1959, would have been pleased to see that his wish was granted, with several of the class later being so named (although at the English end of the system). The other half were, later, to bear regimental names, with Scottish regiments prominently featured, although even that decision was only reached after reversals of policy, as will be recounted.

The Board was informed in March 1958 that the order for twenty-two of these machines, unprecedented in power, had been placed with English Electric at a total cost of £3.41 million (£47.75 million), although the later review of diesel introductions into Scotland gave the net price of the 22 machines as £1.76 million (£23 million). This estimate predicted that the eight regional 'Deltics' would replace eighteen steam engines, and show a net return on capital of no less than 34 per cent. But the Board members minuted their concern that the costings they had received did not appear to include the £50,000-£100,000 they expected to have allocated for servicing facilities in Edinburgh. In the event, the region would have three years in which to arrange this; in practice Class 40 diesels from the same maker would be allocated to the city within two years. These 2,000hp machines, seven of which were expected at Haymarket, would replace fifteen steam engines and show a net return of 23.2 per cent.

In September 1960 the Scottish Board informed the BTC that they would like the 'Deltics' to appear in 'Coronation Blue' livery. This is puzzling, as the former LNER 'Coronation' streamliner sported two shades of blue: Garter and Marlborough. This request was not granted, but a similar request for Caledonian Blue instead of the usual dull green for the Glasgow electric stock then under construction was allowed, as we shall see. The authorities down south, however, were firm on green livery for the 'Deltics', and when in the early spring of 1961 the author saw his first locomotive of the class, silent and stationary at Leith Central depot, its massive nose pointing over the buffer-stop and down the taxi ramp to Leith Walk, it was in dark green, but with a pleasing light green border round the lower, 'tucked-in', body. A flashing headlight, mounted centrally on the nose was a curious, and short-lived, embellishment on this, the then un-named No.D9000.

Unknown to me, the Scottish Area Board had continued debating a naming policy for the class, with the members being told in November 1960 that it would not be possible to employ regimental names. No reason was given, but the former LMS 'Royal Scots' were still engaged on main-line work at the time, and the Eastern Region had definitely plumped for racehorses. The Board's new chairman, Cameron of Locheil, appealed to his Board colleagues for suggestions, possibly of appropriate historical figures or characters in literature. In that same month it was resolved to ask the BTC when these long-anticipated, and much discussed, locomotives were expected to be delivered.

Services within Scotland proposed for conversion to diesel locomotive power in 1959 were Glasgow (Buchanan Street)-Aberdeen and Edinburgh (Waverley)-Aberdeen. Both routes were, according to the Board Minutes, to be served by a fixed number of locomotives (eighteen Type 2s each) and the introductions were budgeted at £1.35 million (£19 million) per line. The accounting practice is curious, as these locomotives could, and did, find themselves operating on other parts of the system. The 1962 Transport Act would bring this kind of fantasy book-keeping to an end. Both the diesel classes involved (Classes 26 and 29) were already being tried out south of the Border, on the Eastern Region. They were tried out to some effect; the '29s' were already making a name for themselves, and not a name of which their makers could be proud.

Although the introduction of diesels on the Aberdeen services out of Glasgow was expected, in June 1959, to bring about an impressive, and impressively precise, 25.92 per cent return on investment, by October Scottish Region was less optimistic. On 14 October, the Scottish Board informed the BTC of its 'regret' that the Region was expected to operate accelerated Glasgow-Aberdeen services with diesels built by North British Locomotive of Glasgow (the class 29), described in the official minutes as 'this unsatisfactory stud' in preference to 'tried and trusted equipment'. The Board insisted that 'NBL should be made responsible for holding spare locos until they had fully proved themselves in service'. Yet the '29' had only been introduced that year! It seems puzzling that Eastern Region ever passed these machines as acceptable if they were so bad as to prompt this *cri de coeur* from Scottish management (these engines are shown in the official registers as 'ex-ER'). Obviously, the reputation of the '29s' preceded them before they returned across the Border, but the decision to pass them in the first place seems baffling. Scottish Region's client status in this matter will be discussed later.

By 1960, with the class attempting to establish itself on former LMS routes in central Scotland, the Board was informed by General Manager James Ness that there had a 'deterioration' in service, and that repeated loco failures was having 'a repercussive effect on other trains'. Ness informed the Board that he had alternative courses of action in mind, one of which was to commission refurbishing some of the class with new equipment. In effect, the Class 29 exactly symbolised its troubled manufacturing company, North British Locomotive.

Lord Reith, a former NBL apprentice, flung himself into the challenge of saving the company after being appointed vice-chairman in 1959, but even he proved unable to save the sinking ship. The *Investor's Chronicle* pointed out in that year that the Glasgow company held loans of no less than £1.75 million from the Treasury, £1.5 million from the Clydesdale Bank, and £500,000 from General Electric, so the company's credit was considered to be good. Indeed, the *Chronicle*, drawing comfort from the firm's apparent ability to raise loans, considered NBL a worthwhile investment. Yet the company went into liquidation in April 1962.

Gourvish records that NBL still held twelve BR contracts worth £15 million (£196 million) as late as 1962, but points out that 'the [BTC] files are full of internal qualms about inflated prices, late deliveries and technical defects'. By that time, the BTC was considering suing the company to recover £300,000 (£4 million) as compensation for late deliveries, and it was coincidentally the very month when the technical press carried a report that a NBL-built Class 29 had been cut up for spares – less than three years after introduction!

The year 1962 was to be an interesting one for the Glasgow-Aberdeen service, as will be discussed later, but the objective observer is forced to wonder why Scottish did not order a second generation of 'Inter City' diesels for this traffic, given the success of the Class 126. Edinburgh-Aberdeen was always going to require locomotive haulage as long as there were through-trains between Aberdeen and King's Cross (before the HST era of course), while, in contrast, Aberdeen-Glasgow was effectively an internal Scottish route, and could surely have benefited from operating the type of long-distance DMU then undertaking 'Trans-Pennine' duties.

In passing, it should be mentioned that the Class 26 diesels, in contrast to the '29s', proved to be worthy additions to the Scottish locomotive stud, from the moment that D5303 joined the Regional complement at Leith Central on 28 November 1958. While soon replaced on passenger services by more powerful units, this class found a new role in heading MGR trains to service such coal-fired powers stations as Cockenzie, being specially adapted with slow speed control to facilitate hopper loading and unloading. Their slightly updated sisters, the Class 27, were to succeed the Class 126s on the Edinburgh-Glasgow passenger run from 1971, and operated on this for almost too long. But BR certainly got its money's worth from the 26s and 27s.

five

PROGRESS (OF A KIND) TO 1962

Before 1960, not a mile of Scotland's rail system was carrying electric train services. This was an appalling statistic for a mountainous country when compared to the electrified railways in Switzerland (97 per cent route mileage electrified on its Federal system) and Norway (32 per cent). Significantly, even as early as 1948, no less than 80 per cent of France's electrified mileage came from hydro-electric power. Scottish nationalists would be quick to point out that those other countries are autonomous states, while the seat of Scottish government, certainly in the 1950s, lay hundreds of miles to the south.

To be fair, a BTC-enforced spending review appears to have compelled Scottish to weigh up the importance of its electrification of North Clydeside against the relative claims of its freight plans. The Board minutes in January 1958 report that 'the electrification project could only keep to schedule at the expense of the Region's new marshalling yards at Millerhill and Perth, together with the new goods terminal at Sighthill [Glasgow] and the new wagon repair depot at Townhill [Dunfermline]'. No decision on the priority of these projects appears in the minutes that year, and it may be that the technical difficulties of the electrification scheme, one of the first to utilise the new BR high-voltage standard, meant that progress was going to be slow anyway. Table VI shows that, unfortunately, by 1958, Scottish was demonstrating considerable arrears in terms of modernisation – at least, measured in terms of traction – and this could have been used as an argument for more favourable investment terms at that time.

And electrification, delayed as it was, could hardly have got off to a worse start.

In February 1959, the Scottish Area Board asked its London master, the British Transport Commission, for permission to depart from the usual

BR livery arrangements in finalising the appearance of new stock for Scotland's first electric main-line railway – the former NBR and LNER North Clydeside lines, known prosaically to the Board as Glasgow Suburban Electrification Stage 1. This was to electrify (by overhead catenary) the network from Airdrie and Bellgrove in the south-east, to Balloch, Helensburgh, and Milngavie in the north-west. As well as eradicating steam from the Stygian gloom of Queen Street (Low Level), it would introduce modern electric traction to the Bonny Banks of Loch Lomond at Balloch.

The Board was given permission to use Caledonian Blue for its new trains, the original suggestion coming from a centralised BR Design Panel, according to Michael Bonavia, and that might explain what railway historians could well regard as a rather inappropriate scheme. Here we had a Caledonian livery being suggested for a former North British line, but such a detail was probably not discernable from London, and seems to have been disregarded in Glasgow as well! But who could honestly say that that the NBR company's olive green, or 'gamboge' as it was known, would have been preferable? In fact, olive green was not far removed from the uninspiring green used on electric multiple-unit stock in and around London, so the Scottish Board was right to seek a striking alternative, particularly since former Caledonian lines out of Central were also intended for electrification.

It would be Scotland's most expensive railway reconstruction up to that time. By the dawn of 1961, after three years of work, and no less than £16.85 million (£234.5 million) of expenditure (the 1954 estimate was £154 million, to include routes out of Central), the new electric trains would have been introduced, and then withdrawn. Steam would once again reign supreme on north Clydeside. What had happened?

On Guy Fawkes Day 1960, BTC chairman Sir Brian Robertson formally opened the north Clydeside electric services, with the public being admitted to the trains on 7 November, the following Monday. The new 25kV ac vehicles, in their imaginative 'new' livery – not seen in Glasgow for three decades, and never seen at Queen Street at all – had experienced some early operational difficulties during trials, and the Board had postponed introduction rather than opting for the suggested alternative, that of operating a service based partly on electric traction while partly retaining steam as well.

BR's determination to go for an entirely new image seemed to have been justified on opening, if media reaction alone is considered. The Board minutes commented that 'press reaction was favourable ... facilitated by a frank presentation of the causes of early "teething trouble"'.

THE RAILWAY EXECUTIVE

RAILWAY REGION OF SCOTLAND.

As from January 1, 1948, the administration of the Railways in Scotland will function as a single entity.

The Chief Regional Officer for the Scottish Region will, therefore, as from January 1st, 1948, assume responsibility for general administration, within the policy and general instruction of the Railway Executive. Clearly, the time factor will prevent the introduction of a complete scheme from January 1, but it is desired that the various steps should be taken as quickly as possible, and the co-operation of all concerned is sought to this end. The aim should be to make the various changes involved as smoothly as possible, and to avoid dislocation of the public service.

The Scottish Region will be organised on a basis which will enable matters local to the region, and coming within the sphere delegated by the Railway Executive to the chief regional officers generally, to be disposed of quickly at the regional level. The regional departmental officers will maintain ordinary day-to-day contacts with one another, but will meet together under the Chief Regional Officer as chairman. This officer will have a co-ordinating function, and will have authority to enable him to ensure the settlement of local questions, leaving only matters of major principle and general policy to be carried up to the Railway Executive. Copies of instructions from the Railway Executive to his regional departmental officers will be sent to him.

With this statement of general principles, the following detailed arrangements will be made :-

(1) Definition of Railway Region of Scotland.

The dividing line between the Scottish and English Regions will be drawn from Gretna to Burnmouth, as shown on the attached sketch.

The motive power depot at Kingmoor, Carlisle, will be under the control of the Scottish Region.

The shipping terminal arrangements at Larne will be under the control of the Scottish Region, though for mutual convenience the Northern Counties Committee may, by arrangement, act as Agents for any part of the work.

Joint Line procedure generally is set out in Appendix I.

(2) Location of Headquarters.

The main headquarters of the Scottish Region will be in Glasgow; the location of the various departmental officers will be determined in relation to the office accommodation available, but it is desirable that as far as possible the Chief Regional Officer and the departmental officers most directly concerned with railway working should be accommodated together in this city. The Chief Regional Officer will make a recommendation accordingly to the Railway Executive, indicating the various departments to be located in Glasgow and in Edinburgh.

(3) Functions of Chief Regional Officer.

The main responsibilities and functions of the Chief Regional Officer will be as follows :-

(a) Co-ordination of departments at regional level in matters affecting more than one department. Instructions as detailed later will be given direct to the regional departmental officers by the Member of

Right: 1. Remit for Scottish Region. This document, produced on an office duplicator, was issued to the new regional managements at the eleventh hour by the Railway Executive at the end of 1947, one of six regional remits originally drafted by Miles Beevor of the British Transport Commission. (National Archives of Scotland)

Below: 2. Modernisation's false dawn? From the autumn of 1948, LMS-designed diesel locomotives Nos.10000/1 operated across the Border into Glasgow (Central) on Anglo-Scottish express trains, but were not allocated to a Scottish depot. Here the Derby-built pair is seen at Motherwell on a Euston-Aberdeen train in July 1958. (James Currie)

3. British Railways was launched on 1 January 1948 with no livery planned for locomotives and rolling-stock, and no corporate design whatsoever for stations and written materials. This lack of image is shown well in this March 1949 picture of a former LNWR 2-4-2 tank engine at Dumfries. The new five-digit number has been applied, but the wording 'BRITISH RAILWAYS' is the utilitarian branding shown on locomotives of the time, although there were some curious variations. (H. Stevenson collection)

4. In the almost ecclesiastical surroundings of Dumfries MPD, a former LNWR 2-4-2 tank is seen at the back end of the shed, still painted in LMS livery and bearing its pre-1948 number of 6639. The picture was taken ten months into nationalised ownership, although this particular engine only lasted in traffic for another eight months, before being withdrawn from Beattock MPD. (H. Stevenson collection)

5. Up 'Waverley' express begins its journey out of Edinburgh's station of the same name, on its way to London (St Pancras) via Carlisle and Leeds in the mid-1950s. Heading the rake of LMS coaches is the last A3 to be built, No.60043 *Brown Jack*, still showing its plain BR emblem on the tender, while D30 No.62424 *Claverhouse* waits to take out a later train. (J.&C. McCutcheon collection)

6. The year 1951 saw the end of operation for no fewer than seventeen Scottish Region lines or services, but Peebles (West) failed to last even that long, being closed in May 1950. Although a dead end for passenger services, this former LMS line extended beyond the station building seen here, and crossed the Tweed to join up with the former LNER line from Edinburgh. (H. Stevenson collection)

7. Biggar lost its passenger services along with Peebles (West) in 1950, but this picture shows a fairly typical branch station, well endowed with two platforms, footbridge, and a signal-box. Parts of this branch were as attractive as anything to be seen in the Highlands and really should have been developed for tourist traffic. Curiously, when track-lifting took place here two decades later, a misunderstanding led to the track being removed on either side of a Class 26 diesel, much to the delight of the local newspaper. (H. Stevenson collection)

8. Neither the LMS nor the LNER rebuilt any passenger stations in their twenty-five years in charge of Scotland's railways, and it was left to BR to open Girvan Station in 1951, five years after the old station buildings were destroyed by fire. Although there have been later station conversions and constructions, none are as architecturally distinguished as this. It has recently been refurbished, and is well worth visiting for its mid-twentieth-century distinctiveness. (Author's collection)

9. Dalmellington in Ayrshire enjoyed rail services until 1964, and unlike many rural branch termini, this was located very centrally in the town. This 1950s shot shows that steam-age equipment was still in use at the time, despite a request from a local government association, forerunner of COSLA, for no closures to take place without modern motive power at least being tried out. (J.&C. McCutcheon collection)

10. Last day at Symington. This deserted wayside station on the West Coast main-line south of Carstairs was once the junction for Peebles via Biggar, but that destination had been unavailable for fifteen years when Black 5 No.45491 pulled out for Carlisle on 2 January 1965. (H. Stevenson collection)

11. While not the most handsome of locomotives, with their inclined cylinders somehow justifying their nickname of 'Crabs', the former LMS 2-6-0 was a popular engine in Scotland. As late as March 1964, No.42737 was to be seen on an enthusiasts' excursion round a number of closed branch-lines, this setting being Wilsontown in Lanarkshire. (J.&C. McCutcheon collection)

12. Strathaven is one of Lanarkshire's most attractive towns and might have been expected to retain its rail service to Glasgow Central as a dormitory suburb. But this July 1957 photograph shows a lack of investment in diesel power, never mind electrification, as Standard 4MT No.80058 runs round its branch train. The line closed in 1964, while the line west of Strathaven had succumbed to closure three decades earlier. (H.C. Casserley)

13. Clackmannanshire is the smallest county in Scotland, and joined the list of those lacking a passenger railway service during the period of nationalised operation. Thankfully, Alloa has seen its service restored, but not so Alva, where J36 No.65323 was photographed heading an enthusiasts' excursion in April 1963. (Author's collection)

14. Suburban trains in both Glasgow and Edinburgh in the 1940s and 1950s were often hauled by Gresley V1 tank locomotives, such as the immaculate example, No.67624. Seen heading west from Haymarket, this appears to be a Fife train, composed of corridor stock. (John Robertson)

15. Neither LNER or LMS invested much in freight traffic, nor were they encouraged to by government, with legislation requiring mineral traffic to be carried effectively at a discount, if rates relief was to be gained by the companies. This held back investment in bulk freight transport as the earning-capacity per train was reduced. Here a 'modern' LNER 0-6-0 of the J38 Class is seen at Niddrie on a mixed freight which might even have included some wagons with a continuous brake. (H. Stevenson collection)

16. A container train leaves Carlisle for the south in the summer of 1965. The containers concerned were designed in the 1920s with a capacity of a mere four tons; the one visible in this picture contained meat, probably from Broughton on the Symington-Peebles branch, bound for London (Maiden Lane). The locomotive, rebuilt 'Patriot' No. 45530 *Sir Frank Ree*, appears to be in less than perfect condition, but that was nothing unusual in BR days. On the left, a 'Derby Lightweight' DMU awaits its next roster deeper into Cumberland. Scottish Region hoped to borrow one of these in December 1955 to placate media unrest at the lack of modernisation north of the Border. (Author's collection)

17. Saved from a watery grave. The 'Austerity' freight locomotives introduced during the Second World War were originally intended to be dumped at sea after the war, but they went on to provide years of service to BR, some lasting into the mid-1960s. Here an unidentified 2-8-0 descends the now-dismantled Lothian Lines loop over the ECML through Joppa and towards Leith with a coal working around 1963. (Author's collection)

18. Former Caledonian 0-6-0 tank locomotive No.56313 is seen at the head of a line of engines at Dalry Road depot around 1961. The line from Merchiston and Carstairs comes in at the right of the picture, but this whole site is now part of a road complex. (Author's collection)

19. Not only has this class of locomotive, the J37 0-6-0, become a thing of the past, but so has the unbraked mineral train on which No. 64605 is seen, while the bridge on which it is running is now demolished. Now the Sir Harry Lauder road runs on this site, crossing the ECML near the former site of Joppa Station. (M. Green)

20. Seafield MPD in 1961, with J37 No.64607 to the fore. The underfoot conditions are fairly typical for a steam-age depot. Shed staff were not protected by the Factories Acts, and before 1948, Britain's railways had no statutory requirement to even provide first-aid for staff injured in such conditions. (Author's collection)

21. The run-down nature of MPDs during the 1950s and early 1960s can be seen from this shot of Seafield shed in Edinburgh. This was home to former NBR J Class 0-6-0s sub-shedded from St Margaret's and, with so little cover, they were left to enjoy the tender mercies of the Firth of Forth, just a few yards away to the left of the picture. (J.&C. McCutcheon collection)

22. The turntable at South Leith, a sub-shed of 64A St Margaret's, and operating locos for docks traffic almost exclusively. The diameter of the table was 50ft, and had to be operated by manpower. This location was described in an official Railway Executive document as a fuelling point for oil-fired steam engines, although the actual fuel tanks were built at Craigentinny in 1947, and probably were never used. Leith docks are out of sight in the background. (J.&C. McCutcheon collection)

23. The former Caledonian and LMS equivalent of the LNER J class 0-6-0s were the Jumbos, seen throughout Scotland well into the 1960s. Here No.57638 is seen on the Carstairs crossover, with the WCML heading off for Carlisle in the distance, in the view taken on 4 August 1955. (J.&C. McCutcheon collection)

24. Car-carrying by train goes back to the invention of the internal combustion engine, but in 1956 British Railways hit on the idea of carrying cars and their drivers and passengers in the same long-distance train. This picture shows the down 'Anglo-Scottish Car Carrier' passing through Joppa on the ECML in 1962, although the car vehicles are out of sight at the rear of the train. A3 locomotive No.60060 *The Tetrach* did not have much more express work ahead of her, being withdrawn in the following year. (Author's collection)

25. Although designed for duty in Scotland, the Standard 'Clan' Pacifics never seemed to make a name for themselves, and perhaps should have had tablet exchange apparatus fitted to increase their range, particularly north of Perth. Here No.72004 *Clan Macdonald* is seen on the former GSWR main-line with a Carlisle-Glasgow parcels duty at Auchinleck in June 1962. (Bill Hamilton)

26. The penultimate steam locomotive on BR books (although not second-last to be built) was 9F 2-10-0 No.92249, seen in the company of Black 5 No.45236 at Carlisle (Kingmoor) MPD as late as October 1966. When the regions were established in 1948, Kingmoor was firmly allotted to Scottish, while the city's Canal depot, just as Scottish in its original company origin, was placed in the North Eastern Region. Both later became part of the London Midland. (Mike Macdonald)

27. One of the last steam locomotives to be withdrawn in Scotland was Standard 4MT No.76000, operating from Motherwell depot until May 1967. It is seen here on a Glasgow (Central) stopping train near Mount Vernon in 1963. (Mike Macdonald collection)

28. The last steam locomotives to operate on a daily basis in Scotland were two members of the J36 class, working from Dunfermline and Thornton depots. Most of the engines in this class passed the seventy-year mark, and served NBR, LNER, and BR Scottish Region. One of the last, No.65288, is seen at Dunfermline on 12 October 1966. (Mike Macdonald)

29. Fastest steam locomotive in the world, *Mallard* was not a regular visitor to Scotland, but worked a number of special trains on the ECML before its inevitable preservation. Here it is seen approaching Joppa, on the eastern outskirts of Edinburgh, on a 1962 working from London (King's Cross), the 'Aberdeen Flyer'. (Author's collection)

30. Viewed through the spectacle glass of preserved D34 4-4-0 *Glen Douglas*, a Cravens-built DMU heads for Edinburgh across the Forth Bridge in 1964. The bridge and its owning company were nationalised along with the rest of Britain's railways in 1948. (Cathkin Barrow)

31. Scottish Region had an ambiguous attitude to loco preservation as the steam era came to an end. Board members decided in 1957 to scrap *Gordon Highlander*, but reversed their decision after coming under aristocratic pressure to preserve the locomotive, and it was felt that there also had to be a former North British representative at the same time. The lucky engine was No.62469 *Glen Douglas*, now to be seen in NBR livery at the Glasgow Museum of Transport. It is pictured here on a special train at the delightfully named Rumbling Bridge on the Alloa-Kinross Junction (Devon Valley) line in the year of the line's closure, 1964. (Author's collection)

32. Saved as a result of a last-minute change of heart, *Gordon Highlander* is seen from the unusual viewpoint of the 'Devon Belle' observation coach running tender-first on the Lockerbie-Dumfries line on a special train in May 1959. Another Scottish veteran 4-4-0, the Highland Railway *Ben Alder* was less lucky, and although officially preserved, was cut up as soon as it reached St Rollox. (W.S. Sellar)

33. 'Locomotives disposed of without replacement' became a regular entry in the Scottish Region Board minutes from around 1960, when steam locomotives began to be written off. Many were dumped, pending sale to scrap merchants, in the open air at two principal locations: Bathgate and Bo'ness. Here V1 No.67619 is seen at the latter site in April 1962. (Mike Macdonald)

34. The railbus seemed an attractive and promising solution to the problem of reduced branch-line revenue. Seen at Hamilton in 1960 is 'Park Royal' vehicle 79972, carrying a LMR prefix after transfer to Scotland, where the usual SC prefix was applied. Unfortunately, these vehicles were so popular initially – showing a 150 per cent revenue improvement on one line – that they stimulated more traffic than they could handle, leading to an immediate downturn within a year. (James Currie)

35. A Swindon-built 'Inter City' Diesel, SC51791, is seen undergoing maintenance under the huge Arrol roof at Leith Central. The Central was earmarked as a diesel depot by the LNER from as early as 1947, when it had another five years to go as a passenger station, but it enabled whole trains to be repaired under cover when converted for opening in 1956. (Bill Hamilton)

36. A Class 126 is seen on Ayr-Glasgow duty in June 1961. These Swindon-built units were responsible for a 28 per cent increase in revenue on the Edinburgh (Waverley)-Glasgow (Queen Street) main-line when first introduced in 1957, and two years later began work in south-west Scotland. (Bill Hamilton)

37. DMU Class 101 was a common sight in Scotland's railways in the later 1950s and well beyond the 1960s. This three-car unit is seen at Dundee (West) depot, with 'Tayport' showing on the destination screen. The services in this area, particularly to St Andrews, showed a handsome increase on revenue when operated by diesels, but that did not save them. (Bill Hamilton)

38. D9000 nameless at Haymarket on 18 June 1961. The production 'Deltics' were nearly three years in design and building, during which time Scottish Region tried to have them turned out in Coronation Blue, and the Board was told by the BTC that they could not be named after regiments. Despite this, D9000 became *Royal Scots Grey* in the following year, in a curious turn-around by the Commission. (Bill Hamilton)

39. An unidentified 'Deltic' heads an East Coast express southwards past New Hailes, where underground workings necessitated a speed restriction for decades. This late 1960s shot shows the removal of occupation loops on the down side. (Author's collection)

40. Not likely to win any prizes for style, a Barclay-built 0-4-0 diesel mechanical shunter D2438 shunts Falkland Junction in its native county of Ayr, in June 1961. (Bill Hamilton)

41. Commonplace throughout BR, Class 08 D3133 shunts Grangemouth docks on a wet August day in 1960. Grangemouth was owned by the Caledonian Railway following its takeover of the Forth & Clyde Canal, and when handed on by the LMS to the new docks administration in 1948, was the only of its Forth ports in profit. (James Currie)

42. While both East and West Coast main-lines took delivery of English Electric Type 4 diesels, the former Midland lines were powered by the BR/Sulzer equivalent, the first ten of which were named after Pennine peaks. Missing the distinction of a name by only five numbers, D15 is seen heading the down 'Thames-Clyde Express' at Kilmarnock in July 1961. (Bill Hamilton)

43. Not allocated to Scotland, and probably running a filling-in turn, D24 heads an Ayr-Glasgow parcels past Falkland Junction in July 1961. (Bill Hamilton)

44. Class 40 D263 climbs Cowlairs bank with QOS in August of 1960, the year when these engines were first allocated to Haymarket depot. The train itself was equipped with new stock from 1962 onwards, although its dawdling course from London to Glasgow via Leeds, Harrogate, and Edinburgh, always made it appear a curious transport option for business travellers. (James Currie)

45. Haymarket MPD with locomotives D263 and D5304 seen on 15 May 1960. The depot had operated 'Top Link' steam engines on such turns as the 'Flying Scotsman' and 'Elizabethan' and was a natural servicing-point for Type 4 and 5 diesels, while St Margaret's was phased out with steam power. (James Currie)

46. Waiting to run light into Waverley Station are the two original Class 26 diesels Nos D5300/1, around 1960. These were used in pairs on the Edinburgh-Dundee-Aberdeen route, which even steam enthusiasts had to admit was best operated by non-steam power. (Mike Macdonald)

47. Side by side at the east end of Leith Central, D5332 and D5117, 16 April 1961, at a time when Haymarket depot was undergoing modification to cater for the new traction. It was at this site, just a few weeks earlier, that the region's long awaited first 'Deltic' was to be seen. It was kept under the overall roof, visible from nearby Leith Walk. (James Currie)

48. A delightful study of a Class 27 diesel, D5363, on a Fort William–Glasgow train crossing at Ardlui with preserved Caledonian No.123 on the 'Oban Railtour' on 12 May 1962. The latter was a veteran preserved by the pre-1948 LMS, along with the Highland 'Jones Goods'. Scottish added two others, but failed to save the Highland *Ben Alder*. (Bill Hamilton)

49. Steam and diesel pairing at Perth, D5341 and 45490, August 1961. Critics of BR motive power policy pointed out that a Type 2 diesel had little in reserve when handling the same work as a Class 5 steam engine, although double-working, with a single crew, was one advantage. (Mike Macdonald)

50. D5117 and D5333 represented express motive power when pictured here at Inverness on 6 August 1963. Scotland is rich in hydro-electricity but no trains are so powered in the Highlands, despite the friendly overtures made to the Scottish Board by NSHEB in the 1950s. (Mike Macdonald)

51. D5116 Polmadie, 1960. Curiously, locomotives of diesel Classes 24 and 25 were omitted entirely from an availability survey carried out for the regional Board in 1966, by which time they had served Scottish Region for some six years. The official records carry no explanation for the omission, but the twenty-eight engines themselves just got on with it! (Bill Hamilton)

52. Class 29 D6149 Haymarket MPD, with small ploughs even as late as mid-April 1961. Scottish was unhappy at having to accept these 'unsatisfactory' locos, as they were described in official documents, and their acceptance by Eastern Region, on behalf of Scottish, seems puzzling. (Bill Hamilton)

53. 'If you want something done properly...' Class 29 D6131 on a mineral train at an unconfirmed location and date. The failure of Scottish Region to test new equipment was a recurring problem, resulting in Glasgow-Aberdeen services having to return to steam haulage, while the Class 17, and Clydeside electrification also suffered. (Mike Macdonald)

54. Class 20 D8081 Polmadie-Falkland Junction freight at Prestwick, 27 September 1961. English Electric proved to be a reliable locomotive supplier (compared to some of its rivals) but design aesthetics were obviously not a high priority. (Mike Macdonald)

55. As with the Class 29, and the pressed steel emus, Class 17 diesels suffered major 'teething troubles'. One was scrapped only three years after the last steam locomotive it was intended to replace. Here, D8517 heads coal empties at Ballieston, 1963. (Mike Macdonald collection)

56. Loch Lomond no longer reverberates to the sound of a paddle steamer carrying passengers round one of Europe's most beautiful areas. This 1964 shot shows the *Maid of the Loch* leaving Tarbet, her decks still thronged, even after disembarking passengers preparing to walk to Arrochar on Loch Long. The vessel is still afloat, but is currently tied up at Balloch. (Author's collection)

57. A variation on the Sulzer-engined 'Peak' Class was the Brush-powered D148, seen here at Joppa in 1962 on an Edinburgh-bound duty. The days of the wayside station on main-lines were fast running out, and Joppa, just east of Portobello, had less than two years of life ahead of it. (Author's collection)

58. The Mound, junction for the Dornoch Light Railway until its closure in 1960. This picture was taken in the 1930s, but little changed in the next two decades. The main-line heads off on left to Wick and Thurso, with the DLR on the right. The regional Board was informed in 1960 that the demolition of this line, despite its lack of buildings and equipment, would release a rich hoard of materials. (J.&C. McCutcheon collection)

59. The Waverley Route was the first main-line to close in Britain, but this view at Riccarton taken on 14 August 1963 shows A1 No.60118 *Archibald Sturrock* (not a Scottish engine) crossing V2 60957, with the crews preparing to change over. The A1's fireman is running ahead, perhaps to buy something at the station's Co-Op! (W. S. Sellar)

60. Last passenger train on Lauder Light Railway, on 15 November 1958. Standard 2MT No.78049 stands at the former terminus with the local Provost addressing the rail enthusiasts. Passenger services on the branch from Fountainhall had ceased before the Second World War, but freight services were continued because of the presence at Lauder of emergency food stores maintained by the government. (W. S. Sellar)

61. Glasgow's St Enoch Station was one of the few to be equipped with colour-light signalling in pre-war days and, not surprisingly, was an efficient and cost-effective traffic point for Scottish Region until closure in 1966. Here, under the impressive overall roof, 'Clan' Pacific No.72007 *Clan Mackintosh* is seen, with former Caledonian 4-4-0 No.54506 on the right, and a LMS-built 2P 4-4-0, a popular design on the old G&SWR system, just visible on the left on the picture, taken on 4 April 1960. (W.S. Sellar)

62. No.42048 on a Carstairs train inside Edinburgh's Princes Street Station on 20 June 1964, fifteen months before closure of a station popular with passengers, including the visiting royal family. Good access for vehicles and pedestrians, but difficult for rail staff to operate – the exact opposite of Waverley! (W.S. Sellar)

63. Tracks on the approaches to Edinburgh (Princes Street) Station seen here on 9 April 1960 from the overall terminus roof. This view will be unrecognisable to anyone born after the 1960s, this site being overlooked nowadays by the Edinburgh International Conference Centre. (W.S. Sellar)

64. The old North British Railway surprisingly failed to establish a hotel in the golfing capital of St Andrews, and it was left to BR Scottish Region to open the Old Course Hotel on the site of the former goods station in 1968. Despite its proximity to the R&A headquarters (seen on the right in the foreground) the hotel struggled financially to begin with, not helped by BR cutting the supply of potential visitors by closing the railway into the town! (Author's collection)

A souvenir brochure was produced to commemorate the introduction, along with a poster featuring the work of none other than Terence Cuneo, showing a Caledonian Blue train (Class 303) beside the Clyde at Bowling.

Public reaction to the introduction of the 303s was little short of sensational – in the first week, no fewer than 400,000 passengers travelled on them, in contrast to the 170,000 using steam-hauled services in the corresponding week of 1959. Saturday use of Queen Street (Low Level) rocketed from 9,000 to 40,000, despite the reduction in platform capacity.

But this early success was soon to be marred. On Sunday 18 December 1960, the decision was made to withdraw all sixty-seven three-car units from service (in fact seventeen were already unserviceable). The Board Minutes itemise three technical problems – 'unsatisfactory and unreliable transformer thermostats', 'failures in the automatic voltage regulators' and 'air blast circuit breakers being tripped by overloading'. Significantly, only the last of these was being investigated by the manufacturers, implying that BR was tacitly admitting that its own acceptance procedures had proved to be flawed.

This rather bald description disguises the fact that there had been a series of five transformer explosions, four occurring when the trains were in service. No fewer than 230 passengers were on board when seven of them, and a guard, were injured in an incident at Renton on 13 December. On another occasion, 250 passengers were forced to evacuate a six-coach unit when an emergency occurred; fortunately nobody was hurt. Clearly, the equipment was too unsafe to utilise in its initial state, and the problem was regarded as serious enough to necessitate a public inquiry, only four days later.

Meanwhile, a 'state of emergency' was declared, and Scottish Region managers and staff went into overdrive to restore the steam-hauled service. A detailed description of how they did this was published in the *BR Magazine* shortly afterwards. It was a highly creditable operation, with many staff reporting voluntarily over that fateful weekend. Forty-two office staff alone were required to type, check, and then duplicate hastily improvised crew diagrams, some of them working until 2.30 a.m. on the Monday morning. The operational problems faced can scarcely be imagined following the clearing of coal, lubricants, and equipment from loco depots such as Helensburgh, to say nothing of the removal of water columns from every trackside location on the routes. This led understandably to a transfer of locomotives with larger water-carrying capacity than the V1 Class which previously predominated – former LMS 2-6-4 tank engines, and three

'Standard' Class 4MT Moguls moved to Parkhead depot, the latter from Corkerhill.

No doubt grateful for the loyalty and flexibility of all staff involved, the Board minuted a suggestion to their PR department that a press release be prepared explaining how professionally the conversion back to steam was achieved. As if the media would be impressed!

The summer of 1961 saw the region (and the LMR) testing the stock following technical modifications, with the Milngavie branch being used for further trials. But there was no immediate remedy; in May the General Manager reported that forty-six trains were suffering so many failures when on trial that 'withdrawal all over again' would be necessary if a public service was restored. All this, six months after initial introduction. Two full-scale trials were held on 17 and 24 September, but only just, in the case of the first date. So bad were the effects of a storm on the day before the first trial that a section of line near Bowling was closed because of 'seaweed on the line', delaying the start of that day's trial until well after 11 a.m.

Reintroduction took place on 2 October 1961 without a press conference, in marked contrast to the previous November's gala. A press statement was, however, issued, although the Region need hardly have bothered. One sympathetic transport journal pointed out that the withdrawal of electrics may have been treated by the media as a national outrage, but their reintroduction was barely reported at all!

The Class 303 EMUs went on to give stalwart service after clocking up 1 million miles by their first Hogmanay in service. They extended their range to services on 27 route-miles out of Central from 27 May 1962, going on to accumulate some forty-one years service to Glaswegians, even into the new century. They began to lose their original livery from around 1968, adopting standard BR blue livery and later the Strathclyde PTE colours. Unfortunately, they became very rough-riding as they aged, and this author recalls an English visitor enquiring if these trains had 'square wheels'. The loss of the forward view over the driver's shoulder, after a refurbishment programme in the 1980s, was also a major disappointment, particularly on the lines running along the north and south banks of the Clyde.

The 303s should have been replaced much earlier than they were, although they were hardly alone in that on modern British railways. An additional difficulty for the staff striving to provide the area with a modern rapid transit system was the lack of investment in accompanying infrastructure. The electric 'Blue Trains' were, particularly on north Clydeside, operating in and out of stations still equipped with gas lighting.

The years 1960 and 1961 must have been dispiriting for Scottish Region managers as they tried to drag their railway into a new decade. The North Clydeside electrification scheme was Scotland's biggest railway project since the construction of the West Highland Railway (no fewer than 119 bridges had been altered, sixty-five of them completely rebuilt) and, with its imaginatively liveried rolling-stock, the 'Blue Train' service should have been a triumph in both British and European terms. But the technical failures put paid to that in the immediate future, and the performance of Glasgow-built Class 29s on Glasgow-Aberdeen services was unacceptable. Both these attempts at modernisation ended with the reintroduction of steam services; an appraisal of the Region's testing and acceptance procedures for new traction was clearly required, but was not addressed. Meanwhile, the much-heralded 'Deltics' still had not arrived.

One rail innovation peculiar to Scotland in the late 1950s and early 1960s was the 'Television Train'. The earliest references to it in the Board Minutes describe this as a CCTV-fitted train, but the press was quick to embellish the whole concept at a time when the introduction of commercial television had made the nation much more television-conscious than formerly. The Scottish TV train, hailed by *Trains Illustrated* magazine as 'the world's first permanent' example, consisted of an on-board studio with a single 'tiny industrial' camera, whose pictures were relayed to TV monitors in each coach. These were also fitted with three loudspeakers each, power being supplied by a diesel generator. The idea seemed to be that the attention of up to 600 passengers could be directed to the passing view, although one suspects that an audio PA system could have done this equally well.

Although the Board Minutes record that the first use of the train was a Glasgow *Evening Citizen* outing to Blackpool, the train was used almost exclusively for schools. Printed handouts instructed children which side of the train to look out of at a particular place, no doubt prompted by the announcer. It has to be said that the prompt sheets issued on the TV train and now preserved in the public archives were poorly produced – duplicated typescripts infested with typographical errors. The author's wife travelled as a primary school pupil on one such train in 1962, from Abbeyhill (Edinburgh) to Crianlarich via Callendar, and although she enjoyed the scenery, the train's TV credentials have not registered on her memory. Later references in the periodical press indicate that the train was used as a stationary exhibition train, principally for the Scottish textile industry.

By 1961, rail closures in Scotland had become so unpopular that Scottish Region made a determined effort to project its point of view on the matter.

The then Board chairman, Cameron of Lochiel, began a 'charm offensive' on the Scottish media by organising a number of lunches for newspaper editors where, presumably, he was able to convince journalists how so much of the country could benefit from losing its rail services. Unfortunately, the Board Minutes do not indicate any discussion about whether the public may have been instinctively right in believing that a policy of closing public transport links, particularly in rural areas, was flawed. Writing about BR's property portfolio up to 1973, economic historian T.R. Gourvish observed that, 'the railways exploitation of their station properties via Railway Sites Ltd [forerunner of BR Property Board] was far from dynamic'. This was not the case in Scotland, however. Indeed, if anything, there was a positive enthusiasm – the description in the Board's own minutes – for the disposal of railway-owned land.

While it is perhaps inevitable that a modern observer might invite charges of cynicism by viewing BR executives' determination to close and dismantle railways as a means of 'liberating' sites for sale to commercial developers, this is to place an inappropriately modern perspective on the diminution of the rail network. It should be remembered that property was not always regarded as so valuable as it is nowadays. The responsibility for providing housing lay with local authorities at this time, and they met this by constructing estates and high-density tower blocks on the periphery of cities. Not until the liberalisation of the divorce laws in the late 1970s did the demand for housing explode, with a much higher proportion of families breaking up and a consequently increased demand for more housing.

But using the word 'enthusiasm' to describe the drive to dispose of railway property in 1960s Scotland is not inappropriate. On 15 November 1965 the minutes record the Board's appreciation of the 'enthusiastic approach of the planning staff' in the matter of disposal where, we learn, 'Scotland has maintained the lead as a Region in this sector'. Stilted prose perhaps, but something of a giveaway to any historian forced to regard the closing of railways as a preoccupation among BR managers who were determined to modernise and cleanse what they perceived as an organism crippled with too much dead wood.

In 1965, Scottish (now headed by a professional railwayman) was considering withdrawing fifty-two passenger services and closing 439 stations. In the previous two years, 486 goods stations had closed, with another 485 slated for closure. This represented removing around 1,400 service points where passengers or goods triggered income for the railway. After taking into account the downright inaccuracy of some of the disposal and salvage figures attached to the closure of particular lines (see Table V, in which it will be noticed that the 1960 estimates, in particular, strain credulity to its limits), it is difficult to understand how Scottish railway managers could believe that they were proceeding fairly in their management of public transport assets.

While it is tempting to speculate that an expanding closure programme was intended to enhance the lucrative potential of Railway Sites Ltd (later the BR Property Board), a projection which is as depressing as it is cynical, it should be noted that, even by the mid-seventies, the Property Board's annual turnover represented barely 6 per cent of the combined total for BR subsidiaries. However, unlike the Freightliner service, just above it in the earnings table for 1973, the sale of BR property was to have a healthy future.

All this was reflected in BR statistics quoted by Gourvish. In the five years up to 1979, income from sites rented out by BR exceeded sales by a ratio of nearly 3:1, but in the five year period to 1990 this statistic was virtually reversed, with sales bettering rental income by 1:2.5, actually £360 million rental to £852 million sales. This is even more damaging than might appear at first sight, since the rental statistic represents *recurring* revenue.

There is, of course, no suggestion of any impropriety, or that BR staff, in Scottish Region or anywhere else, had some kind of a financial incentive in land sales; more of an adoption of a (defeatist) state of mind that the railway could best contribute socially by making land available for redevelopment, especially in city centres. Perhaps the only mitigating factor which Scottish administrators could use in arguing their case for closures was that in Scotland, railways had to pay feu duties to whoever the feudal superior was in the particular area. This will be returned to later.

The response when the Board authorised placing part of the Glasgow (Queen Street) Goods area on the property market late in 1960 was no doubt a pleasant surprise for Scottish Region. No fewer than 100 enquiries were received from interested developers. Buchanan Street, St Enoch, and Princes Street termini were doomed.

Not only landed property was being sold off by British Railways. Steam locomotives were slated for oblivion by the 1955 Modernisation Plan, but as we have seen, dieselisation of Scotland's railways was slow, and electrification even slower. Nevertheless, within a few years, the Board Minutes began to include a recurring item: steam locomotives 'authorised for disposal without replacement'. In September 1962, for example, eighty-six engines were written off at a total 'residual value' of £137,391 (£1.8 million). This paper disposal at approximately £1,600 each suggests that these were comparatively small locomotives, many of them tank engines – although earlier in the year no fewer than eleven V2 locomotives weighing 147 tons each could be found mouldering at a single dump site.

In contrast, many six-coupled freight engines, even seventy-year-old veterans, were still hard at work on the BR system. Indeed, the Scottish Railway Preservation Society had just announced in 1962 that it would concentrate on saving former Caledonian locomotives, as the former NBR J37 0-6-0 class, a favourite for purchase, was still receiving heavy repairs. Regrettably, and despite this resolve, no J37 ever did survive.

Within the year, the value of an express locomotive with tender was reported as around £3,000 (No.60103 *Flying Scotsman* comes to mind). While this price has to be multiplied by a considerable figure to approximate to today's values, such inflation is fuelled by rarity value, and it is curious that more museums did not strive to follow Birmingham's example and procure a locomotive with a connection to their particular community at a time when prices were comparatively low. Scotland's National Museums were particularly indolent in this matter, their failure to acquire any post-grouping Scottish locomotives showing no awareness of the burgeoning interest in industrial and transport archaeology. The Museum's acquisition of the LNER D49 *Morayshire* was by donation; in any event, it was not built in Scotland, unlike, say, a LMS 'Jubilee' or 8F, LNER Gresley A3 Pacific, or a B1. As a result, the impressive Museum of Scotland in Edinburgh's Chambers Street has no locomotive exhibit other than an industrial shunter little larger than the average family car, and even that was rescued by a private individual. Since Glasgow's impressive collection of locomotives is pre-1923, a Scottish-built product of the LMS or LNER would have been a highly appropriate exhibit in the Museum of Scotland – and still would be.

But railway enthusiasts needed no official information about locomotive disposals. For the first time in Britain, locomotive 'dumps' were becoming part of the railway landscape in the early 1960s. Those at Bathgate and Bo'ness were celebrated among railfans, the former catering for Edinburgh's unwanted (forty-nine engines, including the eleven V2s), the latter for Glasgow's (fifty-two), with both these statistics from early in 1962. There was even a mythical Glen Douglas store, where steam locomotives were reputed to be 'mothballed' in case of a traumatic failure of diesel and electric traction nationally, or even some kind of semi-nuclear war where only steam engines would be able to operate afterwards! It is certainly true that in the autumn of 1964, BR installed sidings worth £31,079 (£372,000) in Glen Douglas, but charged the Admiralty an extra £663 at 'trader's rates'.

Presumably the reason for the dumps was a sensible step to regulate the amount of scrap coming on the market simultaneously, and thus keep up the selling price of metal, and in this, the region convinced itself that it was reasonably successful. By early 1964, another 121 steam engines were written off at a cumulative cost of £179,234 (£2.23 million), valued at approximately £1,470 each. Yet whether these prices were subsequently obtained at the scrapyard gates is perhaps questionable. Alternatively, Scottish was possibly scarred by the experience of the Clydeside Electrics failure, and instinctively decided to hold on to its reserves of motive power. However, anyone visiting the forlorn hulks of Bo'ness and Bathgate, where cab fittings, number, maker, and shed plates were being removed almost daily by souvenir hunters, could not imagine any of the engines moving under their own power, ever again.

As if to demonstrate how out of touch they were with public opinion in the Scottish transport community, the Area Board members decreed late in 1957 that the former GNSR and LNER 4-4-0 locomotive *Gordon Highlander* would not be preserved when withdrawn the following year. They reversed their decision within a month, because of 'widespread interest' in the locomotive, headed by the Marquis of Aberdeen.

With the LMS having preserved two, even older, units after withdrawal in the mid-1930s – Caledonian 4-2-2 No.123 and the Highland 'Jones Goods' No.103 – it only required a NBR representative (a D34, *Glen Douglas*) to be similarly saved from the breaker's torch for all the pre-grouping railways to be represented which still had their locomotives in traffic at the end of the 1950s. Unfortunately, this did not include the Glasgow & South Western engines, the last of which barely survived into the earliest days of British Railways. One is preserved at Glasgow's Museum of Transport, but was rescued from industrial use in the 1960s.

Another loss was the former Highland 4-4-0 *Ben Alder* which survived into BR days, but was surprisingly and heartlessly cut up in 1966, at a time when conservation was very much a public preoccupation. From examining the relevant NAS file on locomotive disposal (see Bibliography), it appears that this unfortunate engine, although described in the official ledgers as 'historic', was nevertheless notified by the staff at Kipps shed to the Supplies Manager in the usual way, and was delivered to St Rollox to meet its fate on 18 April 1966. It has been suggested by LMS historians Bob Essery and the late David Jenkinson that preservation of the locomotive was ruled out because it had received a Caledonian boiler and was not therefore 'as new', but an administrative error at Kipps, compounded at St Rollox, seems just as likely.

A unique opportunity for the four preserved steam locomotives to be seen operating again came in September 1959, when Scottish enterprisingly organised a number of special trains to Glasgow for the Scottish Industries Exhibition. No fewer than forty-eight of them were rostered for veteran motive power, working two at a time, and some of these workings went through to Kelvin Hall Station (formerly Partick Central). Supplementing the four was the preserved GWR 4-4-0 *City of Truro*, and the press release issued by the region had no hesitation in awarding the first 100mph on rail to this veteran. The whole exercise was a superb goodwill campaign (popularly attributed to James Ness, although the Board Minutes are silent on this) designed to emphasise the wealth of Scotland's industrial heritage. Needless to say, when this author travelled to Kelvin Hall Station from Edinburgh (Princes Street) on an excursion, I managed to miss the preserved stud of engines, and had to make do with a 'Black 5'!

The unexpectedly slow introduction of 'Deltic' power to the East Coast Main Line has already been remarked upon, with Scottish Board members, deep in argument in 1960 about names and livery for these exceptionally powerful engines, suddenly asking when they would actually be delivered. The answer was March 1961, their final appearance being markedly different from an OO gauge model of a production 'Deltic' introduced by the Hornby Company, which had grown tired of waiting, too! Sensibly, the new locomotives were allowed to work themselves into traffic on existing schedules, with no dramatic accelerations in 1961.

In the summer of 1962 – happily the centenary year of the 'Flying Scotsman' service – the anticipated speed-up resulted. Both the 'Scotsman' and the 'Elizabethan' were scheduled for a six-hour timing between Waverley and King's Cross, and all other expresses were also accelerated. The 'Elizabethan' lost its non-stop riband in this year, the noise and vibration from the 3,300hp engine being too much for an off-duty crew to put up with in the trailing loco cab, there being no means of changing crews through a corridor connection with the train. In this stopping guise, the 'Elizabethan' lasted only a single season.

Scottish Region launched the 10.00 departure of the 'Flying Scotsman' service along with the naming of D9000 as *Royal Scots Grey* in a ceremony at Waverley on Monday 18 June. This was a major step forward in terms of Anglo-Scottish rail travel, although it has to be said that many observers believed that the steam-hauled 'Elizabethan' could have been accelerated by some 30 minutes, especially if the unnecessarily high loading of around 400 tons had been reduced. With the 'Flying' and 'Junior' Scotsman services running behind to handle traffic on route, there had surely been a case for lightening the A4's load in the days of steam, as suggested in this author's book *Non Stop!* In other words, a steam-hauled six-hour journey had been a possibility for the previous five to seven years, but in any event, it was probably not just speed which was to prove the most notable aspect of 'Deltic' performance, but their very high availability.

Curiously, while the 'Deltics' are looked on retrospectively as a success story – they could handle accelerated schedules, achieve impressive 'turn-arounds', and generated a public anticipation of ever-improving journey times – the Scottish Board chairman appeared to need some persuading of their merits. In November 1962, Cameron of Locheil complained about the 'unsatisfactory performance' of the 'Deltics'. One suspects that Scottish Board members were automatically attuned to complaining about diesel and electric performance, and no later mention of Cameron's comment is to be found. History has accorded these 3,300hp diesels a special place in the transport pantheon; perhaps Cameron of Locheil thought the 'Deltics' unsatisfactory, but the 'Heralds' were doing a great job!

Another restoration of steam power came about within the next two and a half years, and represented the exhaustion of the patience of the operating authorities with the NBL diesels. This took place on the Glasgow (Buchanan Street)–Aberdeen line, where a three-hour schedule was introduced in June 1962. Curiously, the poster advertising this improved timetable illustrated a train hauled, not by one of the new diesels, but what appears to be a former LMS 'Patriot' 4-6-0, not rebuilt at that! One wonders if former LMS art-work was used from the immediate pre-war years when a three-hour schedule was introduced for the first time. In fact the locomotives being used in 1962 were larger, but at least the method of traction illustrated was absolutely correct.

Pre-war train names such as 'The Granite City' and 'The Saint Mungo' had been restored to the route in 1949, although not to the same serv-ices as pre-war. In a survey of punctuality in September 1951, the Scottish Regional edition of the *BR Magazine* reported that, of twenty-four arrivals of the northbound 'Granite City' at Aberdeen, twenty-one were punctual. Admittedly, this was on a 225-minute schedule, and, alarmingly, no less than 101 minutes were debited to the locomotives, with 95 minutes being recovered by good station work at each of the six stops. Loads were a good deal heavier than in later years, the standard rake being eleven coaches of 349 tons tare as far as Perth, with a van being attached there bringing the tare weight up to 364 tons thereafter to Aberdeen. Locomotives rostered were described as a Class 6 4-6-0 (probably a 'Jubilee') for the southern half of the journey, and a V2 for the northern. The timetable was revolutionised in 1956, with a regular-interval service being introduced, and a number of intermediate stations closed, particularly north of Perth, allowing an overall acceleration. Even so, this did not include a three-hour timing on the route; the best time was half an hour slower, but with six stops.

Although the much-criticised NBL Type 29s were heading Aberdeen trains out of Glasgow's Buchanan Street into the new year of 1962, it appears that the authorities were not prepared to take a chance on them when introducing a new three-hour timetable in the following June. The arrival of the last of the 'Deltics' at Haymarket – as late as 2 May 1962, in the case of D9021 – triggered a chain reaction involving the allocation of a number of the depot's Pacifics to the former LMS line. The technical press credited James Ness with this initiative; the Board Minutes certainly make it clear that the general manager was left to deal with the problem. Meanwhile, accounting arrangements were changing with the establishment of the British Railways Board in the following year, so the rigid 'line-by-line' costing of diesel power – £1.35 million for the Glasgow-Aberdeen service, for example – was mentioned no longer.

First to move west were A3s Nos 60090/94, although the latter was damaged in a collision at Buchanan Street within six months. But it was the transfer of the A4s that made the headlines in the railway press. No Scottish depot had ever operated them at that time apart from Haymarket.

On 22 February 1962 a trial train was operated in 162 minutes net between the two cities, headed by the newly arrived *Merlin*, sister engine *Golden Plover* having failed shortly before the trial. Aberdeen's Ferryhill had operated East Coast power for many years, with NBR and LNER having 'rented' facilities at this former Caledonian and LMS depot, but St Rollox crews were not so accustomed to Pacifics. A handful of Eastern and North Eastern Region streamliners also found a new lease of life on this former LMS line over the next four years, while ironically, the former LMS 'Duchess' locomotives were destined for the scrapheap, almost certainly because of their tenders' limited water capacity (for a summary of the origin and subsequent allocation of the A4s involved, see Table VII).

Curiously, these lightweight expresses represented exactly the kind of traffic the A4 Pacific had been designed to operate in the first place. From the start, the A4s showed that they had not lost their powers of acceleration, and, reviewing their work four years later, Cecil J. Allen wrote in *Modern Railways* that he had been forced to suppress publication of logs of some

A4 runs on the Glasgow-Aberdeen line. This was because of the 75mph speed ceiling imposed by Scottish Region, and Allen was warned by an inspector that his publication in May 1965 of a southbound trip where No.60034 *Lord Faringdon* had covered 21.7 miles at an average of 82.6mph, could result in disciplinary action for the driver. As this author remarked in the book *Streamlined Steam*, it is ironic that a locomotive class introduced in such secrecy in 1935 should exit from the railway scene some thirty years later in similar circumstances.

... AND OF ANOTHER KIND

At the end of 1961, ten years after the largest number of rail closures in a single year, the question of closing or withdrawing unprofitable services reached a new level. With Scottish officially recognised as BR's worst performing region in terms of turnover and profit, no fewer than 125 passenger services were slated for withdrawal in December of that year, and a further 160 by 6 January 1962. The Peebles branch (strictly speaking, a spur off the Waverley Route) was scheduled for closure to passengers in the following month. Otherwise, many of the worst performing services operated on existing main-lines where there was no question of closure.

Railway employees and enthusiasts alike could only feel a chill of concern on hearing of withdrawals of services in the heavily populated Central belt, including a thinning-out of trains within an existing timetable, indicating that the more remote Oban and Kyle lines were unlikely to survive a similarly forensic approach to rail costings. In 1961, Scottish Region staff, with the newly appointed Dr Beeching looking over their shoulders, produced a list of 'shamed trains', as sampled in the third week of October 1960. It is shown in Table VIII, beginning with the most extraordinary example, the 19.56 Berwick-Edinburgh, whose daily turnover came to a princely 10s!

Clearly, the running of a passenger train over 58 miles of the East Coast main-line to generate the equivalent of 50p revenue was madness, although Scottish initially justified the operation as some seventy-five BR staff used the balancing southbound service (06.50 ex-Edinburgh) to reach their various workplaces. The logical conclusion would have been to run the northbound back eight hours later, in other words turning the train out of Berwick into a workmen's special. If nothing else, some horrendously bad publicity would have been avoided! Notice though, that this train was not the biggest financial loss-maker in the above list; that laurel went to that very outward service which Scottish used as a justification for the 10s earner!

Two Oban line trains enter this listing, the 09.30 out of Oban, and 12 noon from Buchanan Street, but their actual earnings were £84 and £127 respectively, and that was well out of the summer season. So, although operating costs came in at £336 and £275 respectively, the highest in the 'name and shame' list, the origins of an argument to preserve lines for social purposes in comparatively remote areas, can be glimpsed.

On the other hand, the Peebles closure resulted in the biggest rail demolition ever seen in Scotland, generating, at that time, according to the records, no less than £128,240, although this must have been guesswork as this figure was communicated to the Board in November 1963, and the request for closure to freight only followed three months later. The estimate suggests a recovery figure of around £3,400 per mile. This seems enormous, around twice the usual figure, yet bridges were left behind at Cardrona, Eddleston, Innerleithen, and Traquair, the latter two sites having eleven metal spans between them, according to leading industrial archaeologist John R. Hume, writing in 1975 (see Bibliography).

The former Caledonian and LMS line at Peebles, with its station on the west of the Tweed, had closed to passengers in 1950 and to freight some eight years later, but BR could reasonably argue that local people were offered – and had not taken – the chance to sample modern rail travel, following the introduction of diesel multiple-units (class 100s) in February 1958 on the former NBR line. Possibly the linking of Galashiels into the scheme had reduced the train's frequency by lengthening journey times and this, exacerbated by the single line, prevented a more prolific service – at the time of closure there were only seven northbound trains a day. Nevertheless, this remains one of Scotland's most puzzling closures.

The presence on the relevant TUCC of James Amos, the manager of Scottish Omnibuses (effectively the old SMT) was curious, if not downright wrong. After all, SO had complained about this diesel introduction at a meeting with BR in September 1958, and their comment was minuted. Initial use of the DMU showed an improvement of no less than 111 per cent, so the income of the buses must have been affected. It seems impossible to explain how the company's representation on the Committee could be justified. Nor was Mr Amos likely to prove a shrinking violet on any such body; while pioneering bus services in the Borders just after the First World War he did not hesitate to stop his vehicle to 'harangue reluctant passengers', according to the company history.

The 1962 Transport Act abolished the British Transport Commission, and the railways came under the control of a new British Railways Board. The legislation itself disappointed those in the technical media who hoped to see nationalised transport undertaking a more socially responsible role in providing services which were useful, but might require subsidy. As we know, this approach had to wait another six years for the incoming Labour Government to produce its own Transport Act.

One important accomplishment of the 1962 Act was to confirm the legitimisation of the status of the regions within BR. It was always understood that the 1948 legislation setting up British Railways did not provide legal status for the regions within, complicating matters if the region was caught in, say, an employment or property matter which required a resolution in court. As already observed, when Bruce Peebles sued because of fire damage caused by a 3F 0-6-0, the Railway Executive was 'pursued' in the Court of Session, being succeeded in the 'dock' by the BTC from 1956, as the case dragged on.

The new Act removed from the regions any responsibility for policy decisions, including 'the design, procurement, allocation and overall control of rolling stock and ships', as well as workshops, research and development, police, and property disposal. To balance this, there was increased authorisation for works and equipment projects up to £100,000, sales and purchases of property up to £20,000, and appointments of up to £3,000 per annum, not including heads of departments. In many ways, this confirmed the predominance of the professional in the regional boardroom, so a certain process of logic could be discerned.

Anglo-Scottish traffic, both in its timetabling and motive power arrangements, seemed to be an area where the Scots were prepared to accept the dictates of the regions to the south on all three main-lines. Even in the case of internal services where there were problems caused by traction re-equipping, board members seemed to be kept at arm's length, as when General Manager James Ness decided to re-engine the Type 29 Diesel and then replace it with steam on the accelerated Glasgow-Aberdeen services. In this case, the Board's involvement was almost reduced to that of a passengers' consultative organisation. There is reason to wonder if some of its members were perhaps rather too elderly to be involved in the detail of organising a nationalised industry, particularly one having to work with the untried equipment which the main-line diesel effectively was in the mid- to late 1950s.

At the same time, it has to be said that there was no reason why the Board members could not have debated operational policy with more frequency than appears to have been the case. The decision not to electrify the Edinburgh-Glasgow main-line, for example, appears to have been taken on the grounds of economy, with more than a hint of parsimony. Even more extraordinary is the lack of questioning of the region's copious closures policy. Whether railway lines burrowed under the populous centre of Scotland's largest city, or over some of its more barren Border passes, there is a distressing lack of evidence of any debate on whether and how to save such lines as Glasgow Central (Low Level) or the Waverley Route.

The transfer into the chairman's seat of general manager W.G. Thorpe in the autumn of 1964, was, if nothing else, a concession to professionalism. Distinguished economic historian T. R. Gourvish comments on BR's regional structure: 'engineers and 'traffic' managers were dominant, and the only person whose responsibilities embraced both costs and revenues was the Chief Executive (Railways)'.

We have already seen that the initiative for the introduction of new Anglo-Scottish services, such as 'Caledonian' and 'Talisman' expresses, was invariably taken south of the Border. This even led to the incongruous vision of the Scottish Board complaining about the poor timetabling of the first of these trains, which left Glasgow too late in the morning to allow a reasonable stopover time at Euston. Yet the minutes of the mid-1950s discussions in Glasgow make it clear that Scottish Region was still thinking in terms of prestige trains, specifically mentioned as 'High Speed' services, with unique liveries and observation cars, rather than a long-awaited addition to an increasingly accelerated timetable which would soon take on a 'regular-interval' appearance.

Perhaps not surprisingly, in May 1959 the Scottish Area Board decided not to adopt the twenty-four hour clock. Certainly, it was not commonly used on BR at this time, and would not be formally adopted until 1964. But somehow, this Scottish rejection of modern continental practice seems to perfectly sum up Scottish Region's administrators, who at times seemed to be struggling to free themselves from 1930s thinking, particularly when it came to planning a modern timetable for long-distance traffic.

Similarly, the English regions were introducing technical improvements on the main-lines crossing the Border, with the Scottish Board merely being informed of their progress – and asked to help pick up the bill. In December 1957 Scottish Region agreed to pay £3,269 (£47,600) for seven locomotives to be fitted with ATC apparatus for use between King's Cross and Grantham, this out of a total cost of £118,038 (£1.71 million). No operational details were recorded, but one assumes that the seven engines concerned were Haymarket's A4s, which made non-stop runs to and from

London in the summer months on the 'Elizabethan' service. Since many of the 245 express passenger locomotives of the Eastern and North Eastern regions would travel over this stretch of the ECML almost every day, while each of Edinburgh's A4s might only do so once on a theoretical maximum of fourteen days per year (assuming equal rostering of each engine to this three days a week duty), it seems a tad harsh for Scottish to have to pay on this basis! Table VII shows which A4s were allocated to Haymarket up to 1962. If ATC was being speedily installed northwards, such payment would be undoubtedly appropriate; yet only the Edinburgh (Waverley)-Glasgow (Queen Street) line was scheduled for such conversion in 1958, at an estimated cost of £203,585 (£2.8 million).

In practice, it appears that Scottish held a minor role in decision-making on the East Coast main-line, although the *Instructions* booklets establishing the regions in 1948 made it clear that the Railway Executive Member for Operating (originally Michael Barrington-Ward, formerly head of the LNER Southern Area) would 'co-ordinate and control through working between the North Eastern and Scottish Regions'. However, with the Executive now history, ordinances on such technical innovations as cab signalling on the East Coast route would appear to be issued from on high in the south. This was formally the case on the West Coast, where in 1948 the Executive had decreed that: 'the LMR will co-ordinate and control through working between the London Midland and Scottish Regions, and for this purpose will be in close touch with the Scottish Region'.

By the summer of 1959 the Scottish Board Minutes record that the warning system was being extended north from Carlisle on both the former Caledonian and G & SW routes, and also on the Cathcart Circle, at an approved cost of £305,000 (£4.3 million). As with the estimate for the Glasgow-Edinburgh line, the number of locomotives being approved for fitting was not mentioned.

Incidentally, technical manuals made available to Scottish Region in the late 1950s refer to the device as 'AWS' or 'Automatic Warning System' although the later denomination 'ATC' (Automatic Train Control) was probably more correct since there was a control element built into the system from the start. A driver's failure to react to a distant signal 'on' would result in a partial brake application, indicating to the guard that something was wrong. The system also had a built-in fail-safe device which would react to any attempt to tie down the re-set handle, by triggering a brake application within three seconds. Present-day media stories of train drivers succeeding in dismantling ATC systems were obviously anticipated.

In August 1965, Scottish was informed that there was a 'hold' on the installation of CWR (continuous welded rail) on the East Coast Main Line north of Newcastle, 'until its future has been determined'. The minutes record the Board's regret at hearing this news – concerning a line on which they had just shared in a substantial traction re-equipping – and rather bizarrely requested that CWR should be installed anyway, even if the line was reduced to single-track. Curious nowadays to see the ECML referred to in this way.

If the Board thought that diesel failures were a matter of history, there was a rude reawakening in 1963. In April of that year, no fewer than fourteen new diesel locomotives in a single class were temporarily withdrawn because of fractured crankshafts. These were the 900hp Clayton-Paxman locomotives (later designated as Class 17) designed for freight hauling, and 'tested' by the LMR, and their failure prompted a comment in the Board Minutes that this would cause a delay in withdrawing steam locomotives. One imagines that the continued longevity of 0-6-0 goods locomotives – and some of them still had another four years of service in the region – was an embarrassment to an organisation which would liked to proclaim its modernity. Ironically, the first withdrawal of the Claytons took place within three years of the disappearance of the pensioner-aged steam locomotives they replaced!

Obviously, the introduction of these noticeably low-powered machines – and the Board was still complaining about the D8500s at the end of 1965 – was a tacit admission that BR had failed to get rid of the short-distance, unfitted or partially fitted freight working, and that the policy of centring traffic on huge marshalling yards had created a renewed need for such potentially uneconomic workings. Goods being delivered at a city-centre depot would still have to be marshalled into a mixed train (a 'trip' working) and then hauled some 10 miles or so for re-sorting and final transit to the destination – in contrast to a fast freight service with a single destination, a concept which had proved successful since the 1920s.

When, for example, the Board was able to hand over Lothian Road goods station in Edinburgh to the property sellers (a Sheraton Hotel stands there now, along with a new approach road), it was still necessary to spend no less than £81,000 improving the depot known as Leith Walk East. Curiously, the Board was informed that the annual saving from Lothian Road's closure would alone equal this expenditure, although in view of the Leith site's closure in less than fifteen years, this seems improbable. Leith Walk East had operated long-distance fitted freights for many years, but trip transfers to Niddrie were now replaced by trip workings to Millerhill.

The Type 29s were still a long-running problem. Their re-engining was allocated a budget of £1,685,000 (£21 million) in 1964, although twenty were to be so treated before an assessment was made about proceeding with the whole class. Complicating the issue was the demise of their builders, North British Locomotive, who had so completely failed to convert to newer forms of motive power. The Board was particularly concerned that any more investment in the class 29s might not be worthwhile, with no builder able to supply spares. This accounts for the report of a 29 being 'cannibalised' for spares as early as 1962, the year of NBL's closure and within three years of introduction, although this is not recorded in the stock registers. Officially, thirty of these locomotives were 'in store', by the mid-sixties (see Table XI), being condemned at the end of 1967, and another nine by the following summer.

While the Board members were never slow to express their disappointment in many of the early diesel classes delivered, they might perhaps have examined their acceptance testing procedures – if they had any. In an article for *Modern Railways* in April 1962 (see the Bibliography), a member of BR's technical staff pointed out that only four regions tested diesel locomotive, DMU, and EMU classes. Of the remaining two regions, the Southern carried out 'very little' testing and 'Scottish Region does no accepting or testing' at all. Interestingly, the English Electric 'Deltics' (Class 55) were tested at Doncaster, as might be expected, but so was the same company's Class 40, although most of them operated on the LMR. That region in turn passed Scottish-bound units such as the Clayton Type 1s, and the Clydeside Electrics, even although the latter were partially assembled at Paisley. While it may be tempting to suggest that the London Midland's testing procedures were not the most exacting, it appears that it was Doncaster which accepted the worst diesel class of all, the 29.

Of course, the irony of locomotives and EMUs being completed in the Glasgow area, and then heading south for acceptance testing, has surely not escaped the reader. The failure of Scottish to test its own stock may be a legacy of the impressive debut made by the Swindon-built Class 126 in 1957, whose excellence may have obscured the need for Scottish to be more rigid in its acceptance procedures in years to come. If only the later traction units bore the hallmark of Swindon!

In fairness to rail managers on both sides of the Border, it has to be said that there was media pressure to show prompt re-equipping of Britain's railways with new traction – in 1955 the Scottish Board was talking about even just *borrowing* a 'Derby lightweight' DMU to show a critical press that

Scotland was moving in the right direction by embracing new forms of power.

If not unreliable, many diesels were late in reporting for duty. The 'Deltics' were on order for more than three years before delivery, and in the autumn of 1965 the Board was complaining about the late delivery of Haymarket's allocation of what we later learned to call Class 47 diesels. Nine were due at the Edinburgh depot in September, but the first only showed up on 20 October. Many of the '47s' would later bear names, yet in that very year Scottish had already decided that there would no more naming of diesel locomotives beyond those already allocated, owing to the 'expense and loss of locomotive availability' around the time of the naming ceremonies. Obviously, this was another short-lived decision.

Meanwhile, on the main-lines, steam could still do the job when required. In one of the few mentions of a particular steam locomotive type in the Scottish Board Minutes, there occurred a report in August 1965 of the improved timekeeping of the 19.30 Euston-Stranraer working north of the Border, where it was powered by a 'Class 7 Standard locomotive'. Calling it a 'Britannia' was perhaps too train-spotterish! None of the former LNER Pacifics and V2s helping out on former LMS trains south from Aberdeen – including the 'West Coast Postal' as well as the three-hour Glasgow trains – were ever specified by class or originating company in the Board Minutes.

Nevertheless, the technical press commented so frequently and favourably on the work done by former LNER motive power on the Perth-Aberdeen line, that your then-teenaged author set out to sample this for himself in 1964. My choice of a V2-hauled train north from Perth proved to be an unfortunate one; not long after starting, the locomotive developed a fault outside the new (but largely redundant) marshalling yard, and, instead of sending back the few miles to Perth for a new engine, the crew persevered. Dropping time all the way, with your author worrying about his connection at Aberdeen, the V2 finally received assistance from a tender-first 'Black 5', but not until we had struggled as far as Laurencekirk. My eighty minutes in the Granite City was reduced to fifteen, with no apology by BR. The return to Edinburgh was accomplished in a train hauled effortlessly by two Class 26 Diesels. Somehow, sampling former LNER power on the Strathmore line never seemed so attractive again.

By the end of 1966, the number of Scottish locomotive depots capable of operating steam power could be counted in single figures; by September of that year the Board had approved the removal of such facilities at St Margaret's (no doubt much to the relief of the City of Edinburgh's health officers), Carstairs, Ayr, Stranraer, and the complete closure of Hurlford. A handwritten register in the National Archives (see Table X) lists the last steam engines to be notified to the Supplies Manager from most of the above depots in July. These include 73078 from Carstairs, 45177 and 76103 from Ayr, 76108 and 77015 from Hurlford, and 61345 from St Margaret's, where A3 60041 *Salmon Trout* was 'being held for Mr Pegler' (along with 60052 *Prince Palatine*), presumably to provide spares for their preserved sister *Flying Scotsman*. Curiously, Ferryhill depot at Aberdeen was not mentioned in the minutes, but was still turning out two A4s for passenger duties until the closure of Buchanan Street in the following November.

Board members were also told that steam was still operating over the Border on the WCML from the LMR and that some servicing facilities would have to be retained in the meantime at Polmadie, Motherwell, and Perth (these depots' last 'notified' Scottish Region engines in July 1966 being 73063, 44850/81, and 44698 respectively). Facilities would still be required for the 'Britannias' visiting from Carlisle (Kingmoor), whose operation of the Euston-Stranraer boat train north of the Border had pleased the Board so much in the previous year. By the end of the summer timetable of 1966, the majority of the forty-nine 'Brits' existing (on paper at least) were operating out of Kingmoor, but all the 'Clans' – an even newer design, and originally intended for Scottish operations – had gone to scrap merchants.

By this time steam was almost unknown on the East Coast main-line, and the former LMS line out of Glasgow (Buchanan Street) had been the place to see former LNER power for the last few years. But even that was about to end; A4 Nos 60019/24 were still working scheduled services in the summer of 1966, but both were withdrawn in the autumn. The latter, *Kingfisher*, had operated exclusively out of Haymarket for a quarter of a century before being displaced to the former Caledonian and LMS lines, but was not preserved. In passing, it should be mentioned that another Haymarket favourite, A4 60027 *Merlin*, was listed as being retained for preservation by the Edinburgh publisher Mr R.I. Nelson, but was notified to Supplies by St Margaret's on 11 September 1965, its sale shown as cancelled. However, 60019 was luckier. After heading a last special out of Buchanan Street just before its closure at Guy Fawkes weekend 1966, this locomotive survived, but entered into a curious limbo thereafter. The author recalls being astonished to find *Bittern* in steam at Hull Paragon no less than a year later, in November 1967. However, as it was only briefly a Scottish Regional engine, its career should not concern us here.

As mentioned earlier, the last steam locomotive operated by Scottish Region drew its fire for the final time on 4 June 1967 at Thornton depot in Fife, although the Board was told that 30 April was the final day of steam operation. A handwritten BR register now in the NAS (see Table IX) carries an asterisk after No.65345 with the comment 'the last!', although it is noticeable that Dunfermline's No.65288 was withdrawn on the same day. Neither had received a general overhaul for a number of years – six in the latter's case, compared to five for the Thornton engine – but it is not known if this was a factor in the order of withdrawal. The RCTS history of the class, in its excellent *Locomotives of the LNER* series, gives no withdrawal date for either.

Whatever the details, this was almost exactly 150 years after the first steam engine had plied along the Kilmarnock & Troon plateway, terrifying spectators but causing one local mines manager to shout, 'To the tanyard every living beast; flesh and blood cannot stand against that!' In fact, two decades were to pass before the steam engine found its niche in Scottish transport, although stationary engines had been employed in mining since before the Act of Union in 1707. Not only that, but as we know, Scottish was still employing the horse extensively, for road traffic, as late as the end of the 1950s.

Also flying the flag for steam up to the final month were, as might be expected, members of the 'Standard' classes introduced in the early 1950s; May 1967 saw the withdrawal of 5MT 4-6-0s from (nominally, at least) Polmadie, and Corkerhill. The 4MT Moguls which had come to Scotland late, also exited finally at this time, from Motherwell, Corkerhill, and Beattock (see Table IX). All these depots, save the Fife two mentioned above, were still likely to see the occasional LMR steam locomotive, much to Scottish Region's irritation.

Steam was anything but fashionable in those days, and was soon to be barred from BR's main-lines, even for the working of enthusiasts' specials. The minutes of the Scottish Railway Board record the frustration in the boardroom at the delays in finally dispensing with this form of traction in 1967. The last steam-hauled passenger train in Scotland ran on 28 April, recorded by regional official W.A.C. Smith as the 17.03 from Gourock making a punctual arrival at Glasgow (Central) hauled by former LMS 2-6-4 No.42274. Then, after ousting the last J36 from its Fife base, the Board approached the LMR to enquire how long Scottish would have to offer maintenance facilities at Perth and Motherwell for steam workings from that region. These almost certainly comprised 'Britannias' and 9Fs working in from Carlisle (Kingmoor); fifteen of the BR Pacifics were still on the active list in October 1967. Curiously, Scotland was the final destination for no fewer than forty-three of the fifty-five 'Britannias', the largest number of the class, twenty-two, being scrapped at Shettleston in Glasgow. The remaining twenty-one met the breaker's torch at Airdrie, Inverkeithing, Troon, and Wishaw.

The author recalls a visit to Carlisle two years previously where these were almost the only examples of steam traction left, although a rebuilt 'Patriot' was a rare sight, hauling the Broughton meat train southwards (see illustration). Already, the 'Duchess' Pacifics, whose presence at Carlisle Citadel made it a pleasure for the rail enthusiast to visit, were no longer to be seen. None reached the end of 1964 in active service, not even the two outshopped postwar. Scottish Region, which had suffered so much inconvenience and appalling publicity from its *uncritical* embrace of diesel and electric traction, would not have long to wait to rid itself of steam, its servant for a century and a half.

Interestingly, Scottish was also reducing its diesel fleet. Main-line diesels listed by class in Table XI totalled around 400, this being based on information supplied to the Board in January 1967 (and excluding, presumably through clerical error, twenty-eight members of Classes 24 and 25). By the following year, withdrawals in Class 29 had taken place, and Board members were told in June 1968 that the main-line diesel fleet was soon to be reduced from 376 to 352. Of course, this also reflected the reduction in route-mileage still going on. Shunting locomotive numbers were also reducing; from 235 in March 1968 to 210.

Budgetary provision – no less than £305,000 (£3.62 million) in February 1965 – was made to modernise Queen Street for the arrival of Buchanan Street's trains the following year, and diesels would have to be available for the three-hour trains by then. To ensure that they would be, in March 1966 £63,100 (£722,000) was allocated for the installation of diesel maintenance facilities at Aberdeen's Ferryhill depot. The thought of more steam filling the Queen Street tunnel was not a pleasant one. As if to underline the urgency, in August 1965 Board members saw for the first time a model of a building known as Buchanan House.

Containerisation of freight cargoes took on added importance in the 1960s, with the slow but remorseless spread of motorways and the spectre of 'juggernaut' lorries entering from the Continent. Clearly the 4-ton capacity container of 1920s vintage would be inadequate for future needs, and by the mid-60s various experiments in road/rail freight transfer methods, principally the 'Roadrailer', had channelled into the 'Freightliner' concept, based on the universal container registered with the International Standards Organisation.

Glasgow's Gushetfaulds depot was the site of Britain's first long-distance 'Freightliner' service commencing in 1965, following on from its handling of the smaller container type as part of the 'Condor' concept. A 'Freightliner' service to and from London (York Way) opened from here on 15 November 1965, after so many delays that the projected revenue figures for Scottish freight in 1965 were forcibly scaled down by some £190,000 (£2.25 million) before the end of that year. The principal reason for delay appears to have been a shortage of rolling-stock. Only 50 per cent of 'motive units' and no more than 32 per cent of 'trailers' (presumably 'outer' and 'intermediate' wagons respectively) had been allocated at the time of inauguration. Despite this, the Board believed the 'limited' launch to be highly successful, and punctuality to the end of the year was 'exemplary'. Within three years, Glasgow was also dispatching to Aberdeen, Birmingham, Leeds, Liverpool, Manchester and Sheffield.

Also identified as Scottish sites for Freightliner depots in that summer were Guild Street in Aberdeen, Stannergate in Dundee, and Meadows (Seafield) in Edinburgh. Back-up sites were to be Kittybrewster, Taybridge, and Portobello, in the respective cities. Interestingly, the secondary sites in both Dundee and Edinburgh were chosen as the respective city bases for the Freightliner network, while Aberdeen's depot was established at Guild Street, handling traffic for Glasgow and London. Edinburgh's depot was opened at the second-choice site of Portobello in January 1968 and within ten years was moving 2,700 containers monthly. Destinations were Felixstowe and Harwich as well as London, with a 'feeder' service coming in from Corpach in 1968. Despite this, and rumoured profitability, the depot closed in April 1987, allowing a major realignment of the ECML. Ironically, the road organisations failed to get around to erecting directional notices for arriving lorry drivers until 1987, and a week after the depot had closed.

The National Archives contain a typewritten manual on Freightliner operation issued in 1966, giving to the modern researcher an interesting insight into an operational procedure which implied that rail managers had finally abandoned their earlier fixation with marshalling, and were at last taking on the long-distance 'juggernaut'. The stock, comprising 'outer' wagons which coupled to the locomotive or to other Freightliner trains in the usual way using a screw coupling, and 'intermediate' wagons with only pipe connections for the air brake, were assembled fifteen a time into sections nearly 1,000ft in length. Shorter lengths and new technical terms were introduced in later years. Two such lengths made up the average train, which could be hauled only by certain members of the AL6 electric class or by specified members of diesel Classes 40 and 47, those being 370/1/7/8/80 and 1100-11, 1631-81 and 1758-1999. Bell code for the trains was 3-2-5, something which looks curious today and refers of course to the communication system employed between manually operated signalboxes.

That there was a quickening of interest in property marketing by Scottish Region Board members as the 1960s progressed seems unarguable. By March 1963 a Scottish version of Railway Sites Ltd (as BR Property Board was called at that time) was being seriously considered, although one would have thought that this was a legal impossibility, and certainly fades from the minutes in due course. But so interested were Scotland's rail chiefs in property sales, that they soon undertook to sell the very building they sat in!

The Board Minutes for 1963 mention, almost as an afterthought, that the proposed sale of property in Glasgow's Buchanan Street would necessitate a new regional HQ, and the General Manager was asked to prepare a paper on the subject of finding (or building – the record is not specific) a new office block. By November, it was decided that the low rents for office accommodation in Glasgow made leasing practicable while awaiting a new building, and there was no mention at this stage of utilising a former rail site, although that must have been an obvious option at the time. By December, the GM (by now W.G. 'Willie' Thorpe) had announced the leasing of Blythswood House, in the square of the same name, from 1 January 1964 for twenty-one years at £47,000 (£585,000) per annum.

All this would entail the closure and sale of the former NBR headquarters at 23 Waterloo Place, Edinburgh, at one time the administrative home of Scotland's largest railway. In the event, there proved to be too much to be housed at the new Glasgow HQ, so office accommodation was being fireproofed at the Waverley Station by the end of the decade, at a cost of some £68,000 (£688,000). Nevertheless, in 1969, Scottish Board members were clearly delighted at the prospect of disposing of the Waterloo Place site with a potential £120,000 (£1.21 million) price-tag.

One aspect of station closures which the Board had failed to take into account was the loss of the station buffets or 'refreshment rooms'. In 1948 there had been forty-eight of them in Scotland and many of the thirty-eight still working in twenty stations in 1965 were profitable. Board members seem to have been embarrassed to discover that their enthusiasm for closures – in this case eradicating mainly secondary stations in the two main cities, Edinburgh (Princes Street) and Glasgow (Buchanan Street and St Enoch), as well as the irreplaceable Ballater – would lead to the loss of £32,250 (£383,000) profit at these buffets, on gross revenue of £145,600 (£1.72 million). However, the Board was assured that improved facilities at Glasgow (Queen Street and Central) 'will more than recover this loss'. By inference, it appeared that the frozen outposts of Edinburgh and Ballater were being written off!

Reorganisation of Scottish Region had taken place in 1960. The posts of Chief Commercial Manager, Chief Operating and Motive Power Superintendents were abolished, with middle-ranking managers reporting to the General Managers of three geographical divisions – Glasgow and South Western, East Coast, and Northern. Within five years these labels had been shortened or altered to Glasgow, Edinburgh, and Highland.

By 1966, an internal analysis of the management structure showed that Glasgow had thirty-five local managers reporting to the Divisional Manager, Edinburgh nineteen, and Highland eleven. The last-mentioned of these divisional HQs was eliminated in January 1968, with all Highland Area Managers reporting direct to Glasgow. At this time, it was estimated that Scottish Region's staff had effectively halved, from 51,000 to around 25,000, since the beginning of the decade, a mere eight years earlier. Dr Bonavia reported that the annual saving in staff loss and reorganisation was around £200,000 annually.

By the beginning of 1968 Buchanan House was fully staffed, with Blythswood House turned over to Glasgow Division staff, concentrated in a single site instead of being scattered round the city. Four years later, the Board minuted its pleasure at hearing of an MBE awarded to Miss 'Madge' Moore, the head of the region's typing services. She was recorded as having achieved the centralisation of secretarial work with particular assurance by 1968, and the Board was impressed by the high proportion of blind and disabled staff employed in her department – a feather in the Scottish cap.

One regional manager who had made a meteoric rise through the Scottish hierarchy during the final years of the 1950s was a certain Stanley Raymond, whom we last met making a strong financial case for closing the Lauder Light Railway. An orphan with a spectacular war record, by 1959 Raymond had moved from the Commercial department to become Assistant General Manager at Scottish, before succeeding to a BTC post in 1961 and then taking over the Western Region as both chairman and General Manager. He then succeeded Dr Beeching in 1965, one of his more controversial acts being to sack Gerard Fiennes for submitting articles highly critical of BR to a transport magazine, and ultimately publishing his highly readable book *I Tried to Run a Railway*. Incidentally, not long before his fall from grace Fiennes was, as chairman of Eastern Region, a guest at a Scottish Board meeting in January 1967. Raymond was himself sacked in turn by Transport Minister Barbara Castle in 1967, although a recently conferred knighthood possibly sweetened the pill of dismissal.

The regional structure of BR had been itself reorganised by the 1962 Transport Act and, by the mid-sixties, the General Manager would double as the Board chairman, an arrangement which persisted until April 1971. First to hold this combined position was Willie Thorpe, who was appointed as Ness's successor in September 1963, when the latter was assigned to the British Railway Board.

The Scottish Board Minutes record Mr Ness's 'great work' for the region, and few regional GMs could have experienced such a trying time with relatively untested motive power. Surprisingly, Gourvish is critical of Ness, calling him 'a rather paranoid character, who frequently clashed with colleagues'. This blunt assessment overlooks the complexities of running a region with such unique geographical characteristics – Ness was also Managing Director of a major shipping concern – and his problems were hardly eased by the hurried nature of his appointment following Brown's death in 1955 (see Table III).

Thorpe's succession in 1963 was by no means straightforward either. As soon as this former AGM from the London Midland was appointed to Scottish, the LMR asked for him back again in October to substitute as their own General Manager when the latter was taken ill. Mr Gordon Stewart substituted at the Scottish end for the time being.

When Thorpe moved permanently to the LMR in July 1967, Stewart was reinstated to the position of chairman and managing director immediately. He was then confirmed as chairman and managing director of the Caledonian Steam Packet Group of companies. Two salaried positions and two chairmanships occupied by one man – perhaps not an ideal means of administering Scotland's transport by land and sea, but (literally) nice work if you could get it! But more was to come. In the following year, Stewart was awarded a directorship in British Transport Hotels. Later, Thorpe became chief executive to the British Railways Board, while Raymond would succeed Beeching. Scotland was clearly an intensive training-ground for the summit of British railway administration!

Following Stewart's retirement, the positions of chairman and general manager were separated once again. From April 1971, Alex Philip became

GM and Lord Taylor of Gryfe took the chair at Board meetings. A career industrialist, Taylor also served as the highly respected chairman of the Forestry Commission. Curiously, his biographical data suggests that he had held the chairmanship of BR Scottish Region since 1969. He would certainly not be able to reach Glasgow for Board meetings from his local station, Kingsbarns, in Fife. The LNER had closed it forty-one years previously.

Access to the Caledonian Steam Packet files would be revealing to rail administrators about the burgeoning success of their principal rival, the road vehicle. While car ownership had grown annually by around 5 per cent in the early 1950s, BR's Scottish Region could maintain its own index of this source of competition in the increase in vehicles embarked in Caledonian Steam Packet ferries. Over the 1954-64 period, vehicular use of the Clyde ferries went up from 3,493 in 1953 to no less than 118,403 eleven years later. Kyle-Kyleakin increased from 25,158 to 111,812, and Stranraer-Larne from 5,456 to 56,307. This was of course good for BR, since none of these water-crossings could be avoided easily by the motorist, while the Skye bridge, which replaced the Kyle ferry, was not even mooted at this time.

The loss of the Queensferry traffic, after the opening of the Forth Road Bridge in September 1964, was a different matter altogether. Although the Scottish Railway Board was told in 1966 that recoverable assets from the ferry operation came to no less than £194,868 (£2.23 million), the revenue loss was a major blow, registering in the first year of the Forth Road Bridge's operation, 1964-65, at £92,000 (£1.14 million), some £20,000 more than the Board members had been bracing themselves to expect. Presumably, that figure included the transfer of commuter traffic from road to rail, something where BR would have expected to hold their own, particularly in a year when passenger rail travel was actually up by nearly 4 per cent in Scotland.

To make matters worse, the closure 'recovery' figures (see Table V) seem fantastic. The estimate of nearly £200,000 was surely based on the assumption that the four ferries could be sold as 'going concerns'. Yet it was always likely that there would be a shrinking market for such specialised vessels and, in the event, only one, the newest, *Sir William Wallace*, was sold for further service. Shipbreaking records show that one of the 1934 vessels, *Robert the Bruce*, was disposed of for only £2,500, so it seems unlikely that the sale of three of the older vessels raised more than £10,000, say £60,000 including the 1955 ferry.

With the benefit of hindsight, it is easy for the historian to see how Scottish Region could have kept open – and tried to revive – a number of rural railways, while capitalising on the lucrative market for urban sites.

No one would argue that there should be no rationalisation, no eradication of duplicated stations and services, in cities like Edinburgh, Glasgow, and Dundee, but the views of the Association of County Councils, with its concern about rural closures, strike the present-day critic as more attuned to future population and transport needs than the short-sightedness of the railways' governors – assuming they had any concern whatever for social factors – even when there was a reasonable mix of non-specialists and railway professionals attending regional Board meetings from 1955 to around 1963. Those New Towns, and 'unplanned' growth areas, which lost their rail services while their population sizes swelled, included Livingston, Penicuik, and Glenrothes. All this could have been avoided if rail organisation in Scotland had enjoyed a broader base than the two extreme alternatives – either having the railways run by the representatives of the shareholders, as happened before 1948, or having railwaymen in charge who were more accustomed to executing policy than in formulating it, from 1948 until 1955, and again after 1963 to 1971.

A nationalised railway service, established by politicians, should have reflected a more enlightened attitude to public transport, allowing the continuation and improvement of links in rural areas, while eradicating duplicated station and depot facilities, thus freeing up often valuable urban sites. This would have released more 'brown field' sites and lessened pressure on green belts and agricultural land. Apart from anything else, this would also have eliminated the exaggerated and sometimes downright misleading estimates of the value of recoverable material from closed lines, and the critical analysis of the revenue potential of branch lines which had never benefited from diesel travel or a more aggressive marketing campaign featuring re-timetabling and cheap fare deals.

To the outsider, it appears that there was simply not enough enthusiasm for keeping railways going in the 1950s. But the insider may well have divined an over-reaction among senior managers, a leaning towards hard-nosed professionalism which dictated that it was simpler and more convenient to close a branch line than try to make it pay. Dr Bonavia, a former senior railwayman, wrote that in the Beeching era there was, 'a reaction against any concept of public service and even more against the idea that anyone could be in railways because they liked railways. That was 'playing trains' and it was supposed to have been a fault of past generations of railwaymen'. If the railway staff were not enthusiastic enough about their industry, and its need for recapitalisation after 1945, the politicians at Westminster can be forgiven for not being enthusiastic either.

In retrospect, the mid-1960s was probably the most dangerous time for the long-term future of Scottish rail services. While it was a period when passengers lost the chance to travel to Stranraer from Dumfries, to Forfar from Perth, and to Leven from St Andrews, this was as nothing to the losses contemplated as 1964 opened. Effectively, passenger services would have ceased north or west of Dingwall, and the number of stations on the former Highland main-line between Perth and Inverness reduced to single figures. Even Glasgow-Edinburgh services via Shotts would be withdrawn from 2 March of that year, while the closure of *both* lines to Stranraer was tabled, as *Modern Railways* commented, without 'any reference to the Larne boat traffic'. These were proposals too extreme even for the Board at the time, although any resistance to it was successfully accomplished 'behind the scenes', and the Board Minutes of the time reveal no agonised discussion about the wisdom of the Beeching plan.

It would be pleasant to think that the attempted integration of rail and bus services in Glasgow was influential in forcing politicians to contemplate the alternative of a more socially involved transport service. Certainly the transport press at the time believed Glasgow to be in the lead in this matter. Cynics are more likely to point out that a government planning to fight a General Election before the end of that year, 1964, was unlikely to commit itself to such a politically damaging course of action.

Modern Railways appears to have been confident that such draconian closures would not go ahead, at least not at that time and to the extent contemplated, but commented in June 1964 about the thwarted closure of the Far North lines: 'less expected was the prompt and brusque comment from Dr Beeching that the reprieve would cost substantially more that the £360,000 a year quoted by the Minister as the loss on these routes', with the dreaded doctor ordering that routes he had selected for closure be listed separately in future BR account sheets. The reasons for Beeching's unpopularity are not hard to seek!

Gourvish suggests in his massive work on BR's business history, that Labour politicians were unhappy with Beeching because, of all things, they regarded him as too pro-railway! It appears that Wilson's first Cabinet contained ministers, with the exception of Transport Minister Tom Fraser, who were uncomfortable with the doctor's insistence that road and air services should be analysed just as rigorously as the rail system. Not surprisingly, Beeching left within a year, although with the considerable compensation of a peerage.

Nevertheless, if the reader has noticed that the much-maligned Dr Richard Beeching is a marginal figure in the history of Scottish Region, that is because he was. After the 1964 election, a new Labour administration walked a parliamentary tightrope with a tiny majority, and by the time it received an increased mandate from the electorate in the summer of 1966, Dr Beeching had returned to industry. But a policy of withdrawing unprofitable services on branch-lines, and of thinning out stops on trunk routes, was well-established before the good doctor had been plucked from the pharmaceutical industry to head the nation's railways. On one of his first visits to Scotland, he was kicked by an aggrieved railwayman as he made his way through Waverley Station. This was unforgivable: while Dr Beeching undoubtedly raised hackles wherever he went, his policies were already in place.

With steam locomotives having vanished from Scottish tracks by the summer of 1967, the only steam-powered vehicles to be seen north of the Border were breakdown cranes. Of sixty-two cranes on BR by the end of the decade, only two were diesel-powered; the remainder were still to be seen simmering in the largest MPDs on the system, coupled to an accommodation coach for their crew and appropriate support wagons. They were ready to move at any time, but their future was the subject of an all-region conference in May 1969.

Problems facing breakdown crews at that time arose from the introduction of larger tank wagons, in greater numbers, and with a greater variety of loads, many of them dangerous. Modern locomotives were more difficult to move if derailed; while a Pacific might weigh 160 tons in full working order, this could be cut by a third by detaching the tender, and the engine itself could be moved by attaching a hook to the buffer beam, thus halving the remaining weight and bringing it within the ambit of most of the system's cranes. The largest of these had a seventy-five ton capacity, which could be exerted at up to 14ft from the crane centre. The elimination of bufferbeams on diesel and electric locomotives was seen as a major problem, particularly with some diesels weighing more than 130 tons within a single frame. The Class 40 had, in addition, unpowered axles which could be very awkward to rerail.

In Scotland, the only seventy-five-ton crane was stabled at Polmadie, and it was decided at the conference to reallocate this to Eastfield within three years. Cranes with similar capacity could be called on from Carlisle (LMR) and Gateshead (ER) if required. The full Scottish list was as follows:

Lift Capacity	1969 location	Future location
75 ton	Polmadie	To Eastfield by 1972
50 ton	Haymarket	Haymarket
45 ton	Eastfield	To Motherwell by 1972

36 ton	Dundee	Withdraw
30 ton	Inverness	Inverness
30 ton	Ferryhill	Ferryhill
30 ton	Ayr	Withdraw
30 ton	Motherwell	Withdraw and replace with 45 ton
18/20 ton	Eastfield	Withdraw
18/20 ton	Polmadie	Withdraw

Curiously, the steam-powered nature of the cranes did not seem to concern rail management at the time. While coal had to be carried with the crane, it seemed less of a concern than water, which might have to be supplied by the Fire Brigade if a shortage occurred during operations. The understandable loss of boilersmiths from MPDs was, however, a greater cause for concern. Despite this, conversion to diesel power within the existing frames was not recommended. It was an aspect of railway operation rarely glimpsed by even the most avid of enthusiasts.

six

AFTER 1968

One of Michael Bonavia's histories of BR sums up the 1968 Transport Act under the chapter heading 'Mrs Castle's New Railway'. He writes: 'Implicit in the Act was the replacement of reshaping by subsidy. Closures in fact virtually came to a halt…' Except for rail travellers in Scotland! Hawick, Galashiels, St Andrews, Leven, Kinross, all these important towns were still to lose their rail services, as Grangemouth did at the beginning of the year, with three Scottish counties about to be totally wiped from the railway map.

All this was in spite of growing Scottish loyalty to Labour. It was in fact Transport Ministers of that party persuasion, after Mrs Castle had moved on to the Department of Employment, who proved less likely to oppose closure proposals. Gourvish quotes figures which show that, under Labour ministers Marsh and Mulley, no fewer than fifty UK closures were approved in the final twenty-six months of Wilson's Labour Government, while the incoming Conservative Minister of Transport, John Peyton, approved only fourteen in forty-two months. Admittedly, there were less left to close by then!

The 1968 legislation allowed the setting up of Public Transport Authorities (to establish localised transport policy), and Public Transport Executives (to carry this out). But there was also a provision for Scottish local authorities, either acting alone or jointly among themselves 'and with the approval of the Secretary of State [for Scotland], to afford financial assistance for the provision of railway passenger services within, or to or from, their area or areas'. This was tremendously encouraging, and should have begun a revival of rail travel in rural Scotland. The fact that it did not may be a comment on the patchwork state of local government at that time. In particular, it can be inferred that the smaller councils may have lacked the level of administrative expertise that is often taken for granted nowadays, and St Andrews is a good example of this, as will be shown later.

As remarked earlier, after the passing of the 1968 legislation, Scottish service withdrawals were fewer in number, but bigger. None more so than the Waverley Route, the former NBR and LNER main-line linking Edinburgh (Waverley) with Carlisle via Galashiels and Hawick. But the Cowdenbeath-Perth line via Glenfarg was also lost, despite being portrayed in BR's policy documents as viable and worthy of investment. It is appropriate to treat these together for, although they appeared to be in almost polar opposition, they shared the same fate. In neither case was the enlightened legislation of 1968 passed in time to have the slightest effect.

The Scottish Board Minutes hardly mention the Waverley Route until December 1968, when the general manager intimated that he would meet 'Border interests' (Lady Elliot being named specifically) 'to clarify some obvious misunderstandings about the case for closure of Edinburgh-Hawick-Carlisle'. The line was already scheduled to close on the following 6 January – yet this was effectively the *first* mention in the Board Minutes of the biggest rail closure in British history.

The consequence of these 'misunderstandings' can be seen in considerable volume in the files of the Transport Users' Consultative Committee. This body held a meeting at Hawick Town Hall on 16 and 17 November 1966, and the Scottish Borderers turned out in impressive force, and even more impressive unity. Ranged against closure were the County Councils of Berwickshire, Roxburghshire, and Selkirkshire, along with the Town Councils of Galashiels, Jedburgh, Innerleithen, Hawick, Kelso, Selkirk, and Peebles. All but two of these towns had already lost their own railway stations, but clearly believed in the importance of having access to a railhead. These local authorities were weak individually – too small, for example, to operate their own police or fire-fighting utilities – and they collectively retained a firm of Edinburgh solicitors to represent them in this transport matter.

Unfortunately, English local authorities did not join in. Northumberland merely asked the TUCC for it to be informed of any decision made, in case of repercussions on its planning policies, while Cumberland (which was negotiated by one-fifth of the Waverley Route) only drew the Committee's attention to the transport requirements of Arthuret Parish Council in the Longtown area. Yet the English element of the Waverley Route's operations had been increased in 1958 with the decision in October of that year to transfer an additional 11 miles of the line to the LMR, bringing the latter region's area of operations up to Longtown. This was 'considered desirable in connection with the development of a new livestock centre which has been the subject of discussion between the City of Carlisle and the LMR, and will also facilitate the planning of the latter's new yard', as the Board Minutes rather long-windedly put it.

Individuals who commented in writing included David Steel MP, who registered two objections, both as an elected representative and on a personal basis. Mr Steel frequently used the sleeper to St Pancras, but not the down service, whose departure time around 21.45 was obviously too early in the evening for an active parliamentarian. Meanwhile, Lady Trevor-Roper, wife of the illustrious historian, wrote to point out that, without rail access to Carlisle, her husband would be unable to reach Oxford for his professorial duties within a single day if he was to travel by bus from their home near Melrose. This was of course before the opening of the M6 south of Carlisle; unfortunately, at this time, TUCCs were not charged with considering the *quality* of replacement services. One cannot help speculating on their deliberations had they been asked to do so.

For the fact was that the roads at the time, for example the A7, were not appropriate substitutes. Travelling from Edinburgh to Hawick could be accomplished in 78 minutes by train in the mid-1960s. By the 1970s, the bus did the journey in 195. Closure was concluded just before the new Transport Act reached the statute book, requiring TUCCs to be more stringent in their assessment of replacement public services. If the closure decision had been delayed, would the TUCC have been so prepared to abandon Border travellers to the tender mercies of the buses?

In the summer of 1970, a strike of Scottish Omnibus crews was to leave the Borders almost completely deprived of public passenger services. The author was living in Hawick at the time, and can vouch for the fact that the only way to leave the town by public transport was by the (occasional) Ribble service to Carlisle. Around the same time, *The Times* newspaper carried an advertisement, placed by the road haulage industry, citing Hawick as a community which could get along perfectly well without a railway!

Returning to the TUCC evidence, and underlining the lack of a fast road link with the south – to Carlisle, and even between Carlisle and the south – a firm of ironmongers in Hawick advised the committee that rail enabled them to receive specialised supplies from the south in half the time taken by road. The company spokesman added, 'to be threatened with the closure of a main artery of communication is not logical planning at all'. Even Bell's Coaches of Langholm pitched in, 'with no wish to see the railway closed', but were stung into replying to allegations made by a local cleric that there was, 'no real bus service between Newcastleton and Hawick', highlighting the fact that, 'in fact we supply a useful service morning and night'.

Where did the Scottish Board stand on this proposal to wipe hundreds of square miles from the Scottish railway map? As will be shown in a later chapter, both Scottish and LMR working documents assumed, from as early as 1963, that the Waverley Route would definitely close, as proposed by Dr Beeching. By 1969, with the protestations of Borderers swept aside and closure accomplished on 6 January, the only references to the route in the Scottish Board Minutes concern the approach by the Border Union Company for a partial reopening. Here the line is referred to as the 'Waverley' Route for the first time.

There is evidence of immediate track-lifting on one stretch south of Hawick after 6 January 1969, as if to pre-empt any thirteenth-hour approach from would-be resurrectionists. The southern part of the line is also believed to have been used for a simulated rail crash of gruesome proportions around this time, with the unemployed of Hawick being bussed to a remote part of the lineside and then paid to groan loudly and allow themselves to be swathed in bandages. It was hardly what the directors of the North British Railway had in mind 110 years earlier when they forged southwards through barren moorlands to a chorus of (reasonable) complaints from London-based shareholders questioning how remunerative the extension south of Hawick by that route would actually prove. As this author has argued in the book *Rails Across the Border* (also by Tempus Publishing), the Waverley Route should have been built via Langholm.

In 1970 the January meeting of the Scottish Board considered the disposal of the line's 'assets', following a BRB decision to withdraw from negotiations with an un-named consortium interested in re-opening the Waverley Route (presumably the aforesaid Border Union Railway group). The minutes record that: 'Arrangements have now been made to dispose of all assets, other than land and buildings with effect from February 1st'. The Property Board was obviously involved by now. It appeared that an enquiry had already been received for the sale of 'land and buildings stripped of lines and sleepers between Longtown and Lady Victoria Pit [between Gorebridge and Newtongrange]'. The following month's minutes endorse this course of action along with a 'one train working' (what used to be called 'one engine in steam') order between the Pit and Millerhill yard to the north. Recovery was estimated to harvest £283,527 (£2.7 million) worth of materials, although no outlay is recorded, and it would presumably have been major (there were two viaducts in the Hawick area alone which would be difficult and even dangerous to demolish, although the major viaduct at Shankend still stands to this day). Not surprisingly, some track-lifting was taking place near Hawick as early as Easter 1970, the author recalling hearing the unmistakable 'ringing' noise of a Class 40 idling on a pw train in the town's goods yard.

At no stage did the viability of the Waverley Route appear to be discussed by the Board. The alternative of running the line as a branch from Edinburgh to Hawick (as it was for fifteen years after 1847) does not appear to have been considered either. Transport Minister Richard Marsh had made the closure announcement in the summer of 1968, with the *Railway Magazine* deploring the timing, and the 'continuing erosion of the network' despite the fact that the new Transport Act, with its life-giving Clause 39, would become law in October. The minister, however, contended that the Waverley Route was such a terminal case that no subsidy could even be considered. He stated that £700,000 (£7.5 million) would be required annually to support existing operations over the whole route, £400,000 to maintain present services just north of Hawick, or £250,000 to fulfill the latter option but after inflicting the 'most stringent economies'. 'Grants on such a scale could not, in the Minister's opinion', quoted the magazine, 'be justified on a value-for money basis'. One wonders if he was speaking on behalf of, or even with the knowledge of, Scottish local authorities.

Those opposing the line's closure, such as David Steel MP, could hardly adopt the negotiating position of an Edinburgh-Hawick service only, as he had constituents south of Hawick as well as north of there; in other words, if the railway managers were not prepared to pursue this option, the public authorities could hardly do so. But as far as Scottish was concerned it was off the agenda – literally so.

Considering the size of this closure – the UK's biggest until the Great Central was broken up – there is remarkably little about the Waverley Route in BR management files (nor the Board Minutes, as we have already seen) in Scotland's National Archives. Indeed, there is far more about recovery of assets in the event of closure than in discussing how costs could have been reduced by line singling, unstaffed stations and so on, and maximising income by re-timetabling after some kind of public relations survey. Even the option of maintaining passenger services to and from Gorebridge was not discussed by the Board, despite the fact that the tracks were to remain in place within a mile of that station. In contrast, the Great Central was essentially duplicating some of its routes, offering London-Nottingham, and London-Sheffield services in addition to those from King's Cross and St Pancras, for example. The closure of the Waverley Route removed the option of rail travel from hundreds of square miles of Scottish borderland.

Interestingly, closure of the Edinburgh-Perth line north of Cowdenbeath would result in the region's 'financial betterment' (quoting the Board Minutes of August 1968) to the tune of £123,000 (£1.25 million) annually, although passengers would have to put up with a longer journey time. Another beneficiary was the Scottish Development Department, which was able to save £500,000 (£5.05 million) in constructing the new M90 along the course of the trackbed through Glenfarg (the result is perhaps the steepest motorway in Britain).

Yet only five months previously, the Board had authorised singling of the line at a net cost of £79,400, predicting an annual saving of £39,500, indicating a lack of any kind of long-term planning for the route. Grotesquely, the Board members decided to treat themselves to a private excursion along one of the lines in question. On 2 October 1968, they enjoyed a trip from Bridge of Earn to Cowdenbeath along the doomed Edinburgh-Perth link, (presumably in the 'Officers' coach stabled for so many years opposite Platform 19 at Waverley), as well as the Dunfermline (Upper)-Stirling line, due to close five days later.

In passing, how ironic it is that the Kyle, Far North, and Oban lines, so apparently vulnerable to a cold-blooded costing analysis of Scotland's rail services, should survive and prosper, while lines in within 50 miles of the largest cities, were closed forever!

Board Minutes for 1968 exhibit a strange dichotomy in attitudes to Scotland's railway services. In the same month that managers entered the severe portals of St Andrew's House – just round the corner in Edinburgh from the former NBR HQ in Waterloo Place – to discuss subsidy for rural (and some not so rural) rail services, the Board recorded its satisfaction with the closure of the Aberdeen-Inverness service via Craigellachie, and the coastal line through Buckie. This was effectively most of the former GNSR network, and the Board noted that its closure of no fewer than thirty-two stations would save £159,000 (£1.7 million) in working costs. While a service was obviously still possible between the two cities via the remaining combination of Highland and GNSR lines, nevertheless a whole swathe of North East Scotland had lost its trains just as legislation was reaching the statute book which could have preserved them.

The new Act would, according to Michael Bonavia, 'on the passengers side, dissect out the commercial system within the railways, to separate it from the social services that are not self-supporting and maintain these, where required, at the expense of the taxpayer or the ratepayer'. Bonavia also stated that the 'most important part of the 1968 Act ... relieved the railways of the cost of meeting 'social obligations'', although to the outsider, and Dr Bonavia was hardly that, it is difficult to understand quite what he meant since, in Scotland at least, rail managers had never shown any overwhelming concern for popular needs. Unless, of course, Dr Bonavia felt that statutory procedures had inhibited them from closing down even more railways than they actually did!

From a purely Scottish point of view, the Act was noteworthy in setting up the Scottish Transport Group, which amalgamated road and shipping interests, effectively removing the latter from railway control, except on one particular marine route. And the continued existence of this route within the rail system made a nonsense of an otherwise sensible and overdue piece of legislation, as will be related later.

At that first meeting at (Old) St Andrew's House with the Ministry of Transport, which had presumably borrowed accommodation from the Scottish Office, it was decided in June 1968 that 'present levels' of service should be maintained through grant subsidy on Inverness-Kyle, Fort William-Mallaig, Glasgow-Oban, and Glasgow-Fort William routes, for three years, assuming that there were no major road improvements in that time. Within a few years, the Kyle line appeared to be falling through the safety net; 1 July 1974 was slated as the line's closure date, but, with an unusually positive attitude, the Board decided in January 1972 to explore ways and means of stimulating passenger traffic to Kyle.

By 1974 the minutes show that the Board recognised that this beautifully scenic area of north-west Scotland had an unexpectedly rich *industrial* potential. The possibility of constructing oil platforms at Kishorn, and possibly at Drumbuie, meant that the prospect of closure was wiped from the slate. The Board even took Ross and Cromarty Council to the Court of Session over compensation for damage caused by road improvements in the Loch Broom area, celebrations for an early cash award by the court having to be postponed when the Council went to appeal.

In effect, the guidelines suggested by the Association of County Councils to test a line's viability, by combining freight and passenger revenues before assessing the possible withdrawal of the latter, was being put into practice, eighteen years after it had been ignored by the Board. The passage of the 1968 Act was of course a major factor in the continuance of the Kyle line, but it appears in retrospect that the non-railway specialists had the right idea all along.

'Initial consideration' was also to be given to subsidising 'present levels' on Ayr-Stranraer, Glasgow to Ayr, Largs, East Kilbride, and Edinburgh via Shotts routes, with a reduced level on the Glasgow-Kilmacolm service (the only one no longer operating in fact). Two months later, after another meeting at St Andrew's House (often incorrectly captioned as the 'Calton Gaol' in railway books picturing Waverley) no fewer than forty-two applications for subsidy were presented. These included five described as Anglo-Scottish. Among the more surprising candidates requiring support were the North Clydeside electric network, Glasgow-Dundee, and Glasgow-Aberdeen. The upshot was that in 1968 Scottish received a £10 million (£107 million) share of the total initial subsidy of £62 million, an outcome the Board thought 'particularly satisfactory'.

One community which failed to benefit was St Andrews. The town council approached Scottish Region at the eleventh hour about subsidising their last rail service, which was already scheduled for withdrawal from the following 6 January, but this was clearly too late. In December 1968 the Board Minutes record blandly that there was 'an absence of any undertaking by the Town Council'.

The burgh's council minutes reveal a local authority which seemed singularly uninformed in terms of transport matters. When in August 1968 councillors learned from the TUCC that the Minister of Transport had allowed the application to close the town's last remaining rail link, with Leuchars Junction on the Edinburgh-Aberdeen line, their reaction was to investigate other uses for the railway land. They might have reasonably queried the necessity for closure; the introduction of DMUs between Dundee and St Andrews in 1959 had increased revenue by 13.7 per cent. But the councillors were already about to purchase seven acres of former rail property on the south side of the town, on the recently closed line from Thornton Junction via Leven, for a very reasonable £500 (£5,000).

In September, one councillor pointed out that, although Leuchars-St Andrews trains were only intermittently busy, there was already a parking problem in the town, and would rail closure not make matters worse? Belatedly, councillors learned of the potential line-saving Clause 39 of the new Transport Act, and approached the Region about using it as a possible means of maintaining services. In October they received a brusque reply from Scottish warning the councillors that their burgh would have to bear the 'full costs' of keeping the service and, by early November, the region had reinforced the message by announcing an increase in running costs. It was hardly encouraging for the good burghers of St Andrews, who may have realised that their need to introduce controlled car parking around that time would hardly be eased by taking no action to prevent the closure of an existing means of public transport. Not surprisingly, they made a desperate enquiry to Fife County Council about possible assistance with rail subsidy.

To be fair to Scottish, its GM, Gordon Stewart, offered to meet the councillors, but his message was not a happy one: at least £20,000 would be needed annually to maintain the service. Since this was 50 per cent more than the council spent each year on housing, it was clearly not an option for St Andrews, whose council then accepted closure without even waiting to hear from the County. Scottish had hardly made it easy for the burgh's representatives, and there had been no detailed discussion about possible operational economies.

So, rail closure went ahead in one of Scotland's leading tourist centres, the site of a new hotel just opened by British Transport Hotels, an organisation that had as one of its directors the General Manager of Scottish Region, the aforementioned Gordon Stewart! In late 1968 Mr Douglas Brown wrote to the *Railway Magazine*, pointing out that the new hotel not only occupied the former goods station, but was so close to an existing running line that, 'it would appear that the closure of the line was considered when the hotel was projected ... if so, it is regrettable that the hotel was partially contributory to its closure.'

Not surprisingly, the Old Course Hotel, the first built by Britain's railways in thirty years, and opened at 20 per cent over estimate just as the prospect of rail-borne residents was being removed, made a loss for its first three years. In its third year of operations, the deficit came to £60,000 (£600,000) as against a forecast profit of £123,500 (£1,235,000). This was surely inevitable, and the Board's determination to close the railway into the town was perverse beyond belief.

To rub salt in the wound, Scottish Region held a board meeting in St Andrews at the end of July 1970, presumably in their own hotel, having organised on the previous evening a dinner attended by the Provost of St Andrews 'in the furtherance of railway interests'. Quite what these were is difficult to discern, since the railway had been closed to passenger traffic for eighteen months by then. Nowadays, congestion is so bad in this most popular of seaside and golfing resorts that a 'park and ride' bus service is necessary to handle visitors to the town who find it almost impossible to park within its centre.

In an earlier chapter, dealing with the introduction of DMUs to Scottish Region in 1958, the Corstorphine-North Berwick service was discussed, and in particular the closure of the western end of the service deplored. Corstorphine had a serious problem with road congestion, yet the conveniently situated rail terminus there closed at the end of 1967. But the other end of the service continued, and is still open. While it was undoubtedly true that Transport Minister Barbara Castle soon let her civil servants know that she would not welcome recommendations to close lines to holiday resorts, it seems possible to detect a political factor at work in preserving the link to North Berwick. East Lothian has been a Labour stronghold since the mid-1960s (apart from eight months in 1974), while Corstorphine was situated in a Conservative parliamentary constituency until the 1990s, and the city administration was Tory until 1984. Citizens of St Andrews, newly cut adrift from the rail network, could complain in vain to their Liberal MP. Taken with the Waverley Route experience, the political factors involved seem more than just a coincidence. Having newly elected a Liberal tyro called David Steel in the mid-sixties, the Central Borders could expect no mercy.

While the loss of railways running across barren moorland in Liddesdale or Wigtownshire was hardly unexpected, the closure of urban railways at that time challenged logic. In the 1960s there was even greater pressure on suburban transport than nowadays, as commuters' working-hours were more rigidly enforced, and there was no widespread use of flexible working-hours, facilitated by computerised 'clocking-in'. More employees worked in town-centres in those days, anyway, before so many offices moved to out-of-town sites, and there was less working from home too. As a result, rush hours tended to be shorter than nowadays, but were much more intensive. This necessitated high-capacity transport systems capable of shifting a maximum number of short-distance travellers within very brief time-frames. For example, in December 1948, London Transport published appeals for the public not to travel between 0830 and 0930 and between 1630 and 1800, unless absolutely necessary.

It all added up to a major need for urban railways. So, why did Scottish close the Glasgow Low Level lines in 1964? This was perhaps the most mysterious closure in Scotland's transport history for, unlike Edinburgh's Corstorphine, there was no discernable political factor. The Central Low Level Lines had comprised the Caledonian's attempt to match both the North British line running partly underground north of, and parallel to, the Clyde, as well as the city's own Underground system. The Central lines offered a north-south connection through Glasgow, but had always suffered from the use of steam traction in underground locations, and were excluded from BR's electrification schemes for north and south banks. On the last day, 3 October 1964, standard 4MT No.76074 worked the final southbound passenger train under the city, on a line where the principal underground station was so Stygian that it was almost impossible to take photographs in it. The line cried out for new traction and investment, but that went unheard in Buchanan Street. Indeed, in 1967 Scottish Region investigated the complete disposal of what remained of the route, only to be thwarted by the English!

With no thought to a possible reopening in later years, BR property managers went out-of-pocket to the extent of £448 (£5,100) in preparing for piecemeal disposal of the Central Low Lines route, only for the Board to decide that this was unlikely to be approved by the Ministry of Transport before the completion of the then-current Greater Glasgow Transport Study. However, the Board members were assured, according to the minutes in July 1967 that 'steps would of course be taken to bring the availability of the solum [in this case, trackbed] to the notice of local authorities, chambers of commerce, industrialists and other interested parties with land adjoining the Low Level Lines'. This would have effectively ensured the loss of the route through its dissemination among different purchasers. With the new Transport Bill going through Parliament at this time, awarding Scottish local authorities transport-associated powers that England could only envy, it seems incredible that rail managers could be so short-sighted. If this was the disgraceful way that a Glasgow-based organisation treated an internal Glasgow line, what hope was there for the far-away Waverley Route, still open at that time?

In 1966 Scottish could console itself with nearly £3 million worth of property sales, with the Board Minutes recording particular satisfaction that the amount saved on feu duties on the properties would now come to nearly £10,000 (£114,000) per annum. This was a problem peculiar to Scotland, since society north of the Border remained feudal until the opening of the Scottish Parliament at the end of the twentieth century. In other words, all Scottish landowners had to pay a tax to a feudal superior, very often the Church of Scotland, although this could be aggregated in a single payment in later years. If English readers think this medieval, which it was, literally, they should bear in mind that the Westminster parliament had some 290 years to reform the antiquated system of Scottish land ownership, but could never quite find the time.

Another peculiarly Scottish aspect to BR's property management arose in 1966, when new local government legislation increased rating on railway property. Even advertisement sites were now rated, something which did not happen south of the Border.

The fact that local authority rates financed road improvements (directly benefiting rival buses and lorries) was a continuing thorn in the flesh of railway managers, and was a problem which could have been addressed by Westminster at the time of nationalisation. In 1948, railways and railway-owned canals in England and Wales were assessed for £1.85 million (£37 million) in local government rates, following a revision two years earlier. The Scottish figure was a theoretical one, since the then-new legislation did not apply north of the Border, but the figure suggested for Scottish railways and canals (the latter in the central belt only) was £110,735 (£2.21 million). Scottish looks slightly 'under-rated' in the 1948 figures, whether assessed as a percentage of UK rail mileage, or by the 'Barnett' formula later used by government to assess government finances relating to the funding of the Scottish Office.

At St Andrews for example, the burgh spent £28,000 (£275,000) in two years in the late 1960s on road upkeep and improvement, although there was always the prospect of recovering some of that expenditure by introducing controlled parking. By the end of the decade, the town would receive no rates income from BR, except of course through its Hotels Division.

The target for property disposal in 1967 was £1.9 million, with the Board members seemingly rubbing their hands in anticipation at the large station sites being 'liberated' for sale. At the same time, the minutes record that the disposal of branch lines had not quite reached the levels expected. To 628 miles of redundant railway available at the end of 1965, 209 miles were added up to April 1967 (totalling 837), but only 80 miles had been sold – less than 10 per cent. At this time BR also owned 2,902 houses in Scotland, but Scottish was aiming to dispose of nearly half of these by the end of the year.

Yet the question of why Scottish was so dedicated to land disposal still remained to be answered. In 1971, income from commercial rentals brought £393,000 (£3.41 million) into Regional coffers, with an increase to £406,000 expected in the following year. It was hardly negligible, and represented a land bank which BR itself might have need of someday.

In 1955 Scottish Region had listed its major stations in order of size. Those in the two largest categories are listed below, in no particular order:

1st category

Edinburgh (Waverley)
Edinburgh (Princes Street)

Glasgow (Central)
Glasgow (St Enoch)
Perth

2nd category

Aberdeen
Dundee (Tay Bridge)
Dundee (West)
Glasgow (Buchanan Street)
Glasgow (Queen Street)
Inverness
Paisley (Gilmour Street)

The above classification was actually devised in order to achieve fairness in administering a 'Best Kept Stations' competition, but it will serve as an introduction to a brief history of the fate of Scotland's most important railway passenger stations. The most obvious omission from the above list was Carlisle, which had been owned jointly by the Caledonian Railway with (originally) the Lancaster & Carlisle. To this day, the Caledonian crest can be seen above the main entrance to the station, and it includes the strangest-looking lion rampant you will see anywhere! But the omission of Carlisle, 9 miles into England, and the London Midland Region, needs no further explanation.

Of the above twelve stations listed in 1955, four are now closed, so their fate is worth examining. In December of that year, the possible closure of Edinburgh's Princes Street was already being discussed at Board level, along with the 'combination' of services at Glasgow Queen Street and Buchanan Street. (BR had already closed Leith Central three years previously; its size would undoubtedly have qualified it for the second category.)

Edinburgh's Princes Street terminus was well situated in the West End of the city, although hidden from Lothian Road by the Dumfriesshire sandstone façade of the Caledonian Hotel. It was highly convenient for passengers, who could access and leave it at ground-level, and there was road access from Rutland Street. It was however less convenient to operate than Waverley, particularly with its lack of through tracks being made worse by the omission of 'run around' loops. Scottish inherited a track layout signalled with semaphores by the LMS, despite re-equipment taking place as recently as 1937 (when the LNER was signalling Waverley with colour-lights). In addition, the turntable just outside the terminus was too short for the largest Pacifics. One of the author's earliest railway memories, from around 1950, is of seeing former LMS 'Princess Royal' Pacific *Princess Margaret Rose* standing among her Gresley counterparts at Haymarket shed where she had been sent to turn.

If BR wanted to integrate former LMS and LNER services, the city's rail map would have to be redrawn in at least two places. While services from Princes Street to Stirling could access the direct route via Polmont at Haymarket West junction (over what is now part of the Western Approach Road, and how No.46203 reached Haymarket depot), there was no reciprocal means for Waverley's outbound trains to reach the former LMS until the Duff Street connection was completed in 1962, costed at nearly £700,000 (£7.8 million) in that year. Meanwhile, the Slateford-Craiglockhart spur, costed by BR at £698,808 in June 1956, allowed the exchange of freight traffic between the two former systems (in place of steeply inclined connection at Granton), as well as the immediate running of Sunday traffic from Carstairs to Waverley via the former NBR Suburban Circle. This was a preliminary to closing Princes Street, which lost its recently introduced DMU service to Leith in 1962. There were no outstanding arguments for retaining Princes Street Station once the above adjustments had been made to the rail map of the capital, but one wonders what the royal family thought. They made no secret of their preference of this now-vanished terminus over the gloom of Waverley.

St Enoch is a name now known to Glaswegians for its pyramidal shopping centre. Yet it was the location of a rail terminus on the north bank of the Clyde before Central, and this former GSWR headquarters once boasted Britain's biggest signalbox, one of 488 levers before the LMS installed colour-light signalling in 1933 (a certain Mr Nock was involved).

This terminus operated cheerfully and efficiently until the end of its working life; if it was in decline, the downward path was a slow one. In the last full year of the LMS's existence, 1947, St Enoch handled 1.26 million outgoing passenger journeys and this had fallen only to 1.23 million in its final full year of operation, 1965. This was exclusive of season ticket sales and parcels revenue; the value of St Enoch to the public transport network was undeniable.

Not surprisingly, a TUCC was set up to investigate this closure proposal, although it was always fairly obvious that diversion to Central was a practical possibility, while the Saltmarket connection would not be enough to save the station (although the viaducts are still largely intact). Privately, the Board was being told that closure of St Enoch would 'save' no less than a remarkable £252,000 (£3.2 million) in annual operating costs alone. But, more realistically, £34,000 would have to be spent in altering Central's signalling to deal with the traffic transferred. Closure was complete by 27 June 1966.

Buchanan Street seemed to bestir less affection, and was looked on as a likely closure target from 1955, if not earlier. In December of that year, the new Scottish Board discussed the possible 'combination' of Queen Street and Buchanan Street. Unlike St Enoch, Buchanan Street was not its owning company's principal station in Glasgow before 1923, and its rebuilding by the LMS in the 1930s was half-hearted, with second-hand platform canopies being used. No major realignment of rail access was required within Glasgow, since trains to former Caledonian and LMS destinations in the north could reach there from Queen Street at Castlecary. However, as mentioned elsewhere in this volume, some modernisation was required at the latter terminus before Buchanan Street could be handed over to the developers after closure in November 1966.

Dundee once had three main-line railway stations, two of them termini. Dundee (West) was operated successively by the Caledonian and LMS railways, much of its traffic being with the similarly doomed Glasgow (Buchanan Street). A connection at Buckingham Junction enabled traffic from Perth to reach former LNER metals into Tay Bridge Station, so no great hardship to passengers resulted, and BR was able to plan the routing of all its Glasgow-Aberdeen and Euston/Crewe/Carlisle traffic via the city of Dundee, instead of the more sparsely populated route through Forfar. Although the latter was well-laid-out for speed – as the A4s demonstrated 'illegally' for four years from 1962 – its elimination from the rail network could now be planned. Meanwhile, Dundee (West) closed on 1 May 1965, and is now submerged beneath an improved road network.

Those major stations not closed began a process of reorganisation. With steam traction no longer present to darken stone and glass, it was possible to clean up Britain's railway stations, although the technology of stone-cleaning appears not to have been perfected until the 1970s at the earliest. One station which underwent a major refurbishment at the end of the 1960s was Edinburgh Waverley. With one eye on the forthcoming 1970 Commonwealth Games, it was decided to redesign the very heart of this, what was once the NBR's – and perhaps more surprisingly, the LNER's – largest station. The central booking office, a magnificent wooden structure centred in a hall paved with the NBR's coat of arms in the corners, and with a grandeur almost enough to discourage the traveller in quest of a ticket, was demolished and replaced by a modern travel court. This had no booking office element at all, the latter being tucked under the arcade on the south side of the hall. Meanwhile, the passageway leading the ticket-holder to the eastbound platforms was closed off. This was not considered a problem, since the Waverley Route, most of the Berwick line stations, and almost all suburban services had been closed. Where forty-six stations had been reached eastbound less than 15 miles from Waverley in 1910, only three existed seventy-five years later. Westbound, the figure slipped from nineteen to twelve, but the latter number of stations included those formerly served within 15 miles of the Princes Street terminus.

Transporting cars with their drivers proved to be a worthwhile enterprise in the form of the 'Anglo Scottish Car Carrier', but it was not the only example of Scottish Region undertaking the transport of road vehicles by rail. Two Government schemes for the dispersal of jobs in the automotive industries meant the opening of two Scottish factories, far from the West Midland area normally associated at the time with road vehicle production. The first was the British Leyland factory at Bathgate in 1962, the second the Rootes Group car factory at Linwood, Renfrewshire, in the following year.

Neither was to become a permanent part of the industrial landscape, and the former soon became a growth area for Scottish nationalism, with BR and associated road services delivering parcelled components from the Midlands bearing racist messages from workers down south who felt that the Scots were being 'feather bedded' by government. From a strictly transport point-of-view, Bathgate was responsible for assembling lorry chassis which were then sent southwards again, often via the Waverley Route to Carlisle. All this would have fed criticism of any industrial dispersal scheme, with its inherent reliance on costly long-distance transport. At least with Linwood, the complete vehicle – for much of the factory's life this consisted of the Hillman Imp – was moved out by rail, although only 40 per cent of factory input, in 1968. But even such a self-sufficient operation could not survive a transfer to foreign owners at the end of the 1970s. Scottish Region could at least be complimented on its targeting of these two markets, undoubtedly assisted by the lack of motorway connections which could have eased the movement of car and truck transporters.

Perhaps one of the saddest aspects of 1969 – a year which saw a legal apparatus of subsidy engage to save the existence of railways in parts of the country, such as the Far North, Mallaig, Kyle, where closure had seemed inevitable – was the fact that Scottish failed to share in the sudden upturn in BR's fortunes. Within a UK-wide operating surplus of no less than £48.5 million, of which the net profit was £14.7 million, Scottish made a loss of £7.3 million. Admittedly, this was the region's best performance in thirteen years – itself a melancholy fact.

Accidents on Scotland's railways should not be omitted in a regional history such as this, and are listed in Table XIII, although in fact the safety record of Scottish Region was mercifully good. While Scotland has been the location for the worst rail and air accidents in British history – Quintinshill in 1915, only a mile from the English border – from 1948 onwards the worst railway accidents took place on railways to the south.

The 1950s saw two major railway accidents in the London area which merited the description of 'disaster' – at Harrow in 1952 and Lewisham five years later – but no Scottish incident involved death-tolls in double figures. Eighteen passengers and staff died in Scottish Region rail accidents up to 1968; in that period, exactly 500 passengers died on BR nationally, with staff figures not included. Statistically, with Scottish Region making up approximately one-twelfth of total BR mileage at nationalisation, this means that fatalities in operational accidents in Scotland were less than half of what might have been expected.

Scotland's first accident, if one discounts the spectacular fate of the tanker train on the Highland main-line (mentioned in Chapter 2), took place at Lamington on the WCML on 7 March. Unfortunately, there was a blowback on the locomotive hauling a Glasgow-London express which killed one crewman and badly injured the other. The minister himself took questions about this in Parliament eight days later, one MP asking if this shocking accident had taken place on a coal or an oil-fired locomotive. Obviously, it was the former, since oil-fired engines – and, in any event, the former LMS had not converted any express passenger types – had a sealed firebox. If the questioning MP had been hoping to press this point, he was not given the opportunity to do so. A ministerial inquiry later heard no fewer than forty witnesses. Tragically, it appeared that the crew had decided to proceed south from Carstairs knowing that locomotive No.6224 had a defective water-gauge.

The highest death-toll in Scottish rail accidents over this period was no more than five. This happened at Beattock in June 1950 when a cigarette-end carelessly dropped apparently ignited chemicals from upholstery, accumulating in a fireball, affecting two carriages of a Birmingham-Glasgow express nearing Beattock Summit. It seems possible that the dead, who included two children, had been asphyxiated before the fire reached them. Curiously enough, there had been an accident the previous year, again involving fire, at Penmanshiel, on the ECML. On this occasion, cellulose lacquer used in décor varnish was ignited on a southbound express train, the heat generated sufficient to melt the windows, and although there were no fatalities, seven people were burned or injured. In both cases the ministry's inspector commended rail staff for the way they had minimised death and injury by their swift handling of the accidents.

Perhaps the worst Scottish accident in terms of 'preventability' was at Glasgow Queen Street in November 1951. Here, in yet another runaway incident on the Cowlairs incline, where four people died and no fewer than sixty-five were injured in 1928, the lack of safety provisions at one of Britain's worst main-line locations was highlighted, fortunately without any loss of life on this occasion to underline this chronic omission.

Although not the worst in numerical terms, the Wormit accident of 1955 was perhaps the most distressing in regional history, concerning as it did a train of Sunday school picnickers. On this occasion, a tender-first 'Black 5' hauling an eight-coach train returning from Tayport to Dundee, came off the track in Wormit tunnel, causing three people to lose their lives. The footplate crewmen had visited a pub before setting off on the return journey, although no witness reported them drunk, but they had allowed three unauthorised visitors to travel on the footplate. The driver was found by the subsequent ministerial inquiry to have travelled too fast on the approach to Wormit, although to say that there were attenuating circumstances would seem to understate the matter. He had never driven a '5' before, his view was obscured by the tender, and, needless to say, the locomotive carried no speedometer.

In the circumstances it was incredible that the unfortunate driver – who admitted his breach of operating rules – should have been forced to stand trial for culpable homicide (manslaughter in English law), when British Railways had failed to observe their full responsibility of care to paying passengers. No attempt had been made to test or train the crew in the use of the brake arrangements – which BR admitted were different on a 'Black 5' from those on former LNER locomotives normally driven by the accused – while the use of tender-first engines on passenger duties was never satisfactory. With a locomotive so configured, the driver had constantly to divide his attention between the (partly obscured) road ahead and the cab controls, which needless to say, would not tell him what speed the train was doing. Not surprisingly, the driver was acquitted.

seven

SCOTLAND'S RAILWAYS AT SEA

Scotland's railway companies – including the LMS and LNER in the quarter-century from 1923 until nationalisation in 1948 – had always comprised
more than just the permanent way. Three of the five pre-grouping companies had operated ferries or pleasure vessels during the twentieth century,
with no less than two-thirds of the Clyde shipping business being railway-
owned in 1922. The three canals in the central belt had been acquired by
CR and NBR and passed to the LMS and LNER respectively, while all
but the largest docks in Scotland were railway-owned. All the companies
had owned hotels, the Highland and the G&SWR more than the others.
The LMS and LNER in Scotland had invested heavily in Scottish Motor
Traction – and most lucratively too – although the measure of control
sought over Scotland's buses was never attained.

The maritime work of the railways tended to fall into two categories:
ferries and seasonal passenger cruising. The new British Railways inherited both aspects of this maritime world in 1948, which was something of
an anomaly. Why should the new legislation take away hotels, docks, and
canals from railway managers, as well as the lucrative financial partnership
with bus services, but leave ferries and pleasure steamers? Addressing his
BTC colleagues on 29 September 1947, Sir Cyril Hurcomb was recorded
as saying: 'The operation of existing steamer services should continue to be
linked with the Railways, of which they are in effect a projection across the
narrow seas'. In any event, it could have been worse if the Internal Docks
and Waterways Executive had not been instituted. Most Scottish docks
were not economical – with the prominent exception of Grangemouth
– while canals were a blot on the landscape (as far as the railways were
concerned).

In 1948 the BTC took over some 100 ships in addition to terrestrial forms of transport, and nearly one-quarter of these came from the two Scottish railways, or their marine operating divisions. In the previous year the LMS and LNER had operated Clyde services which lost a total of £84,000 (£1.68 million) between them, but these maritime operations were estimated to generate £286,000 (£5.72 million) in rail income. In any event, twenty-five ships were doing the work of thirty-five in use nine years earlier. The LMS had utilised an 'arms-length' concern called the Caledonian Steam Packet Company – its previous owning railway can be guessed – while the LNER had a more direct operating policy, on the Clyde at least. The two worked together on Loch Lomond.

The Caledonian fleet was the larger of the two in 1947, comprising nine passenger vessels, one dredger, and four short-distance ferries. Pride of the fleet were the steam turbine-powered 'Duchesses' - *Duchess of Montrose* and *Duchess of Hamilton*. Dating from the 1930s, both had rendered valuable war service, with sister vessel (although a paddle steamer) *Duchess of Fife* making no fewer than four crossings to rescue troops from Dunkirk in 1940. These veteran vessels were able to continue Clyde cruising well into the 1960s (for a list of ships taken over by BR, and later ordered by the railway authorities, see Table XII).

The LNER's Clyde fleet had been unlucky in war, with both the *Waverley* and *Marmion* being lost to enemy action. The company ordered a replacement for the former, and *Waverley* – the fourth to bear the name – entered service just before nationalisation, joining the *Jeanie Deans* and *Talisman*. The *Waverley* is, of course, still sailing today, an excellent investment for £125,000 at the time! An older vessel, *Lucy Ashton*, only just made the transition to public ownership, being already in her late fifties!

Hurcomb saw no problem with the fleet services in Central Scotland. But he told his colleagues in October 1947 that, 'there remains the troublesome matter of MacBrayne services, in which we shall become half-owners in succession to the LMS and in partnership with Coast Lines'. What was 'troublesome' about this was the promise made by the LMS to purchase half the shares in a new £100,000 issue, designed to pay for new tonnage. In April 1948 the BTC Comptroller (a Scot!) recommended that this transaction should be proceeded with. Taken with a 1950 Modernisation Plan for seven new railway-owned Caledonian Steam Packet vessels (see below), this represented a major investment in Scottish shipping, on a scale that the corresponding Scottish Region rail network could only dream about.

Three years into nationalisation, the BTC announced a £1 million (£20 million) modernisation plan for its Clyde fleet – considerably more than it was spending to modernise Scotland's railways (as shown in Table II). Indeed, one historian has pointed out that, so generous was the budget for ship replacement, it completely distorted the investment figure for railway services, disguising how bad the level really was 'inland'. The ship's programme involved constructing four twin-screw passenger ships, along with three general-purpose vessels. Servicing passenger routes were the four 'Maid' vessels – *Maid of Ashton*, which, with the 'Maids' of *Argyll*, *Skelmorlie*, and *Cumbrae*, entered service in 1953. Significantly, two of these were converted to car ferries before their careers were over – an indication of how Scottish marine transport was to develop.

Three ferries dubbed 'general purpose', and known as the 'ABC' class, began work in the following year (with the *Cowal* being delivered after the *Arran*, but before the *Bute*, it should have been the 'ACB' class). But the concept of the vehicle ferry was slow to be adopted, as could be expected under rail ownership, with the first of the class requiring cars to reach the main-deck by a time-consuming electric lift. This was despite increasingly overwhelming evidence that road traffic was burgeoning. As shown elsewhere in this book, while Clyde ferries carried 3,493 vehicles in 1953, this figure had ballooned to 118,403 eleven years later.

The Kyle-Kyleakin passage was in profit at the time of nationalisation and, in the 1950s, BR introduced the *Lochalsh, Broadford,* and the *Portree* on to this short route. None of these could accommodate more than four cars, while a new (actually second-hand) ferry, the *Coruisk*, had no vehicle accommodation at all. This was on a station where vehicle transport was to quadruple within fifteen years. By the 1960s, the need for vehicle ferries was being more realistically addressed, but not before time.

In November 1955, the Scottish Board debated the possible conversion of seven (unspecified) vessels from coal to oil-firing. This was because of difficulties in recruiting firemen and also 'the more stable price of oil than coal'. Within a year there was petrol-rationing; in less than twenty years the price of oil was to rocket. While there are railway historians (including this one) baffled at the failure of BR to fit mechanical stokers to the larger steam locomotives, it would surely have been worth considering such an improvement for the nationalised shipping fleet. Coal was indigenous and comparatively cheap. Its only demerit was dirt, yet this was not given as a reason for conversion to oil.

BR's seven new vessels, launched following the 1950 Modernisation Plan, were all diesel-powered, so the seven planned for conversion to oil-burning were presumably the *Jeanie Deans, Waverley, Caledonia, Jupiter, Queen*

Mary II, and the two remaining 'Duchesses'. The coal-fired *Marchioness of Graham* was approaching her final cruise at this time, and was withdrawn after the delivery of the diesel-powered *Glen Sannox*.

The year 1957 saw a reorganisation in Scotland's railway ships, with the reinvigoration of the Caledonian SP Company as, 'the organisation through which their various steamer and ferry services in Scotland shall be controlled', as the official press release announced. This encompassed operations on the Clyde, Loch Lomond, and at Kyle. The railways' general manager (James Ness) was made chairman and managing director of Caledonian, whose general manager, Alex Stewart, had responsibility for day-to-day operations. The press release conceded that there had been a certain loss of identity in the nationalised shipping off Scotland's western coastline when under the nominal aegis of an intermediate holding company, Clyde Shipping Services.

The relationship between BR and Caledonian came under serious review in 1959, following a tragic accident at Kyleakin. Four car passengers drowned when their vehicle crashed through the rear ferry doors of the *Broadford* on 13 April of that year. The Scottish Board recommended that these doors be lashed shut with rope in future, while Caledonian felt that this was an admission of liability which could prove costly if a court case resulted. Sir Ian Bolton is recorded as saying, quite reasonably one might think, that his Board members 'have given their opinion as asked'. No further action is quoted in the railway minutes, so the shipping company was clearly being left to decide its own course of action. But, tragic though this was – and there had been an unhappily similar accident at South Queensferry in 1957, although caused entirely by unsafe operating – it all seemed as nothing compared to the loss of the *Princess Victoria* in 1953.

Until Lockerbie in 1988, this was Scotland's worst transport accident since Quintinshill in 1915. Technically, the service was operated from Euston by the London Midland Region from 1952 to 1961, possibly because it had been found inconvenient in terms of administration to have the LMR operating the Belfast ferry facilities, with Scottish running Larne's, as originally envisaged in the 1948 *Instructions*. But the loss of this vessel united Scotland and Northern Ireland in grief.

The *Princess Victoria* was a postwar vehicle ferry on the Stranraer-Larne run and was fitted with rear vehicular doors. She had just cleared Stranraer with 170 people on board on 31 January 1953 when she ran into a severe storm. Her stern doors, which were not designed to seal the hull or superstructure, appear to have given way and she tragically foundered with the loss of 133 lives. From available evidence, it seems that the captain fatally delayed giving the order to abandon ship, allowing a list to become so severe as to prevent the launching of lifeboats on one side, although his reluctance to commit passengers to the stormy water is perhaps understandable when he believed, wrongly, that help was near at hand.

A court of inquiry subsequently held in Northern Ireland was critical of the BTC for operating a vessel so clearly defective in design. There had been problems before with the *Victoria's* stern doors, but one incident had not even been reported to the marine authorities. Additionally, and fatally, the vessel had twice demonstrated an inability to drain her vehicle deck quickly, one of the previous incidents involving, of all things, quantities of spilt milk. The BTC appealed the court findings and the High Court of Northern Ireland, in a judgement handed down in November 1953, was more specific in assigning blame. Unfortunately, it appeared that the Scottish Region Marine Superintendent, who controlled the vessel from 1948 until January 1952, was deemed to have failed to address the ship's design problems. The individual concerned, Captain Harry Perry, had served the LNER as Marine Superintendent before moving up to the Regional post, and was being criticised for not noticing the defects of a LMS-designed vessel. It might have been that, following nationalisation, the post was simply too exacting, with responsibilities for marine services on both Scottish and Irish coasts. Of course, moving the control of the Stranraer-Larne service to Euston in 1952 was hardly much of a solution, particularly with the LMR not appointing a manager at Stranraer until *after* the disaster. A.L. Pepper was appointed District Marine Manager there in June 1953.

By that time, Scottish, although not the direct ferry operator, was finding itself haunted by this tragedy. After the publication of the initial inquiry's findings in June 1953, the media were not slow to seek scapegoats for the disaster. The *Daily Express* seized on the 'remoteness' aspect, asking why it had been necessary for the beleaguered captain 'to get into telephonic communication with the headquarters in London, some 400 miles away' – although the transcript of radio messages from the doomed ship indicate that raising London was hardly in the radio operator's mind as he desperately tried to summon help. Incidentally, the wireless operator of the *Victoria*, David Broadfoot, was posthumously awarded the George Cross for remaining at his post without thought for his own safety. Meanwhile, the *Daily Mail* asked pointedly if Harry Perry would now be suspended, this even before the BTC appeal was lodged, although the ship's Registered Manager, Captain J.D. Reed, based in London, did not escape media opprobrium either.

Four years later, Scottish GM James Ness quashed a suggestion from
his own PR department that they should co-operate in a BBC radio programme about the *Princess Victoria* and, two years after that, took legal advice
about an enquiry from the *Sunday Dispatch* about compensation paid to the
families of Northern Ireland Deputy Premier, John Sinclair, and Sir Walter
Smiles MP, two of the more prominent victims. Since it was suspected that
the newspaper might mischievously compare this compensation to sums
paid to other passengers' families, the advice received was to declare such
information confidential.

It seems incredible to the modern reader that the authorities had been unable,
on that day in 1953, to locate this sizeable vessel, in daylight in a comparatively
narrow channel, in time to render it assistance. Radio communications with the
lifeboat service were so complicated as to make the accurate passage of messages
almost impossible, while the Royal Navy attempted to co-ordinate its rescue
attempts from far-off Plymouth, with an unexplained forty minute delay rendering useless a gallant rescue attempt by the destroyer HMS *Contest* venturing
out into the storm at near-fatal speed from Rothesay Bay. The Portpatrick lifeboat set out on a rescue mission before any other vessel, but was so misdirected
by inaccurate radio messages that it arrived at the site of the sinking last of all.
Not surprisingly, the Minister of Transport told Parliament in December 1953
that search and rescue procedures at sea were to be reviewed.

On a happier note, Loch Lomond had been served by a joint railway
approaching from the south, run by, firstly, the Dumbarton & Balloch Joint
Railway, which was supported by both the Caledonian and the North
British railways, and then by their respective successors, the LMS and LNER.
Balloch was also approached by the erstwhile Forth & Clyde Junction
Railway, which was operated firstly by the NBR, then by the LNER.

At the time of nationalisation, Loch Lomond services were being operated profitably by two elderly paddle steamers, the *Princess May* and *Prince
Edward*, and the new authority (strictly speaking, the BTC), noting their
ages as fifty and thirty-seven years, decided to retire these two existing vessels and replace them with a new steamer on this most attractive of inland
waterways (on paper, the Loch Lomond and Kyle services were not transferred to the Caledonian SP Company until 1957). The new *Maid of the Loch*,
launched in 1953, was also a paddle-steamer, and is described by maritime
historians Duckworth and Langmuir (see Bibliography) as 'in many respects
an anachronism', with the coincidental closure of Luss Pier removing one
of the last reasons why a more modern type of vessel was not ordered.

Unfortunately, the limited season militated against the service being profitable; in particular, 1964 was a bad year, incurring a loss of no less than £11,300 (£140,600). Not surprisingly, in 1965 the authorities embarked on a promotional campaign to boost patronage, although this may have had something to do with the discovery by the Scottish Board, in March 1963, that any attempt to withdraw the Loch Lomond sailings would have to be referred to a TUCC. Surprising on the face of it, as the service was seasonal.

At least the 1965 campaign reduced the loss to £1,600 (£19,000). No sailing figures were placed before the Board but it is believed that 192,000 passengers were carried in that year. Interestingly, one author writing on lake steamers has commented on the poor level of steamer patronage which the Scots have shown at Balloch over the years, compared to Windermere. Despite the latter being much farther from a conurbation, no fewer than half a million sailings were notched up there in 1964.

Despite this cavil, the *Maid* inspired great affection among her passengers, who were able to watch her massive pistons operating from a viewing platform above the engine-room and, although withdrawal from service has become a reality, the vessel still exists at the time of writing, tied up at Balloch pier as a floating restaurant. There cannot be many European countries where such a major scenic area is not served by waterborne transport.

In contrast to Scottish Region's determination to ruthlessly hunt out and close those railway lines showing negative returns (and even sometimes positive returns), the Board members seem to have found their shipping division to be a source of real pleasure from time to time. In June 1968, the Board learned of the 1,240 column inches of newspaper coverage for the introduction of the *Antrim Princess*, this in addition to 61 minutes of TV time, calculated by Scottish as worth £500 a minute in terms of advertising. At the close of 1970, the Board recorded their satisfaction at hearing of the launch, in Venice, of the *Ailsa Princess*, by Mrs Stewart, the wife of the chairman. A new vessel could always represent a 'clean slate' on a particular service, since any improvements in horsepower, loading methods, and capacity, were unlikely to be reduced, or even nullified altogether, by an antiquated infrastructure. In contrast, we have already seen the Blue Clydeside electrics serving stations still illuminated by gas.

Curiously, the 1968 legislation was intended to remove shipping from the clutches of railway management in Scotland, with the establishment of the STG. This did not include the Stranraer-Larne Station, probably because it was not internal. But it created an anomaly, as shown later.

Clyde steamer services declined under nationalised ownership. By 1960 there were only six pleasure steamers remaining, with the 'Maids' and the 'ABCs' being joined by the *Glen Sannox* on the Arran Station. By 1974, there was only one seasonal steamer, the *King George V,* by which time, ferry services had been taken over by new owners following the 1968 Transport Act, one shipping enthusiast commenting: 'A lot of mud was frequently thrown at the railway-owned Caledonian SP Company, which ran all the steamers and the ferries from its Gourock offices. Well, the enthusiasts got more new broom than they wanted when the Scottish Transport Group took over...' Effectively, the ships, including *Maid of the Loch,* were now owned by a bus company ('more steamers went, more piers were closed' according to the above historian), which seems a curious progression considering that the original transport legislation of 1948 was intended to create five separate executives for all transport except air, but never quite established a clear-cut, mutually exclusive, network. The 1968 legislation seems to have created an echo of the confusion from twenty years earlier.

In 1968, while the marine (and freshwater) services from Central Scotland went into the new STG, the Stranraer-Larne passage found a new master, or more accurately a former one. This important service, operated by the London Midland Region for some years after nationalisation, had found itself under a renewed Scottish aegis in 1961. This transfer had been anticipated by the BTC; in August 1959 the Commission 'had taken cognisance of the remoteness of Euston from Stranraer', and resolved to place the service under Scottish control once again (at least, the Commissioners did not regard Stranraer as 'remote' from Euston!). In 1968 the route came under a new corporate title: British Transport Ship Management Ltd (Scotland). Its Board Minutes are preserved in Scotland's National Archives, which is just as well, as BR's historian Dr Bonavia, does not mention the company in either of his published accounts of that period (see the Bibliography).

Its chairman also being the Scottish Region's GM, the new company held its Board meetings in Glasgow (Buchanan House), a Stranraer hotel, and in Belfast, and hurriedly sought to secure a company seal, as if to confirm its identity, despite the fact that it was nominally part of BR Shipping and International Services (SIS) Division.

Misconceived as it appears to have been, the new BTSM company was crippled by bureaucracy from the start; in best civil service tradition, its employees appear to have been required to answer to two masters. At one of the first Board meetings of the company, General Manager John Thomson was empowered – by BR's SIS Division – to spend up to £3,000 (for the year 1970), with no more than £500 on any one item, and this was not to include expenditure on ships, vehicles, or office machinery. The historian is tempted to ask what would be left for a shipping official to spend money on! But in fact Thomson later committed to expenditure on loading equipment, even before Board permission was obtained. He could not have found it easy to work to SIS management down south while following Scottish Region management instructions, 'unless obviously inapplicable and until SIS produce their own instructions re delegation of authority'.

Overcoming this handicapping of senior staff, and genuine doubt in the Boardroom about the extent of Scottish authority, the new company enjoyed a healthy trading history; despite the outbreak of civil unrest in the Province from 1969, commercial traffic used Larne as an Irish point of entry, and egress rose from 12,000 vehicles in 1967 to 43,600 in 1973. The Board Minutes commented in November 1969 that: 'The carriage of commercial vehicles had not been affected by the disturbances'. Passenger takings certainly declined over 1969-70, but started to recover by the mid-seventies. While pleased with this, the BTSM Board members were only too aware of their monopoly, and in 1970 minuted their 'growing concern that the success of the Stranraer-Larne route could well encourage severe competition from a British or foreign shipping line by the development or introduction of service between Cairnryan and Ireland'.

Three years later, their concerns proved to be correct, with the Atlantic Steam Navigation Company placing the *Ionic Ferry* on the (shorter) Cairnryan passage in July 1973. Curiously, the minutes show that traffic statistics for the new crossing seemed freely available to the Board – possibly because Atlantic came under the ownership of the National Freight Corporation at this time, spawned, like BTSML, from British Railways. And Atlantic appeared to represent less of a threat than the Larne harbour authority. Larne now announced a 30 per cent rise in harbour and loading fees, no doubt in order to maximize its own share in this successful trade.

It must be emphasised that the creation of the BTSM Company went against the grain of the 1968 legislation which took away the ship services operated by Scottish Region, awarding them to the new Scottish Transport Group, while services south of the Border became part of the new SIS division. Meanwhile, the region was expected to carry on this important British-Irish passage, without the benefits that might have accrued from any economies of scale in ordering supplies and equipment for a larger shipping group. Its Board Minutes make it clear that BTSM was administered virtually as an independent company, with little or no mention of any part in

BR shipping operations. This company's existence can only be regarded as a total anomaly within the UK's transport network.

An excellent history of the Stranraer-Larne ferry services has been written by Fraser MacHaffie (see Bibliography), and he highlights the anomalous position of this Scottish-controlled company, which operated ferry services while, technically, owning no ships. Also, in 1971, Professor MacHaffie and a friend had complained about the poorly stocked café at the Stranraer terminal, claiming 'it's always the same with British Railways catering', only to be told in no uncertain terms that the service might be terrible, but it was British Ship Transport Management service!

Incidentally, this text is being written around the time when regular ferry services in and out of Stranraer are scheduled to be transferred up the sea loch to Cairnryan, probably with an unhappy knock-on effect for the Girvan-Stranraer rail route. At the time of writing, it looks as if Stranraer will be superseded, just as it once superseded Portpatrick, and the railway may face the same future as the latter's branch.

On the other side of the country, the Granton-Burntisland ferry failed to survive the Second World War. At one time this was a train ferry carrying passengers and rail vehicles between Edinburgh and Fife, but was superseded by the opening of the Forth Bridge in 1890. Although both NBR and LNER continued it as a vehicle ferry, it failed to re-emerge after being suspended during the war. Two efforts have been made to resume service since then – on one occasion using a catamaran vessel – but both were private ventures, and not operated by British Railways. At the time of writing, a major bus company is considering reintroducing the ferry service here.

To the west of Granton are the Queensferry Narrows, and Scottish continued railway responsibility for the road ferry here. In 1934, the Dumbarton firm of Denny's had suggested a modern car-ferry, but the Forth Bridge Company declined to purchase this and instead leased the passage to the firm. So the Dumbarton company supplied two side-loading ferries with chain-driven paddles, and these craft, the *Robert the Bruce* and the *Queen Margaret*, became part of the Forth seascape for thirty years, with a third (using a different form of propulsion) supplied to BR by Denny in 1949 (the *Mary Queen of Scots*), and a fourth (*Sir William Wallace*) in 1955. Demand for deck-space increased year on year but, when Denny proposed in 1958 to bring in a fifth vessel, the MV *Rupel*, available for £50,000 (£700,000) in Belgium, Scottish refused.

The ferry operated until 4 September 1964, when the Road Bridge opened, much to the detriment of Scottish Region's rail traffic. As mentioned earlier, the Board was assured in February 1966 that the 'way and structure assets' – which presumably includes ships – was worth nearly £200,000. The ownership of the ferries had passed from Denny's following that firm's passage into voluntary liquidation in 1963, with the final year of service being completed efficiently by the liquidators. The ships were now transferred to the Caledonian Steam Packet Company but, considering that three of these ferries were sold for scrap (*Robert the Bruce* for only £2,500), and the jetties found only occasional use, it is difficult to see how this impressive valuation could have been arrived at by Scottish officials. The fourth member of the fleet, the *Sir William Wallace* of 1955 vintage, operated in the Netherlands until 1970.

The LMS and LNER had owned no fewer than twenty-eight docks and piers in Scotland, from the 16,000ft of quayside at Grangemouth docks to the 64ft-long quay at Kentallen on the Ballachulish branch. Some of these could be classed as 'packet' stations, the remainder being 'trade harbours'. In 1948, all passed to the Docks and Inland Waterways Executive.

In 1951 the BTC carried out a survey of the 'trade harbours' which had come into public ownership through rail companies, and it made interesting and sometimes depressing reading. With one notable exception, nearly all the former railway docks in Scotland had fallen on hard times, mainly due to the collapse in the export of coal. Grangemouth had seen coal exports fall from one quarter of its turnover to one eighth in the previous ten years, while Bo'ness shifted only 19,000 tons in 1949, and Burntisland even less. Even Methil, which was completely geared to coal-handling, exported less than 1.5 million tons in 1949. To be fair to Methil, its loss in 1949 was only £5,000 (£100,000) on a turnover of some £168,000 (£3.36 million). Of the former rail ports on the Firth of Forth, only Grangemouth made a profit, and that was thanks to oil imports.

Comparative figures for the Clyde were not available in this BTC report, as a special working party was studying the possibility of an overall ports administration (which became the Clyde Ports Authority, but which did not include the Ayrshire harbours, as proposed at that time). The docks at Leith, Kirkcaldy, Dundee, and Aberdeen, were all owned by local authorities or non-profit-making commissions at this time, but Silloth was an interesting exception. Although a solid part of the Cumbrian shoreline, its harbour had been owned by the North British Railway, and might have been expected to join the Scottish fold for administrative reasons. This did not happen; indeed, the branch was passed from the North Eastern to the London Midland region within the first six months of nationalisation, and its 'Scottish' origin appeared to be unknown to the authors of the BTC report.

Harbour installations were inevitably expensive to maintain, with Scottish having to take responsibility for those facilities servicing ferry routes, while attempting to defray its costs at every opportunity. In 1965, after spending £27,000 (£321,000) on repairing the Fisheries Pier at Mallaig, the Board immediately ordered an approach to DAFS (then the Agricultural wing of the Scottish Office) to recover the investment. Three months later, in April of that year, a further £30,000 was spent repairing the facilities at Wemyss Bay, but this was charged to the marine subsidiary, the Caledonian SP Company, which in turn was expected to raise its pier dues on both passengers and freights in order to defray the cost. Similarly, new buildings for Irish services would be leased to Caledonian at 'appropriate commercial rates'.

The working of piers was to remain with Scottish until 1 August 1971, when the new Scottish Transport Group took over the operation of all former railway piers, apart from those configured as rail terminals, from thirty BR staff. Unfortunately, the Scottish Board noted that 'liaison arrangements between the Region and the Caledonian Steam Packet Company were not as close as they might be', and the General Manager was asked to seek improved links with the shipping concern (this, despite the fact that the railway GM was chairman of Caledonian). In that same year, railway harbours (presumably those with rail connections) were shown to be making a profit of only £4,000, but on a turnover of £21,000 this hardly indicated a major profit failure, or indeed a highly intensive aspect of the industry.

Two dock installations which were not taken over by the new Executive were Military Ports 1 and 2. The year 1948 was only seven months old when the BTC was offered, and declined, control of these wartime emergency dock areas, at Faslane and Cairnryan. These had been constructed in case such major ports as Liverpool had been bombed out of commission, although they had fortunately not been required to any major extent. On 15 July, the BTC minuted that its members 'saw no prospect of these bases ever becoming commercial ports and it would not be proper to take them over from the government'. The lack of a commercial future would come as a surprise to P&O, which uses Cairnryan nowadays. Unfortunately, the demolition of the former Cairnryan Military Railway means that there is no rail connection to this Irish ferry port. Meanwhile, Faslane has become the most important naval base north of Portsmouth.

The history of canals after 1948 need not delay us long, as those owned by the 'Big Four' companies passed out of railway control in that year – in theory anyway. In practice, as a BTC document advised in December 1947, there does appear to have been a delay in establishing a canal administration, and 'existing arrangements on [railway-owned] canals and docks will continue for the time being'. Nevertheless, this interregnum cannot have been lasted more than a year. In Scotland only the Caledonian and Crinan canals were not controlled by the LMS and LNER, but the Firth & Clyde, Union, and Monkland were transferred from railway control to the new BTC (and later the British Waterways Board). The last of these three waterways has some call on our attention, however, as it was the subject of a long series of negotiations between the LMS and the City of Glasgow, and then through the nationalisation period before involving, curiously, docks administrators at Grangemouth.

The saga began in 1934 when the Monkland was finally closed to navigation, although its continued existence was required as a water supplier to the Forth & Clyde to the north. Worried by the costs of maintaining the Blackhill Locks, the LMS hit on the idea of handing over, free of charge, the canal and twenty-five acres of its hinterland between the Provan and Cumbernauld Roads in Glasgow to the city for non-commercial purposes, provided the local authority paid for piping the supply northwards. This was by no means a negligible area, being wide enough to accommodate the site of a former inclined plane. The transfer was agreed in principle, the *Glasgow Herald* commenting approvingly in October 1942 on the friendly nature of the negotiations.

But the newspaper was premature in its congratulations. In 1954 the East Coast Scottish Ports Manager, based in Grangemouth, wrote to the City of Glasgow asking when the agreement for piping was to be implemented, since he had to be assured of water supply for the F & C. A voluminous file of correspondence exists in the National Archives relating to this matter, which obviously outlasted the LMS, and would not legally concern its successor, British Railways.

It appears that the kernel of the problem was that the Ministry of War Transport could not, or would not, grant an abandonment order for the Monkland Canal before it lost its own identity at the end of the Second World War. It was a minor problem for the LMS, and one can understand the relief of railway managers at losing responsibility for inland waterways when the intricate, and almost irresolvable nature of this kind of problem is exposed. It was probably a fairly typical complication for the canal-owning railways before 1948; to put this in a national perspective, in January 1947, Britain's railways had generated revenue close to £20 million; roughly 400 times what thirty-four canals, totalling 976 miles, earned in the same month in tolls and freight charges.

Railway ownership of bus industry capital has not perhaps been fully appreciated by transport historians over the years, and is due for reassessment. At the end of the Second World War, the 'Big Four' rail companies owned no less than £9.6 million (£211 million) worth of shares in bus companies, at a time when the market was depressed because of the powerful disincentives for the British public to move around their own country. In addition, as indicated earlier, the four companies had £4.7 million (£103.4 million) invested in their own fleets of parcels and goods road vehicles, plus £2.7 million (£59.4 million) worth of garages and stables. There was also investment totalling £3.1 million (£68 million) in rival road concerns.

If 'Big Four' railway managers had hoped that their investment in bus companies, following the passing of the 1928 Railway Road Powers Act, might allow them some measure of control over a thrusting new competitor, they were soon disillusioned. However, no railway shareholders could ever complain that such investments were unwise financially – the Train soon came to receive a handsome income from the Bus. Even during 1944, the last full year of war, SMT 'earned' the LMS and LNER £67,065 each – the second highest dividend received by any UK rail companies from their bus investments in that year, and worth £1.87 million nowadays. This fails to take into account some secondary investment in other transport concerns in Scotland, Alexanders, Central and Lanarkshire, all associated to SMT. The LMS also had a 50 per cent interest in both Highland Transport and David MacBrayne. In their final year of existence, LMS and LNER drew the equivalent of £11 million in dividends from SMT. All this ended with the 1947 Transport Act.

So important had bus dividends been to the railways that, in 1948, the BTC was notified that the 'Big Four' were unable to finalise their accounts because these could not include dividend figures from bus companies operating to a different financial year. As already observed, the BTC, in February 1948, gave a written assurance to the companies' auditors that it would, 'give provisional approval of any figures produced if the amounts were arrived at by applying the normal accounting practice of each of the Main Lines concerned'.

At the same time as nationalising railways, the 1947 Transport Act seemed to take a somewhat relaxed view of passenger road undertakings, and the road nationalisation process was less rigid than that applied to the railways. David Maxwell Fyfe, later a Conservative Home Secretary, commented at the time that 'passenger road services are left very much up in the air'. In contrast to rail shareholders receiving shares in British Transport Stock, although even this was over-valued, according to some Labour politicians, SMT sold itself directly to the Government. It is difficult to avoid the conclusion that the Labour Government took a paternalistic attitude to such methods of transport as canals and railways, which were either fighting to remain profitable, or not profitable at all, while treating the owners of more lucrative transport industries with kid gloves.

The SMT sale involved the transfer of some 722 passenger vehicles, 133 of them double-decked. By mid-1949, 3,800 buses were reported in the national fleet, including SMT subsidiaries. As mentioned earlier, the engineering side of SMT retained the name, while the passenger transport element took on the generic title of Scottish Omnibuses.

Another twist in the convoluted relationship between bus and train became clear in later years. Following the 1930 Transport Act, railways had right of appeal to newly appointed Traffic Commissioners over proposed bus routes, although the then-recent investment in buses by railway companies might inhibit any such objection to the activities of a mode of transport which was offering an immediate and handsome financial return. But by the 1950s, the boot was on the other foot. Where BR closed down a rail service, local bus companies could claim grant assistance for incorporating a former rail-served community into their route network following a TUCC hearing (at which, as we know from the Peebles proposal, Scottish Omnibuses could well be involved in the decision-making). And who would pay the grant? Why, BR Scottish Region of course! In January 1966, the Scottish Railway Board considered the 'subvention of the Scottish Bus Group for additional miles operated in replacement of rail passenger services withdrawn or curtailed'.

Since this does not exclude the possible retention of freight services on the lines concerned, it would seem more logical to have maximised line occupation by continuing the passenger trains, while finding ways to make them profitable, and to avoid strengthening a rival operating within a monopoly. But no, the same entry in the region's minute book records that this grant support for a (successful) rival would be granted, although negotiated annually, and subject to a time-limit of payment.

Road freight undertakings had been nationalised in 1947, but were 'set free' by the subsequent Conservative administration. Meanwhile, the railways lost a formidable amount of revenue from investments, in both passenger and freight road transport, which had represented either a botched attempt to control rival transport concerns, or, depending on one's point of view, were a means of securing a 'nice little earner'. In addition to the bus holdings already mentioned, the LNER owned £84,808 worth of shares (£2.4 million) in Curries of Newcastle in 1944, while the LMS held no fewer than 143,000 shares in Wordie's, the major Glasgow transport firm. In December 1947, the BTC bought an exactly similar number of these shares for £381,333 (£8,008,000) from an investment company, as the LMS had undertaken to do on request, but presumably the taxpayer-supported railway system benefited not at all from its own share disposal. Nationally, the 'Big Four' had £3.1 million (£67 million) invested in Hay's Wharf Cartage in 1944, of which the famous contracting firm of Pickford's was a subsidiary, as was Thomas Cook & Son.

The historian is tempted to ask if the railways' road investments in commercial road concerns, shrewd as they were in terms of revenue, might have been better used in funding the equipping of the nation's railways with the most up-to-date technical advances, paying patent fees if and where necessary, in order to introduce as many innovations into rail operations as possible, and thus strengthening themselves in competition with their road rivals.

In Scotland the new Road Transport Executive set up three freight divisions, headquartered in Glasgow, and with offices in the other three cities. Twenty-three haulage firms were taken over immediately, comprising 960 motor vehicles and 440 horses, although this was expected to increase by the end of 1949 to 286 companies operating 4,500 vehicles.

Although the spread of the railway network had inspired the construction of some of the UK's finest hotels, there was a conviction prevalent in the late 1940s that these should be separated from the railways when nationalisation took place in 1948. Sir Cyril Hurcomb explained it to the Railway Students Association in March of the following year: 'Hotels had been separated from the railways at Executive level [in 1948], because they were a specialised industry and required individual management, but the excellence of the hotels would be a means of increasing traffic'. The comment is somewhat confusing, in that the last part appears to contradict the first by emphasising the relationship between train and hotel.

Mention Scottish railway hotels, and the (older) reader thinks of Gleneagles, and the large Caledonian and North British establishments in both Edinburgh and Glasgow. But the ominous-sounding *Physical Condition of British Railways* report drawn up early in 1948, concentrated on the lesser-known hotels, and former hotels, whose condition caused concern. While these were about to pass to a separate Executive in that year, they would return to railway ownership before long.

Aberdeen used to have two railway establishments, but the Palace Hotel had been badly damaged in a fatal fire in 1941, and the 1948 hotel review ruled that the site was now to be sold off. The Station Hotel had now passed out of government control, but its refurbishment was approved. The Cruden Bay establishment was to be disposed of, the experience of acting as an army barracks proving too much for it and its unique tramway. Dornoch's Hotel could be refurbished, but only if petrol rationing was lifted (why, one wonders, as there was a perfectly good rail connection to Dornoch at this time). Strathpeffer's Hotel was still in the hands of the military. As for Turnberry's, its 'future is subject to the reinstatement of the golf courses'.

On a more positive note, the Railway Executive reviewed its compliment of thirty-three active hotels by April 1948, in time for the coming summer season, with Sir Cyril Hurcomb querying whether Gleneagles was worth holding on to. This is surprising to say the least, but the BTC chairman may have been under the impression that the famous hotel was not rail-connected. Irrespective of Sir Cyril's views, Gleneagles had opened for the 1948 season a few days earlier, on 25 March.

In 1948, the establishment of a separate Hotels Executive was clearly not keeping pace with that of its railway counterpart, with its history going back to 1914. In the meantime, the *Instructions* booklet which acted as a written remit for Scottish Region, was positively Delphic in its ruling on how Scottish railway hotels were to be run in the first half of 1948: 'As from January 1, and until further advised, the Chief Hotels Superintendent, LMSR, will continue his existing activities for the London Midland and Scottish Regions'. A similar, confusing, instruction was given for former LNER hotels, again naming an official from a company on the point of being wound up as the manager of such establishments as the NB and Caledonian hotels in Edinburgh and Glasgow, and Gleneagles! Just to show that this was no misprint, *Instructions No. 1* also carries a footnote: 'The Hotels Superintendent, Scottish Area, LNER, will also cover LNER refreshment rooms in Scotland'.

While it is true that the final AGMs of the 'Big Four' were not held until around the end of the 1947-8 tax year, it remains a curious anomaly in the files of the nationalised railways, and one wonders what kind of 'job security' the officials, allocated the responsibility of running major hotels and all station refreshment rooms, could expect.

The new Hotels Executive was formally established on 1 July of that year under the chairmanship of Lord Inman, and with a woman as one of its part-time members – the only example of the fair sex to make an appearance in transport documents of the time (this was Mrs Ella Gasking, who had built up Batchelor's Peas into a major canning industry from the age of twenty-two). Executive and Commission showed no reluctance to sell those hotels they regarded as surplus to requirements, a curious practice for administrative bodies charged with safeguarding the public's property.

In 1948, hotels were classified into three categories according to size, with Scotland having four in the 'top ten': Glasgow Central, the NB and Caledonian in Edinburgh, and Gleneagles. The only Scottish members of the B classification of thirteen establishments were the NB and St Enoch hotels in Glasgow, while the C category listed six Scottish hotels out of nineteen, at Ayr, Dumfries, Perth, Inverness, Kyle of Lochalsh, and the Dornoch establishment whose continued existence had previously been thought dependent on petrol availability.

All of the above underlines the indisputable fact that Scotland's railway comprised more than just sleepers, rail, and ballast.

eight

INTO THE SEVENTIES

Amidst the record of closures and falling revenue, there were some bright points. New ships always seemed to raise the spirits of Board members (as mentioned in the last chapter), and the 1970 minutes also dealt with the opening of a spur to the Clyde Container terminal at Greenock from the existing Wemyss Bay line. This was costed at £101,834 (£970,000), although the Clyde Ports Authority was likely to find the bill amounting to £146,534 at 'private party rates'!

In the following year, the relocation of Fort William passenger station to a point slightly to the north of the town was costed at £100,000 (£900,000), looking curiously cheap at that price. However, Scottish Board members were clearly enthusiastic, as BR seemed committed to pay a mere tenth of this, with the rest to be debited to the Scottish Development Department (then responsible for road improvements) at the dreaded 'traders' rates'. By 1973 the commitment made by Scottish was (on paper at least) £125,000, but it appeared that the SDD would be billed for £142,500. Suffice to say that the transaction was convoluted, and was certainly overdue. In 1963 Cecil J. Allen had noted how cramped the existing station layout was at Fort William when vehicles arriving at the rear of a train from the south, and lacking steam-heating pipes, had to be shunted on to the rear of a train awaiting departure for Mallaig.

The year 1970 also brought good cheer when the Board was able to rejoice in the news that the West Coast Main Line electrification was to be extended from Weaver Junction to Glasgow. This had been mooted for some years, and the National Archives contain two prior assessments of the economic and engineering aspects of the proposal. While the announcement of electrification was probably made with one politician's eye on the

General Election expected that summer, there was nevertheless the feeling that changing between electric and diesel traction at Crewe on every passenger journey on the WCML was simply inappropriate on what should be seen as a continuous route.

The first detailed study of extending the catenary north of Weaver Junction (where the Liverpool line left the basic WCML) was completed in January 1964. Entitled 'Appreciation by London Midland Region and Scottish Region working parties on the linking-up of electrification between Weaver Junction and the Glasgow suburban scheme' (the latter of course already utilised the higher-powered voltage adopted as BR standard in 1956), the report centred on 680 single route-miles, but without costings. Edinburgh was not included in the report's remit, and its published maps assumed the closure of the Waverley Route and Settle & Carlisle line, the latter being retained only as a single line south from Horton-in-Ribblesdale to service the quarries there. One wonders what Border inhabitants would have thought if they had known that the closure of the Waverley Route, then only a Beeching proposal, was taken as inevitable by BR managers in the early 1960s! Also to be singled was the former G&SWR line from Gretna through Dumfries as far as Kilmarnock. The Moffat and Dumfries-Lockerbie lines were to vanish altogether.

On a practical level, steam traction was to be eliminated from the route (belying the document's NAS catalogue date of 1967), and electricity feeder stations were to be established at Ecclefechan and Beattock Summit. These would be used in addition to existing Scottish feeders at Eglinton Street and Parkhead in Glasgow, and Motherwell, although the latter two were described as in need of extra capacity. Interestingly, Beattock Station was to be retained.

A later report, dated July 1967, did at least consider Edinburgh for possible electrification from Carstairs, the additional cost being approximately 11 per cent on top of the projected £22.8 million (£2.55 milliards) for the basic Weaver-Glasgow conversion. However, Glaswegians would have been delighted at the report's suggestion that 'Glasgow greatly outweighs Edinburgh', on grounds of larger population, greater industrial capacity, and the fact that the Scottish capital already had its own main-line to London. In that case, it was a pity that the report's remit was not elastic enough for it to consider electrifying the former G&SWR route north of Gretna.

If Edinburgh was not be included in the West Coast planned electrification (and it would not be until 1991, obviously not as part of this scheme), and Perth, Dundee, Inverness, and Aberdeen can all be reached from there by ECML trains, it would surely have been worth concentrating on the England-Glasgow traffic by electrifying through Dumfries and Kilmarnock instead of through Annandale. These towns would generate considerably more revenue than Beattock and Lockerbie (indeed, BR eventually would not even bother to keep Beattock open, although it was rumoured at the time to be making a small profit), while the old 'Sou West' main-line, as well as accessing the Ayrshire coalfield, could also have enabled Euston-Stranraer traffic to be hauled by electric power, to and from the south, well into Ayrshire. Extra travelling time on expresses between Euston and Glasgow via Dumfries would hardly be critical for travellers between these cities, where the option of air travel was established even before the Second World War, and restarted very soon thereafter, thus catering for those travellers for whom time was at a premium. As early as December 1972 the Scottish Board noted with approval that it had taken £165,000 (£1.34 million) in student fares that year. Students, families and retired people, were hardly going to worry about an extra hour on the train if the fares were kept low. But perhaps that was asking too much prescience from rail managers, who were, after all, simply being asked to cost out the job.

The 1967 report contained more detail on traction matters. While recommending electrification to Glasgow only, the document conceded that the Carstairs-Edinburgh section would require only three extra electric locomotives, or four Type 4 diesels if left unconverted. If the entire programme did not go ahead, then the favoured form of motive power to operate the line north of Crewe was to be pairings of Type 4s of 2,750hp, with one sufficing for night trains. 'Deltics' were dismissed as being unsuitable, as the Class 55 seemed to have established a reputation for being ill-at-ease on freight duties.

It was clearly assumed that electricity would be the favoured choice of traction; in practice twinned Class 50 diesels operated trains north of Crewe until electrification was complete in 1974. Introduced from 1968, this class made a good impression from the start, although one *Railway Magazine* correspondent pointed out that their engine fittings were not standardised, resulting in one engine crew at Glasgow (Central) desperately topping up their locomotive's cooling fluid with buckets of cold water, as the station hoses did not fit.

One penny (½p) was predicted as the price per unit of electricity, with the cost of supply expected to fall annually by 2 per cent over the 1971-78 period, after 'discounting the effects of inflation'. This was a bold, if not reckless, projection, at a time when the oil reserves of the North Sea were still unknown to the general public, and, one assumes, to railway managers. Oil was certainly the fuel of choice for the generating stations which would supply the line, and the report considered, but dismissed, the idea of BR opening its own power stations (they would probably have less reserve cover in the event of plant failure). Natural gas was briefly considered as a fuel, as opposed to the manufactured gas then in use, but was dismissed on the grounds of insufficient information on which to base financial estimates. Nevertheless, the report recommended proceeding with electrification from Weaver to the Glasgow area at a cost of £22.8 million (£2.55 milliards). This was a bargain when the cost of upgrading the line at the present time is considered.

Unfortunately, the four-year conversion period was a dangerously long one considering the existing speed advantage of air travel – a more potent rival to rail over 400 miles than the 200 or thereabouts between London and Liverpool and Manchester. Nor, in the event, were the Class 50s, despite the high opinion they engendered, able to keep the services north of Weaver to time during the conversion period. At the height of the 1971 summer, punctuality between Euston and Glasgow had plummeted to 38.2 per cent. Liverpool/Manchester-Glasgow was even worse at 34.4 per cent, although Birmingham-Glasgow achieved 43.1 per cent of punctual arrivals. Punctuality did not improve in the following year, by which time the Board Minutes carried a comment about the 'low availability' of the Type 50s on the West Coast Main Line.

These problems vanished with the opening of the entire West Coast Main Line to electric traction from 6 May 1974. A royal visit followed two days later, and the Board members were able to glow with appreciation at the regal comments made. Railway enthusiasts from an older generation had to come to terms with the idea of trains ascending the 10 miles of Beattock Bank at the same speed that they could achieve coming down!

By 1987 *Modern Railways* was to refer to the route north of Carlisle as a 'dead duck'. The need to change traction on trains travelling to and from destinations north of Glasgow meant that long-distance routing via Edinburgh was more remunerative, a factor compounded by the lack of income from the long station-less stretch south of Carstairs. Some life has been breathed into the corpse by privatisation, with the lack of stations (only Lockerbie in the 73 miles between Carstairs and Carlisle – surely a British record) proving an advantage for operating long-distance services at *continuously* high speed. But the modern rail enthusiast must wonder if engineer Joseph Locke was right, back in the 1840s, when he pronounced in favour of building the Beattock route so unconvincingly that one railway director at the time said that, 'Mr Locke is arguing against his own convictions'. Glasgow's main-line from Carlisle should have been electrified through Dumfries, in this author's opinion.

As the 1970s opened out, Scottish Region Board members were able to minute their thanks to Scottish staff for their handling of the potentially tricky problem of decimalisation. The changeover for £ s d to £ p took place on Sunday 15 February 1971, although managers had expected more of a problem on the following day. In fact, the public had been well briefed on the changeover (although conspiracy theorists detected a virtual doubling in some retail costs) but transport matters were helped by 40 per cent of weekly Scottish season-ticket holders purchasing their tickets before the changeover weekend.

Meanwhile, something had to be done about the region's flagship line, between Edinburgh (Waverley) and Glasgow (Queen Street). After pioneering inter-city DMU traction from January 1957, the service badly needed modern traction and stock as the 1970s dawned. One would have thought that, with its potential for high-speed connections from one city-centre to the other, there was surely a good case for electrification (a case recently emphasised by the former head of ScotRail). This certainly was not debated at Board level; perhaps there were too many engineering obstacles for cheap or easy catenary installation on this, one of the oldest inter-city lines in the UK– not least on the lengthy Almond viaduct or through four tunnels, those between Queen Street and Cowlairs, at Falkirk, Winchburgh, and Haymarket (not to mention the Mound).

One comparatively cheap solution was to utilise a diesel locomotive at each end of a fixed rake of six coaches, with a driver controlling both engines through a control cable running the length of the train. Class 27 diesels were tested at up to 90mph as early as the spring of 1968 to assess this possibility, one which appeared unique to Scottish, and as a result encountered considerable delay. Obviously, Scottish lacked testing expertise, as we well know. 'Push-pull' working was also being attempted in April of that year, a Class 37 being tested, and the official papers reveal an intention to try out a Type 4 diesel (presumably a Class 47) as well, in order to enable a forty-five minute timetable. In the event, two 27s could trim 2 minutes off even that timing. Parallel with stock testing, improvements were made to the permanent way. In 1967, 75 per cent of this line had been re-laid with continuous welded rail (CWR), with the Board being assured of programme completion by the end of that year.

Nine weeks after the new service had opened on 3 May 1971, Scottish managers found that the new motive power was coping with demands, punctuality being 'extremely high', even with the journey time pared to 43 minutes, and with patronage up 18 per cent on the previous year. This increase was nevertheless less than expected, although the capital costs would hardly appear high enough to impose an insurmountable threshold for viability.

By the end of 1971, punctuality was 'not as good as desired' but, after fifty-two weeks, passenger journeys were up by 11.7 per cent between the cities, with receipts showing a healthy improvement of nearly 25 per cent. In April 1974, the Board was told that the 'revised total outlay' on the Edinburgh-Glasgow 'High Speed' service was £1,930,352 (£12.3 million), including an inflationary £20,000 (£128,000) on heating costs over the previous autumn and winter. Hardly exorbitant amounts, given the timeframe which appeared to cover technical adjustments made over three years, and bearing in mind the improvement in both the number of journeys and increased revenue generated by then. The region had succeeded in introducing – one might even say, improvising – a new service without expensive capital costs, but one capable of pushing up speed levels.

Unfortunately, the new train sets did not include buffet cars, as a colleague of the author discovered to her cost after tottering (in the then fashionable stiletto heels) the length of the moving train in mounting disbelief that such a popular aspect of the service had been dispensed with. Interestingly, restaurant cars were far from popular with regional managers. In 1971, onboard catering made a loss of £58,000 (£504,000) in Scotland, expected to increase to £60,000 in the following year. This should come as no surprise; Michael Bonavia records that 'the restaurant cars of BR always lost money'.

Scottish had, rather belatedly, recognised the need for a less formal approach to onboard catering on its trains, and BR as a whole was experimenting with a service less regimented than seating diners in a restaurant car, while still a million miles away from the trolley service so common nowadays. In September 1953 two 'Cafeteria' cars began operations on Edinburgh-Dundee, Edinburgh-Glasgow, and Glasgow-Dundee lines. Soon, griddle cars were in use elsewhere on BR, and in 1965 Scottish decided to have three 'surplus' standard coaches converted into this newly fashionable type of catering vehicle by the Workshops Division.

This became a somewhat protracted episode, with Scottish lodging a complaint in May 1965 with the General Managers of both Workshops and Hotels Divisions regarding delays and a budgetary increase of £15,400 to £43,950 (£522,000). Whatever reply was received from the GMs is not recorded, but it apparently caused Board members 'displeasure and regret' in July. In the following month we learn that work would progress – while Scottish loaned three such cars (presumably those it was waiting for) to the Western Region. Perhaps Scottish was resigned to missing the peak travelling season north of the Border by then, but whatever the outcome, it illustrated how complicated stock ordering was becoming. Any earlier Board of Directors of a Scottish railway would simply have asked their GM to place an order at Cowlairs or St Rollox.

As the 1970s progressed, the Board found itself in the unusual position of closing down a diesel depot. With the commercial failure of so many DMU services on the east of Scotland, it was decided to eliminate the pioneering diesel depot of Leith Central from the MPD list. It is easy to underestimate the significance of Central in the modernisation of Scotland's railways, but it allowed the maintenance and repair of DMUs in a sheltered environment where cleaning could also take place, all at limited capital cost to the region (Leith Central has featured frequently in this history. Perhaps the author can be excused for this; my father, a painter, worked among the Arroll roofbeams during the conversion of the former terminus, coming home stinking of diesel).

The closure entailed transferring 100 drivers to Haymarket in April 1972, even though this came at a time when there was overcrowding at other depots in the national motive power network. For example, Glasgow's Eastfield had a locomotive allocation of 173, instead of its planned capacity of 140. One wonders if the sheer size of Leith Central – one of Scotland's twelve largest stations and a source of wonder to local councillors when planned at the end of the nineteenth century – had come to the notice of the BR Property Board in Glasgow! Yet, when this author asked the BRPB for advice about the station site's eventual purchaser (in fact, the local authority), the staff were unable to find the file on the matter. Needless to say, this proved a suitable conclusion to an article entitled 'The station nobody wanted' (see Bibliography)!

While we have seen the Scottish Railway Board exhibit little more than indifference to the Glasgow Central Low Level line, the local authority was rather more concerned with urban transport matters. It was always obvious that the Glasgow area was a logical site for a Passenger Transport initiative of the kind launched by the 1968 Transport Act. This introduced a two-tier administration of local transport with the Passenger Transport Authorities and the Public Transport Executives below them. While taking our story beyond its present timeframe, it is worth recording that the Greater Glasgow PTA was Scotland's first (and only) example, becoming operational in July 1972, the fifth in the UK. It covered 662sq. miles, and its governing body comprised thirty seats, of which thirteen were allocated to the city, and five to representatives of the Secretary of State for Scotland. From 1974, British Rail, as it became, provided the Strathclyde PTE with rail services.

One recurring factor in the working life of Scottish Region was the painting of the Forth Bridge. Popularly believed to take three years, with the painters then having to restart immediately, the task begins to appear in the regional Board Minutes from the late 1960s onwards (prior to 1948 of course, it was the responsibility of a separate company, the Forth Bridge Railway Company, nationalised in that year). Interestingly, cleaning and painting estimates placed before the Board between 1970 and 1972 show an increase of 14 per cent in just three years – £72,000 (£583,000) in 1972 – indicating the aggregating nature of the problem in maintaining one of the world's greatest engineering structures. Health and safety legislation passed later in the same decade was to make this task even more expensive.

The story of Scotland's railway company workshops (as opposed to commercial builders, like NBL) differs from that south of the Border. 'In house' locomotive building ceased in Scotland in 1924, with the LMS and LNER concentrating their new construction down south. A curious decision, as Glasgow was still the outstanding centre for new commercial construction, with members of such famous locomotive classes as the LNER A1 Pacific, LMS 'Royal Scot', and SR 'King Arthur', seeing the light of day for the first time at North British Locomotive before the 1920s ended. LNER 'Sandringhams' and (later) LMS 'Jubilees' and 8F 2-8-0s followed, to say nothing of the Riddles 'Austerity' types, and postwar LNER designs such as the B1 and L1.

Nevertheless, the two main companies were prepared to dissipate their own construction expertise away from Cowlairs and St Rollox, although overhauls and repairs could still be carried out there, and at such smaller works as Inverurie (LNER), and Lochgorm and Kilmarnock (LMS). We have already seen, in the 'rainbow' display of new liveries and linings in Scotland in 1948, that there was a healthy spirit of independence in the nationalised rail system's smaller workshops.

The 'Standard' programme of new construction for BR, which began with 'Britannia' in 1951, was exclusively undertaken at BR works, from Darlington in the 'north' as far south as Brighton, with commercial firms finishing off the construction of such classes as former LMS 'Black 5s' and ex-LNER B1s. This went on up to nearly five years into BR days, and the private companies, excluded from the Standard programme, were not slow to complain that there was insufficient stimulus in the home market for new diesel and electric traction. NBL, as we know, hastened to buy in German motor technology when BR's 1955 Modernisation Plan was launched, but the Glasgow firm never adjusted to the demands of the new motive power. One curious result of all this was seeing the first of the 80000 tank class, fresh from construction in the pleasant seaside resort of Brighton, allocated to depots in the city which was the leading loco manufacturing centre in Europe. Yet, the LMS and LNER had announced that Glasgow was too isolated for their own construction programmes, making manufacturing there too expensive, while Brighton continued to prosper under both commercial and nationalised concerns.

BR's own workshops faced a major challenge to adjust, and more rationalisation became essential as traction changes took effect. In 1963 the new British Railways Board reduced the number of workshops in the UK, from twenty-eight down to sixteen, setting up a separate Workshops Division. By the end of the 1960s, St Margaret's and Perth had their wagon repair departments transferred to Townhill, with work from Kipps and Craighead going to Motherwell. Workshop reorganisation took on momentum, the 1968 Transport Act freeing BR to bid for outside work. Two years later, British Rail Engineering Ltd was formally set up, with fourteen workshops nationally, two of them in Scotland, at Glasgow, formerly St Rollox, and at Barassie, although the wagon works at the Troon site lasted for only a further two years. The latter's mantle was taken by the Townhill works near Dunfermline, a plant whose future was threatened in the spending review at the end of the 1950s.

Those shops which failed to survive long after the run-down of steam power on Scottish Region included Inverurie, the former GNSR plant which was still undertaking repair work up until 1969 at a time when larger works, such as Cowlairs, had closed. The latter lasted until 1968, its demise coinciding with the end of steam in the UK, and remaining repair work in Central Scotland was transferred to nearby St Rollox (in later years, this became known as Springburn, a district which once contained no fewer than three major locomotive plants). By 1964 the site of Lochgorm Works at Inverness was accommodating a diesel MPD. Meanwhile, Kilmarnock had ceased to repair locomotives in 1952, continuing actively for another seven years in repairing cranes and in the scrapping of locomotives and boilers.

Following the 1968 Transport Act, Freightliners were now administered by a separate concern – a source of some bitterness among BR management, after their careful nurturing of the service through the 1960s – but at least the railway maintained a major shareholding interest. The service had certainly won the approval of the rail community, with the Scottish Railway Development Association calling in 1969 for no fewer than fifteen additional Freightliner service points by the mid-1970s. However, by August 1973, the Scottish Board was told that punctuality on the Glasgow-London service was poor, not helped by crane failures at the northern end, although since loco-hauled passenger expresses hit a nadir in that month with only 50 per cent punctuality, this was hardly an exceptional performance.

Meanwhile, the idea of dedicated train loads had been applied to the most basic cargo: coal. In May 1968, the Board was pleased to have confirmation that the new power station at Cockenzie in East Lothian received 38,000 tons of coal in forty-five train-loads at the rate of nine trains per day. These came from the Bilston and Monktonhall collieries only a few miles away, although Gourvish comments on the problem raised in 1964 by the NCB's insistence of levying a toll on rail cargoes – presumably, and this is not evident from the minutes – because transport by road would not necessitate the same hopper-loading system which would be required to be constructed at Monktonhall (yet this was one of the Lothians' newer pits; bulk loading does not appear to have been considered at the time of commissioning). The system of MGR (merry-go-round trains, which theoretically never stop, both loading and unloading while on the move) was of course extended when these pits closed, and coal had to be brought from elsewhere.

As well as Freightliners, BR lost control over coastal shipping. In the case of Scottish, there must have been some disappointment, at the very least, over the assignment of Caledonian SP to other hands, after Scottish had, figuratively speaking, steered the company through the economic storms of the early 1950s, into more tranquil blue water. In November 1965 the Board had been told that a working loss of £139,882 (£2.5 million) in 1953 had been converted into a working profit of £640,000 (£7 million) in 1965. Even if it was not clear if the earlier figure carried some mark against capital for the seven ships entering the fleet at the time, it was nevertheless an encouraging sign.

Meanwhile, one packet route fell back into the hands of Scottish Region. This was the Stranraer-Larne passage, on which the *Caledonian Princess* was reported to have made a cumulative profit of £1.8 million in four years.

This unexpected bonus was previously covered in more detail in the chapter on BR shipping, and comprised yet another twist in the tortuous story of public transport workings in this part of the UK. This route is now operated, commercially, by a new generation of ferries. At the time of writing, the attractive lines of the Dumbarton-built *Caledonian Princess* can still be seen as she languishes on the Tyne in Newcastle city centre, renamed the *Tuxedo Princess*.

Scottish Region was born in 1948 of political parents, so it was only reasonable that the Board members should continually be aware of political developments. In 1972, the Board discussed the likely effects of the UK's impending entry into the Common Market, as the European Union was called at that time. Discussion centred principally on road haulage regulations – it was recognised that the European norm for increased road lorry dimensions could be damaging to BR's freight interests, but that the requirement for tachographs in lorry cabs would be helpful to rail as it would regulate the hours of drivers and thus inhibit the growth of the haulage industry (not so you would notice, is the cynical comment in retrospect). There seemed to be no discussion on the effects of Value Added Tax, surely a more pressing matter.

Two years later, in 1974, a year of two General Elections, there was much talk of devolution for Scotland, and the Board members felt that they should place on record their reaction to the idea. The September Board Minutes state that:

> the break-up of the United Kingdom railway management structure by the creation of a detached organisation for Scotland would be indefensible … [although] if funding was made available, through an Assembly, for Scottish industrial development, it would be the duty of railway management in Scotland, supported by the Regional Board, to press for an allocation of funds to the railway business.

A neat compromise! In fact, political devolution was not to become a fact for another twenty-five years, prompting the contemporary joke that the difference between evolution and devolution was that that latter takes longer! By the time of the 1999 elections to the new Scottish Assembly at the Mound, British Railways had ceased to exist anyway.

So, Scottish Region reached its twenty-fifth anniversary in 1973 (unnoticed by the Board) with a system slimmed down considerably from the 3,730 route-miles inherited from the LMS and LNER in 1948. The staff complement had declined by no less than two-thirds. The counties of Selkirkshire, Roxburghshire, Peeblesshire, and Kinross-shire were wiped from the railway map by Scottish, along with the county towns of Wigtownshire, Kirkcudbrightshire, Berwickshire, East Lothian, Clackmannanshire, Sutherland, and Angus. Such important burghs (and even recently enlarged towns) as Bathgate, Biggar, Callander, Castle Douglas, Dalkeith, Galashiels, Glenrothes, Grangemouth, Hawick, Kelso, Leven, Musselburgh, Penicuik, and St Andrews, found their way into the category of 'passengers no more', although some later had their rail links restored.

One main-line and two minor lines connecting with England – the principal source of tourist income and the largest ready market for Scottish products – were closed. Glasgow had at long last seen the introduction of electric trains, although the loss of the Central Low Level lines was a serious mistake, yet to be rectified by 1973. Edinburgh, meanwhile, lost two termini and almost all of its suburban services, largely because of the appallingly inaccessible Waverley Station, bereft of investment in escalators or moving pavements (it still is!). Journeys within Scotland were quicker than ever before in some areas, between, say, Glasgow and Edinburgh, and Glasgow and Aberdeen. But Edinburgh to Perth was slower, and Edinburgh or Glasgow to St Andrews or to Hawick was impossible. In particular the failure to use the 1968 legislation to rescue so many parts of the country from losing their rail services, has to be deplored.

Scottish Region might have done well to listen to the SRDA in 1969. Pointing out that £250 million (£2 milliards) had been spent on Scottish roads and motorways in the decade just ending, the association called for comparable investment in the nation's rail infrastructure. As well as fifteen new Freightliner service points, the pressure group called for stations to be reopened at Bathgate, Livingston, and Cumnock (they predicted three out of three!), escalators at such termini as Waverley, while deploring the lack of interchange facilities between new bus stations built close to railway stations in Perth and Aberdeen.

Perhaps more controversially, the association called for a union between Scottish Region and the STG – an amalgamation which would fly in the face of a policy of creating mutually exclusive transport bodies – but it could be argued that such a policy had never been attained since nationalisation anyway, the then-recent creation of the BTSML being evidence of the inconsistency. Suffice to say that the association made a useful and informed contribution to British transport policy and helped pave the way for our time when no closed line can escape the fever of reopening scrutiny.

When Dr Michael Bonavia published his 1981 survey of British Railways as seen by a senior member of staff, he employed a quarter of a century as the timescale for his account. This brief history of Scottish Region has of course been written by an 'outsider', who started his association with railway matters as a lineside enthusiast, became an increasingly occasional rail traveller (my local station, Joppa, closed in 1964), and unavoidably developed into a critic about the way that Scotland's railways were run. In particular the seemingly indiscriminate, and sometimes downright illogical, closures programme has never ceased to be a personal source of dismay, as the reader will have gathered by now, and will hopefully share the disappointment.

But this book's twenty-five year time-scale has been dictated by the current law on official document disclosure. Since it was my objective in this book to recruit official Board Minutes as a commentary to, and occasionally a complete contrast from, what was going on at 'grass roots' operational level, this approach could only succeed if there was complete disclosure of BR documents when required. The current 'Freedom of Information' regime promises this disclosure, though governments (or more precisely, opposition parties hoping to succeed to government, as in 1970) have often promised greater freedom to historians and researchers, but without delivering. It seems that the present administration may be more broad-minded; and this author has at least managed to read the previously closed file on the Dornoch Firth Bridge (see below).

During this research, however, 1973 has perforce been my cut-off date, and this forms a neat twenty-five-year span. Significantly, Scottish Region did not celebrate its twenty-fifth year of existence, so this book has attempted to assess it over that period. Incidentally, when enquiring about access to the Board Minutes of the North of Scotland Hydro-electric Board, whose members played such a creditable part in seeking new sources of branch-line power, I was told by a modern Hydro official that there would be 'no question' of my being allowed to see their Board Minutes for 1956! This was a misunderstanding, soon ironed out by National Archives staff. Even the current regulations are not as restrictive as that!

If the reader is wearied by the author's apparent fixation with closures, then a postscript should be added. After the final frenzy of closures at the beginning of 1969, few Scottish railways have closed to passengers, Kilmacolm being an obvious exception. But what of the future? At the time of writing, Stranraer is about to lose its last ferry operator, Kyle is no longer the gateway to Skye since the opening of the bridge, while another new structure, the road bridge over the Dornoch Firth, has compromised the future of the Wick and Thurso line, leaving the rail network with a mean-der inland almost as unrewarding as the West Coast Main Line between Lockerbie and the Motherwell area.

Incidentally, the official file explaining the exclusion of a railway from the new Dornoch Bridge was, until recently, to be closed until 2016. This author has now examined it under the 'Freedom of Information Act', and it reveals that the crucial factor in the Secretary of State's decision not to sup-port a rail link directly across the Firth was BR's insistence that the detour inland would have to be closed.

The lines to Stranraer, Kyle, and the far north may be threatened once more. Who is to say that the 'closerati' who run Scotland's railways may not strike again? And what arguments could be marshalled for rail retention in the near future if the roads in these particular areas are demonstrably better than the 'way' which, in Scotland, has been anything but 'permanent'?

TABLES AND LIST OF SOURCES

TABLE I
COMPARATIVE PERFORMANCE OF SCOTTISH REGION, 1948-68

	Sc	NE	E	South	W	LM
No.of route miles (1948)	3rd	6th	4th	5th	2nd	1st
No.of staff (1948)	4th eq	5th	3rd	4th eq	2nd	1st
Train miles per annum (1946)	5th	6th	2nd eq	2nd eq	2nd eq	1st
Profitability performance to 1956	6th	1st eq	1st eq	4th	5th	3rd
1956-68	3rd eq	2nd eq	1st	2nd eq	3rd eq	3rd eq

Sources: Data combined from tables from Bonavia and Gourvish (see Bibliography below). From the above, it can be seen that Scottish compared poorly with other Regions, particularly North Eastern.

TABLE II
INVESTMENT PROGRAMMES WITHIN SCOTTISH REGION, 1948-1968

	1948	49	50	51	52	53	54	55	56	57	58
Modernisation Plan announced (ships)			√								
Modernisation Plan announced (rlys)								√			
AWS/ATC											√
Diesel traction (main line)										√	√
Electric traction											
Roller-bearing stock											√
Continuous welded rail											

	1959	60	61	62	63	64	65	66	67	68
Modernisation Plan announced (ships)										
Modernisation Plan announced (rlys)										
AWS/ATC	√	√	√	√	√	√	√	√	√	√
Diesel traction (main line)	√	√	√	√	√	√	√	√	√	√
Electric traction			√	√	√	√	√	√	√	√
Roller-bearing stock	√	√	√	√	√	√	√	√	√	√
Continuous welded rail								√	√	√

TABLE III
GENERAL MANAGERS, SCOTTISH REGION, 1948-74

(Post entitled Chief Regional Officer, 1948-55. Combined with chairmanship of Board, 1964-71)

	Year appointed	Previous post/employer	Then
Thomas F. Cameron	1948	Area GM, LNER Scottish Area	Retired
A.E.H.Brown	1955	Scottish Region	Deceased
James Ness	1955	Scottish Region	To BRB
W.G.Thorpe	1963	London Midland	To LMR
Gordon Stewart	1967	Scottish Region	Retired
Alex. Philip	1971	Scottish Region	Retired 1974

TABLE IV
SCOTTISH REGION PASSENGER SERVICES DIESELISED IN 1957-58

Date	Service	Diesel Type	Revenue improvement v. Steam	
			1st year	2nd year
7.1.57	Glasgow (Q St)-Edinburgh (Wav)	126	28.0%	5.1%
3.2.58	Corstorphine-North Berwick	100	65.8%	9.5%
17.2.58	Edinburgh (W)-Peebles/Galashiels	100	111.5%	4.3%
21.4.58	Aberdeen-Ballater	Battery RC	64.9%	11.5%
5.5.58	Edinburgh (P St)-Leith (North)	100	41.9%	-18.7%
9.6.58	Edinburgh Sub O Circle & Rosewell	100	22.7%	15.2%
9.6.58	Edinburgh-Musselburgh & I Circle	100	30.2%	11.5%
15.9.58	Gleneagles-Crieff-Comrie	Wickham Railbus	158.1%	-29.5%
3.11.58	Aviemore-Elgin Park	Royal Railbus	88.5%	-19.1%

Source: BR/RSR/18/18. Data combined from three separate tables therein.

TABLE V
SCOTTISH REGION ESTIMATES OF MATERIAL RECOVERY FROM CLOSED RAILWAYS

Year (Reporting)	Line	'Recovery' figure	Per route mile	Note
1955	Aberfoyle & Kilsyth branches	£126	£6.50	1
1958	Symington-Peebles	£37,984	£1,999	2
	Morningside, Shotts-Benhar & East Benhar branches	£6,849	£311	3
1960	Dornoch Light Railway	£11,000	£1,447	4
	Lauder Light Railway	£29,500	£2,950	4
	Ladybank-Auchtermuchty	£8,000	£1,882	
	Auchterhouse-Newtyle	£7,500	£1,863	
	Jamestown-Drymen	£11,000	£1,833	
	Lennoxtown-Aberfoyle	£22,500	£1,800	5
	Muir of Ord-Fortrose	£24,000	£1,714	6
	Stirling-Port of Menteith	£24,000	£1,846	7

1963	Hawthornden-Peebles-Galashiels	£128,240	£3,465	
1965	Gleneagles-Crieff-Comrie	£18,571	£1,259	
1966	Inveramsay-Turriff	£30,774	£1,709	
	Newton Stewart-Whithorn	£29,132	£1,513	8
	'Stirling-Alloa-Kinross-Perth'	£19,204	£1,129	9
	Queensferry passage	£194,868	N/A	10
	Dumfries-Lockerbie	£25,074	£1,700	11
1967	Dumfries-Lockerbie	£19,116	£1,296	11
	Leven-Crail-St Andrews	£34,534	£1,233	12
	Maxwelltown-Dunragit inc.Kirkcudbright	127,047	£1,649	12
1968	Stanley Junction-Forfar-Kinnaber Jnct. inc. Justinhaugh	£84,658	£1,693	12
	Crianlarich (Lower)-Killin-Dunblane	£78,944	£917	13
	Almond Valley Jnct-Crieff	£17,854	£1,115	12
1969	Muir of Ord-Fortrose	£36,002	£2,571	6
	Elgin-Craigellachie & Aberlour-Boat of Garten	£90,538	£2,057	12
	Turriff-Macduff	£23,095	£1,924	12
	Ladybank-Auchtermuchty	£8,641	£1,920	12
1970	Ferryhill Jct-Ballater	£82,536	£2,013	14
1971	Riddings Jct-Lady Victoria Pit ('Waverley Route')	£283,527	£3,831	15

KEY TO NOTES

1 Distance not specified in BR Board Minutes. If taken as only Kirkintilloch-Kilsyth, and Buchlyvie-Aberfoyle, the total comes to 19 miles. But see also 5 below.

2 Not clear from Board Minutes if this included dismantling of bridges; the viaducts at Lyne and Neidpath were, in the event, left in situ. In September 1960, the Board was told that the recovery outlay was £59,113 against an authorised £38,139; this was described, in a totally confusing passage, as 'underspending'.

3 Mileage calculated at twenty-two.

4 Built as a Light Railway, with minimal earthworks and buildings. Assets recoverable, especially on the Lauder line, seem inexplicably high (see text).

5 Appears to cover much of the 1955 Aberfoyle/Kilsyth estimated area.

6 Appears in Board Minutes in 1960 and 1969. By the second appearance, the net figure had increased by 50 per cent in nine years.

7 Average recovery per mile for the 1960 intimations = £1,916. Without Lauder Light = £1,757.

8 Net figure, after subtraction of necessary costs. This 'outlay', as communicated to the Board, was no less than £41,866, for no specified reason. It could not have involved a subvention to the local bus company, as passenger services ceased in 1950. In any event, the latter type of grant-aid is not costed in the Board Minutes in relation to any particular closure.

9 Net figure, after subtraction of £45,473, for 'alterations to pw and signalling'. The exact alignment route of this recovery presumably covers the Devon Valley line only, and the mileage figure given above is calculated on that basis.

10 Although reported after the opening of the Forth Road Bridge, whose financial effect was massively damaging to Scottish, the 'recovery' figure seems excessive, and was presumably based on valuing the

ferries as 'going concerns'. In fact, three of the four ferries could only be sold for scrap, one of them known to have fetched only £2,500.

11 1967 estimate for Dumfries–Lockerbie line is for recovery of underbridges only, and is a net figure after outlay of £5,958. No such outlay was notified to the Board in the previous year, when the gross figure was reported.

12 Net figure, after unspecified outlay.

13 Net figure lower perhaps because of recovery difficulties. Part of this line was closed by landslip.

14 Net figure, after estimated outlay of no less than £70,552. In January 1973 the Board learned that there had been an 'underspend' of £88,983 on asset recovery on the Ballater line – rather more than the original estimate.

15 Entry in Board Minutes (RSR/1/40, January 1971) appears to give net figure for recovery from LMR boundary to Lady Victoria Pit, the latter sited between Newtongrange and Gorebridge.

Allowing for change in monetary values, the four highest estimates for recovered material, per mile, are: 1) Hawthornden-Peebles-Galashiels; 2) Lauder Light; 3) Waverley Route [at pre-decimal values]; and 4) Muir of Ord-Fortrose [1969 estimate].

Sources: BR/RSR/1/18-32 and 38-42. The above list is not exhaustive, but is based on what was reported to the Board. Any errors in mileage calculations are the author's responsibility entirely.

TABLE VI
TRACTION CONVERSION ON BR REGIONS BY MARCH 1958, THREE YEARS AFTER MODERNISATION PLAN

Region	Steam	DMU	Main-line Diesel	EMU	Others	% improvement
Scottish	2,128	105	0	0	1 BMU by April	5
North Eastern	2,068	382	0	162		26
Eastern	2,675	214	8	429		20
London Midland	4,907	470	4	864		21
Southern	1,359	138	0	3,587		73
Western	3,625	341	1	0	1 Gas Turbine 5 Narrow-gauge steam	9

Source: Based on summaries in *Railway Yearbook* with some data added. The right-hand column, '% improvement', indicates new traction units (including unpowered DMU and EMU carriages) as a percentage of all traction methods. Percentages are rounded to nearest full number. EMU figures for LMR, NER and SR include pre-1948 introductions, confirming that the lack of Scottish modernisation was a chronic factor.

TABLE VII
ORIGIN AND ALLOCATION OF GRESLEY A4 PACIFICS OPERATING THREE-HOUR SCHEDULES ON GLASGOW–ABERDEEN ROUTE, 1962-66.

	To Glasgow (St Rollox)	To Aberdeen (Ferryhill)
Original depots, 1961:		
From Edinburgh (Haymarket)	60027/31 (also A3s 60090/94)	60004/9/11/12/24
From Gateshead		60005/16/19/23
From King's Cross		60006/7/10/26/34

Sources: Contemporary transport journals. The Haymarket A4s are believed to have been the first Scottish locomotives fitted with AWS/ATC in 1957, at the request of the Eastern Region, for operating between King's Cross and Grantham on non-stop services (see text).

TABLE VIII
REVENUE & OPERATING LOSSES OF SCRS LOWEST-EARNING SERVICES (SURVEYED OCTOBER 1960)

Service	Income	Operating cost	Deficit
19.56 Berwick-Edinburgh (Wav)	10s (50p)	£164	£163.10s
08.32 Lanark-Glasgow Central	£6	£113	£107
05.48 Kilmarnock– Dumfries	£7	£176	£169
09.50 Glasgow (St E)- Kilmarnock	£12	£103	£91
12.00 Carstairs-Muirkirk	£14	£106	£92
20.00 Glasgow C – Lanark	£17	£120	£103
06.50 Edinburgh (Wav)-Berwick	£22	£218	£196
09.30 Oban-Glasgow (Buch St.)	£84	£336	£252
12.00 Glasgow (Buch St.) – Oban	£127	£275	£148

Source: Based on *Modern Railways*, Vol.15, 1962, p.4.

TABLE IX
WITHDRAWAL OF LAST STEAM LOCOMOTIVES ON SCOTTISH REGION, 1967

Month	Type	Number	(Nominal) depot
May	BR 5MT	73059	Polmadie
		73060	Polmadie
		73064	Polmadie
		73079	Polmadie
		73100	Corkerhill
		73146	Corkerhill
	BR 4MT	76000	Motherwell
		76002	Motherwell
		76046	Corkerhill
		76093	Corkerhill
		76094	Beattock
		76098	Beattock
		76104	Beattock
June	J36 0-6-0	65288	Dunfermline
		65345	Thornton 'the last' (as indicated in BR register)

Source: Based on BR/RSR/5/85

TABLE X
'LAST' SCR STEAM LOCOMOTIVES NOTIFIED BY MPDS
TO SUPPLIES MANAGER FOR DISPOSAL, 1965-66.

Depot	Loco No.	Date of notification
Glasgow (Polmadie)	73063	2.7.66
(Corkerhill)	73009/80007	16.7.66
(St Rollox)	73152	18.12.65
(Eastfield)	44970	25.9.65
Aberdeen (Ferryhill)	60528/60009 (without tender)	4.6.66
Perth	44698	16.7.66
Dundee	61403	16.7.66
Stirling	73007	16.3.66
Thornton★	61103/64606/65910	16.7.66
Dunfermline★	64610	12.6.66
Edinburgh (St Margarets)	61345 +60041 'retained'	16.7.66
(Dalry Road)	61134	9.10.65
Bathgate	65243	16.7.66
Hawick		No notification
Dumfries	46450	29.1.66
Beattock	42260	4.6.66
Carstairs	73078	16.7.66
Ayr	45177/76103	16.7.66
Hurlford	76108/77015	16.7.66
Motherwell	44850/81	16.7.66
Greenock	42264	16.7.66
Grangemouth	64580/90553/46468	23.10.65
Kipps	54398	15.1.66

Source: BR/RSR/5/98. This handwritten register is incomplete and probably does not record the last steam locomotives allocated to the depots listed above, or even serviced there (as we know with Dunfermline★ and Thornton★ – see Table IX), but hopefully the reader will find it useful as an official sample record of locomotive distribution shortly before the final withdrawal of steam power in Scotland.

The Kipps advice concerned former Highland 4-4-0 *Ben Alder*. Although listed as a 'Historic locomotive' in the ledger, it seems nevertheless to have been notified to Supplies management, being delivered for disposal on 18 April 1966 (see Chapter E). Dundee Tay Bridge was holding 46464 on 27 August 1966 for Dundee Art Galleries & Museums at the request of Mr I.N. Fraser. 60041/52 were described as 'retained for Mr Pegler', presumably to provide spare parts for 60103 *Flying Scotsman*, while an attempt to preserve 60027 failed.

File GD344/5/60, although a Diesel register, shows former Dumfries-based ex-LMS 2P 40670 retained for the Midland & Great Northern Joint Railway Society before being scrapped, and J39 64950 held at Inverurie. Two N15 0-6-2s, 69128/38, both from St Margarets, were shown as held for an unspecified customer. The SRPS was believed to be interested in possible purchase of an N15, but none of these four locomotives was preserved.

TABLE XI
SCOTTISH REGION DIESEL AVAILABILITY: ACTUAL 1966 & PREDICTED FOR 1967
(Shunting locomotives excluded)

Class	Nos in service	In store	Actual 1966 %	Predicted 1967 %
55	8	0	78	80
47	9	0	83	80
40	19	0	73	75
37	23	0	87	87
24	9	0	Not recorded	
25	19	0	Not recorded	
29 1	13	0	65	75
29 2	15	30	79	70
26/27	134	0	80	80
20	75	0	88	87
17	99	0	66	68
17 3	2	0	79	75
126 Power cars (pc)	88	0	85	83
126 Trailer cars (tc)	44	0	91	90
126 Pc 4	8	0	83	85
126 Tc 4	14	0	87	90
DMUs (various pc)	251	0	87	85
DMUs (various tc)	172	0	93	90

1. Re-engined with Paxman equipment.
2. With original M.A.N. equipment.
3. Re-engined with Rolls-Royce equipment.
4. Described as 'cross-country', used in reduced formations.

Sources: BR/RSR/1/31, January 1967, and 1969 Register of ScR Diesels, GD344/5/60. The former source is the 1967 Board Minute Book which omits Classes 24 and 25 from the availability survey, for no apparent reason, although the latter class had been in service with the Region since 1960. One 25 was damaged in a 'mishap' at Castlecary and condemned on 29 September 1968.

TABLE XII
BR (SCOTTISH REGION) SHIPS AND FERRIES, 1948-59

Taken over in 1948	Introduced 1948-59	Withdrawn from Scottish service
Caledonia		1969
Countess of Breadalbane		1989
Duchess of Argyll		1952
Duchess of Fife		1953
Duchess of Hamilton		1970
Duchess of Montrose		1964
Queen Mary II		1977
Glen Sannox (I)		1953
Jupiter		1957
Jeanie Deans		1964
King Edward		1952
King George V		1974

Taken over in 1948	*Introduced 1948-59*	*Withdrawn from Scottish service*
Talisman		1966
Lucy Ashton		1949
Marchioness of Graham		1958
Marchioness of Lorne		1954
Waverley (IV)		1973
Princess May		1953
Prince Edward		1954
Coruisk (I)		1951
Lochalsh (I)		1957
	Maid of Argyll	1973
	Maid of Ashton	1972
	Maid of Skelmorlie	1972
	Maid of Cumbrae	1977
	Arran	1979
	Cowal	1977
	Bute	1979
	Maid of the Loch	1981
	Glen Sannox (II)	1989
	Lochalsh (II)	1973
	Portree	1965
	Broadford	1967
	Mary Queen of Scots[1]	1964
	Sir William Wallace[1]	1964

Excludes Stranraer-Larne ferries (LMR, 1952-61). Nominally, former LNER vessels were not taken into Scottish Region's maritime concern, the CSP, until November 1951, with Loch Lomond and Kyle services following in May 1957.

1   Property of William Denny & Co. until 1963, along with *Robert the Bruce* and *Queen Margaret*.

TABLE XIII
ACCIDENTS ON SCOTTISH REGION 1948-73

Date	*Location*	*Killed*	*Comments*
7.3.48	Lamington	1	Firebox collapse
17.7.48	Ardler Junction	2	Collision
31.1.49	Glasgow Cross	Not known	SPAD
26.5.49	Douglas Park	Not known	Signalling irregularity
23.6.49	Penmanshiel Tunnel	Not known	Fire on train
27.11.49	Strathmiglo	1	Derailment during pw work
8.6.50	Beattock	5	Fire on train
10.1.51	Alloa Junction	2	Collision after storm affected signalling
21.4.51	Pollockshields/		
	Queen's Park	3	Breach of signalling rules
14.11.51	Glasgow (Queen St)	Not known	Collision following brake failure
17.12.53	Longniddry	1	Derailment – obstacle on line
28.5.55	Wormit	3	Derailment following breach of rules
20.5.58	Arkleston Junction	1	Collision following breach of rules
17.8.57	South Queensferry	2	Ferry accident
13.4.59	Kyleakin	4	Ferry accident

2.9.60	Castlecary	Not known	Collision following signalling error
13.12.60	Renton	Not known	Transformer explosion
6.9.62	Glasgow (Buchanan St)	Not known	Collision following brake failure
29.9.68	Castlecary	Not known	Collision
15.6.69	Lamington	Not known	Derailment – buckled rail
6.10.71	Beattock	1	Collision following brake failure
30.8.73	Shields Junction (Glasgow)	1	Collision following SPAD

Sources: Issues of the *Railway Year Book*. Statistics given therein were subject to later adjustment, if, for example, an injured victim later died; for that reason, even blank figures in the *RYB* are treated as 'Not Known' in this table. Later editions of this yearbook listed no accident incurring fewer than five deaths, and there are no entries for Scottish after 1950. Some information has been added from Board Minutes and GD344 files, but no centralised list of BR Scottish Region accidents has been located in NAS.

Eighteen passengers and staff died in Scottish Region rail accidents up to 1968; in that period, exactly 500 passengers died on BR nationally.

Excluded from the above is the loss of the MV *Princess Victoria* in 1952, as this service was an LMR operation at the time. Also excluded are personnel accidents not involving moving rail vehicles.

All tables, © A.J. Mullay, 2004.

LIST OF ABBREVIATIONS

ac	Alternating current
ASLEF	Associated Society of Locomotive Engineers and Firemen
ATC	Automatic Train Control
AWS	Automatic Warning System
BMU	Battery Multiple Unit
BR	British Railways (later British Rail)
BRPB	British Rail Property Board
BTC	British Transport Commission
BTSMC	British Transport Ship Management Company (Check)
CME	Chief Mechanical Engineer
CR	Caledonian Railway (to 1923)
CRO	Chief Regional Officer
CWR	Continuous welded rail
dc	Direct current
DMU	Diesel Multiple Unit
ECML	East Coast main line
EMU	Electric Multiple Unit
ER	Eastern Region
FB	Flat bottomed (rail)
FBR	Forth Bridge Railway Company (to 1948)
GM	General Manager
GNSR	Great North of Scotland Railway (to 1923)
GWR	Great Western Railway (to 1948)
G&SWR	Glasgow and South Western Railway (to 1923)
HP	Horsepower
HR	Highland Railway
KV	Measure of volts in 1,000s
LMR	London Midland Region
LMSR	London Midland & Scottish Railway (to 1948)
LNER	London & North Eastern Railway (to 1948)
MPD	Motive Power depot
MGR	Merry-go-round (Continuously circulating coal trains loaded and unloaded on move using hoppers
MV	Motor vessel
NAS	National Archives of Scotland
NBL	North British Locomotive Company
NBR	North British Railway (to 1923)

NCB	National Coal Board
NER	North Eastern Region
PS	Paddle steamer
pw	Permanent Way
RE	Railway Executive
SMT	Scottish Motor Transport
SO	Scottish Omnibuses
SPAD	Signal passed at danger
SRDA	Scottish Railway Development Association
STG	Scottish Transport Group
TUCC	Transport User Consultative Committee
WCML	West Coast main line
WR	Western Region

BIBLIOGRAPHY

NATIONAL ARCHIVES

BR/BTC/1/1-7. Minutes and meeting papers of the British Transport Commission, August 1947 – April 1948. [Includes the Railway Executive remit document Instructions No.1 Scottish Region, the first BTC Monthly Report, and 'Physical Condition of BR', all January 1948].

BR/BTC/5/1 The coal: oil conversion scheme on British Railways, 1945-48. Railway Executive, 1949.

BR/RSR/ 1/18 – 32, 38 – 43 BR Scottish Area Board Minutes. [From 1963, known as Scottish Railway Board; from 1969 Scottish Board].

BR/RSR/1/143 'Appreciation by London Midland Region and Scottish Region working parties on the linking-up of electrification between Weaver Junction and the Glasgow suburban scheme'. January 1964 [catalogued as 1967].

BR/RSR/4/12 Ballater branch closure proposal. Undated [1963?].

BR/RSR/4/81 'Television Train' documents, including children's questionnaire. 1962.

BR/RSR/4/93 Report of the Regional Committee on the electrification of Glasgow suburban lines. 1954.

BR/RSR/5/45 Minute of a meeting of the BR Mechanical Engineers' Committee, 8 January 1948. ('Interchange of locomotives between the regions').

BR/RSR/5/85 Register of steam locomotive repairs and withdrawals [1967].

BR/RSR/5/98 Disposal of condemned locomotives. [1966].

BR/RSR/8/1 'Service for motor cars between London (King's Cross) and Edinburgh (Waverley)', 1956.

BR/RSR/8/7 and 8/9 Berwickshire goods traffic receipts, 1958.

BR/RSR/18/12 Breakdown trains and re-railing equipment, 1969.

BR/RSR/18/18 'Report on the progress of Diesel schemes in the Scottish Region', 1960.

BR/RSR/32/3 Board Minutes, British Transport Ship Management (Scotland) Ltd., 1969-75.

BR/RB/2/223/1&/2 'Load[ing]s of passenger trains with relative instructions'. 1957.

BT2/20302 Board of Trade papers re liquidation of London Scottish Transport Ltd.

GD344/3/13 Technical manual on Automatic Warning System, 1959-60.

GD344/3/99 List of snowploughs, issued by Motive Power Office, Glasgow, October 1952.

GD344/5/60 Register of ScR Diesels, 1969.

NSE1/13 and /14. North of Scotland Hydro-electric Board Minutes for early 1956.

RCC6/27/1-3 TUCC files on Waverley Route closure.

BOOKS (TRANSPORT TITLES)

Allen, C.J. *New light on the Locomotive Exchanges.* Ian Allan, 1948.

Allsopp, S.G. *Diesel Multiple Units; early developments* [cover title *Short and sweet*]. Midland Counties Publications, 2005.

Bonavia, M.R. *British Rail; the first 25 years.* David & Charles, 1981.

Bonavia, M.R. *The organisation of British Railways.* Ian Allan, 1971.

Brodie, I. *Steamers of the Forth.* David & Charles, 1976.

Cox, E.S. *Locomotive panorama.*Vols I and II, Ian Allan, 1965/6.

Duckworth, C.L.D. and Langmuir, G.E. *Clyde river and other steamers.* 3rd edition. Brown, Son & Ferguson, 1972.

Foster, C.D. *The Transport Problem.* Croom Helm, 1975.

Glaister, S. and Mulley, C. *Public control of the British bus industry.* Gower, 1983.

Gourvish,T.R. *British Railways 1948-73: a business history.* C.U.P., 1986.

Gourvish,T.R. *British Rail 1974-97: from integration to privatisation.* O.U.P., 2002.

Hajducki,A.M. and Simpson,A. *The Lauder Light Railway.* Oakwood, 1996.

Johnson, J. and Long, R. *British Railways Engineering 1948-80.* Mechanical Engineering Publications, 1981.

Larkin, E. *Illustrated history of British Railways workshops.* OPC, 1992.

McCrorie, I. and Monteith, J. *Clyde piers.* Inverclyde District Libraries, 1982.

MacHaffie, F.G. *The short sea route; Portpatrick-Donaghadee, Stranraer-Larne, Cairnryan-Larne.* Stephenson & Sons, 1975.

Millar, A. *British PTEs : Strathclyde.* Ian Allan, 1985.

Ministry of Transport. *Final report on the accidents and failures that occurred in multiple-unit electric trains in the Scottish Region and Eastern Region, British Railways.* HMSO, 1962.

Railway Correspondence and Travel Society. *A detailed history of British Railways Standard steam locomotives.* Vol.1. 1994.

Robertson, C.J.A. *The origins of the Scottish railway system, 1722-1844.* John Donald, 1983.

Sixsmith, I. *The Book of the Coronation Pacifics.* Irwell, 1998.

Thomas, D. St J. *The Rural Transport problem.* Routledge, 1963.

BOOKS (NON-TRANSPORT TITLES)

Barry, E.E. *Nationalisation in British politics: the historical background.* Cape, 1965.

Hume, J.R. *The industrial archaeology of Scotland. 1. The Lowlands and Borders.* Batsford, 1976.

McIntyre, I. *The expense of glory: a life of John Reith.* HarperCollins, 1993.

Robertson,A.J. *The Bleak Midwinter 1947.* Manchester University Press, 1987.

Rolt, L.T.C. *Landscape with figures.* Alan Sutton, 1992.

ARTICLES

Elliot, J. 'An account of stewardship'. Presidential address, 5 October 1953. *Journal of the Institute of Transport,* 25, (7) 1953, pp.243-52.

Evans, R.K. 'The acceptance testing of Diesel locomotives'. *Modern Railways,* Vol.15, 1962, pp267-70.

Missenden, E. 'Some thoughts on railway motive power'. *Journal of the Institute of Transport,* 23, (8) 1951, pp230-7.

Mullay, A.J. 'Leith Central, the station nobody wanted'. *Blastpipe* (SRPS journal), nos 73-75, 1986/7.

Robin, G.H. 'Glasgow Queen Street'. *Trains Illustrated,*Vol.9 (1), 1956.

Robin, G.H. 'The Cathcart circle'. *Trains Illustrated,*Vol.11 (117), 1958.

Also, articles in various issues of *British Railways Magazine (Scottish Region), Glasgow Herald, Modern Railways, Monthly Bulletin of the Railway Research Service, Railway Magazine, Railway Observer, Scotsman* and *Trains Illustrated.*

Retrospective valuations of currency are taken from the Internet site 'EH.net', edited by Samuel H. Williamson, although your author balked at the idea of a bottle of whisky costing the equivalent of £78 in 1948, and halved this particular valuation!

INDEX

If you are interested in purchasing
other books published by Tempus, or in case you have
difficulty finding any Tempus books in your local bookshop, you can also place orders
directly through our website

www.tempus-publishing.com